**DO NOT REMOVE
CARDS FROM POCKET**

The Novels of Barbara Pym

GARLAND REFERENCE LIBRARY
OF THE HUMANITIES
(VOL. 901)

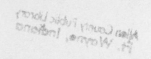

THE NOVELS OF BARBARA PYM

Katherine Anne Ackley

Garland Publishing, Inc. • New York and London
1989

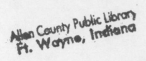
Library of Congress Cataloging-in-Publication Data

Ackley, Katherine Anne.
    The novels of Barbara Pym / Katherine Anne Ackley.
        p. cm. — (Garland reference library of the humanities ; vol.
901)
    Bibliography: p.
    ISBN 0–8240–5621–3 (alk. paper)
    1. Pym, Barbara—Criticism and interpretation. I. Title.
II. Series.
PR6066.Y58Z53   1989
[GV1595]
823'.914—dc19   88-34699
                                                                                              CIP

Printed on acid-free, 250-year-life paper
Manufactured in the United States of America

For Heather, Laurel, and Jeremy

CONTENTS

ACKNOWLEDGMENTS

I am grateful to my colleagues in the English Department of the University of Wisconsin at Stevens Point for making possible my sabbatical leave in order to begin work on this book. I am also grateful to the University of Wisconsin at Stevens Point for a grant that enabled me to travel to Oxford, England, in order to read the Pym manuscripts at the Bodleian Library.

Thanks are due the staff of Room 132 in the Bodleian for their kind assistance, and to Hazel Holt and the Bodleian Library for their permission to read the manuscripts and to quote from them. My special thanks to Hilary Pym for graciously consenting to talk about her sister with me.

Acknowledgements are due E.P. Dutton, a division of NAL Penguin Inc., and Jonathan Cape Ltd. for permission to quote from *Some Tame Gazelle*, *Excellent Women*, *Jane and Prudence*, *Less Than Angels*, *A Glass of Blessings*, and *No Fond Return of Love*; Macmillan London Ltd. and E.P. Dutton for permission to quote from *An Unsuitable Attachment*, *Quartet in Autumn*, *The Sweet Dove Died*, *A Few Green Leaves*, *A Very Private Eye: An Autobiography in Diaries and Letters*, *Crampton Hodnet*, and *An Academic Question*; and Macmillan London Ltd for permission to quote from *Civil to Strangers and Other Writings*.

Many thanks to Eleanor Ligman for her assistance in preparing the manuscript for printing. For reading the manuscript and pointing out where more felicitous wording was needed, I am grateful to Heather Schilling; for their frequent cheerful inquiries into the progress of my work, I thank Laurel White and Jeremy White. Finally, I am most thankful for the constant encouragement of my husband, Richard Ackley.

INTRODUCTION

Interest in Barbara Pym has been growing rapidly since 1977, when she was the only living writer to be named in a *Times Literary Supplement* feature as the century's most underrated writer. During her lifetime (1913-1980), Pym saw the publication of eight of her novels. Five more have been published posthumously, thanks to Pym's longtime friend and literary executor, Hazel Holt. Other than reviews at the time of their issue, relatively little was written about Pym's books when she was alive. Since her death, scholars have been making up for that neglect with zeal. Pym would appreciate the irony.

Chapter one in the study that follows is an overview of Pym's novels, a general introduction to her works. The six subsequent chapters each in turn discuss a specific theme, with many of them overlapping. Chapter Two explores male-female relationships and Pym's particular comic stance toward what she viewed as the often ridiculous nature of those relationships. Chapter Three examines the effects of a male-centered world on women's friendships, and Chapter Four looks at the effects of mothers on their grown children. Chapter Five follows with a discussion of the ways in which Pym's characters cope with isolation and loneliness. Chapter Six examines Pym's treatment of the subjects of the past and the future and the ways in which her characters respond to possibilities for change. The final chapter is a detailed analysis of the connection Pym saw between literature and life, answering the question put to Dulcie Mainwaring in *No Fond Return of Love* about her love of literature: "But what does it lead to, Miss Mainwaring?"

My study takes into consideration all of Pym's novels, including the posthumously published works, but focuses primarily on the nine novels Pym readied for publication herself.

ABBREVIATIONS

Page numbers are noted in parentheses within the text. I quote from Dutton editions of Pym's novels throughout, with the exception of *Civil to Strangers and Other Writings*, for which I have used the Macmillan edition. I use the following abbreviations:

STG	*Some Tame Gazelle* (1950; rpt. 1983)
EW	*Excellent Women* (1952; rpt. 1978)
JP	*Jane and Prudence* (1953; rpt. 1981)
LTA	*Less Than Angels* (1955; rpt. 1980)
GB	*Glass of Blessings* (1958; rpt. 1980)
NFRL	*No Fond Return of Love* (1961; rpt. 1982)
QA	*Quartet in Autumn* (1977; rpt. 1978)
SDD	*The Sweet Dove Died* (1978; rpt. 1979)
FGL	*A Few Green Leaves* (1980)
UA	*An Unsuitable Attachment* (1982)
VPE	*A Very Private Eye: An Autobiography in Diaries and Letters* (1984)
CH	*Crampton Hodnet* (1985)
AQ	*An Academic Question* (1986)
CS	*Civil to Strangers and Other Writings* (1987)

Note: CS is also used for citations to *Gervase and Flora*, *The Home Front Novel*, and *So Very Secret*.

MS PYM Pym's private papers, which are housed in the Bodleian Library, Oxford University. Manuscript numbers are indicated within parentheses in the text.

The Novels of Barbara Pym

ONE

SOME ASPECTS OF THE NOVELS

During the jubilant period following her "rediscovery," Barbara Pym wrote to Philip Larkin that a photographer had come to take her picture. She tried not to smile too much, she said, adding: "I would really like to achieve a dark brooding expression but don't think I ever could" (**VPE** 302). This comment might just as easily apply to her novels, particularly the later ones, for although the tone of the novels written during the period when she was not being published is darker than the tone of her other novels, Pym never achieved a "dark brooding expression." No matter how serious her subject matter--with illness, aging, decay, and death explored at length in the last three novels--she always managed to treat her characters and their experiences with humor and detachment. Even *Quartet in Autumn*, perhaps the grimmest of all her novels, Pym regarded as "by no means a depressing book" (**MS PYM** 165, fol. 101). The subject of most of her novels--how intelligent but plain unmarried women manage to live with dignity in an uncertain and disillusioning male-centered world--does not seem a likely subject for comedy. Yet Pym successfully turns it into humorous material by balancing the sad and indefinite aspects of her characters' lives with objectivity and wit. Her central character heroines may realize the necessity for settling for second best and finding compensations where they can, but they have a wise and comic vision of their world. They are sensible and compassionate women who do the best they can under difficult circumstances, women who harbor hope in a cheerless environment.

Eight novels were published during Barbara Pym's life, the first six of which appeared in rapid succession from 1950 to 1961: *Some Tame Gazelle* (1950), *Excellent Women* (1952), *Jane and Prudence* (1953), *Less Than Angels* (1955), *A Glass of Blessings* (1958), and *No Fond Return of Love* (1961). Then in 1963, her seventh novel, *An Unsuitable Attachment*, was rejected by Jonathan Cape, the publishing house which had brought out her previous novels. Thus began a period of fourteen years during which no one would publish her work. Pym continued to have admirers during that period, however, among whom was Philip Larkin. Their correspondence, begun ironically when Larkin wrote requesting permission to review her next novel--the one that was never accepted by a publisher in her lifetime--continued to the end of Pym's life. It was in large part Philip Larkin's doing, along with the fortuitous help of Lord David Cecil, that Pym was rediscovered.

Perhaps "discovered" is the more appropriate word, for none of her first six books brought her the kind of recognition scholars are now giving her. When Larkin and Lord Cecil named Pym the most underrated writer of the century in a January 21, 1977, *Times Literary Supplement* article, Pym found herself the center of attention, with publishers rushing to print her new work and reissue her old, the media interviewing her, and critics and scholars praising her. Macmillan brought out *Quartet in Autumn* (1977) and *The Sweet Dove Died* (1978); *A Few Green Leaves* (1980) was being readied for print when she died. During the last three years of her life, Barbara Pym not only had the very real satisfaction of becoming once again a published novelist but found herself on the best seller list and had a wide audience thirsting for new Pym novels. While she had always received letters from grateful readers, after her newfound fame letters poured in from all over the world, from South Africa to Canada and many

American states. The sentiments expressed by all of these letter writers reveal a profound appreciation for her quiet humor and witty insights. They must have been enormously gratifying to Pym after the long, bitter years of anonymity.

Pym's final novel, *A Few Green Leaves*, is the only one written when she knew a large readership was waiting for its publication. In it, Pym returned to her favorite themes. Having been rediscovered and once again publicly acknowledged a writer--and a good one at that--she was free to go back to the subjects that gave her the most pleasure. Curates, spinsters, male-female relationships, cozy village life and death, and anthropology appear once again in this quintessential Pym novel. Emma Howick, an anthropologist retreating to her mother's cottage to write up her notes--"something to do with attitudes towards almost everything you could think of in one of the new towns" (9)--never quite gets around to finishing her project. Rather, she becomes interested in the goings on around her and from time to time conjectures the kind of thing she could write about the people here: "'Some Observations on the Social Patterns of a West Oxfordshire Village'" (38). The entire novel is in one sense a summary of Pym's own observations of social patterns, for in the course of her life in this village, Emma witnesses the range of events and people Pym wrote about in all of her previous books. It is a tour de force, this final work by a dying writer who finally was getting the critical acclaim she never dreamt possible but fully deserved. Pym makes references to previous characters and themes, indeed, to all aspects of her novels, not in the way a tired imagination might use old material but in the way one conscious of tidying up loose ends, of touching base with old friends and old pleasures, might do. It is a wonderful book to end a reading of all the previous novels; it is also an excellent introduction to her works.

To the continued delight of her followers, few writers have been as prolific following their death as Barbara Pym. When she died in January, 1980, she left six finished novels, parts of three novels, and twenty-seven short stories unpublished. Some of these works were written in the 1930s, 1940s, and 1950s. During the fourteen-year period when she was not being published, from 1963 to 1977, Pym wrote several new novels, occasionally worked on old material, and tried to revise *An Unsuitable Attachment*. Since the publication of *A Few Green Leaves*, through the wise and intelligent editing of her literary executor, longtime colleague, and friend Hazel Holt, four more novels and a collection of parts of novels and short stories have appeared. Working in the same office at the International African Institute in London for twenty-five years, Pym and Holt often discussed characters and situations in Pym's novels. Furthermore, Pym kept notes on her works in progress which enabled Holt to prepare manuscripts for publication. *An Unsuitable Attachment*, which Pym had sent to dozens of publishers after Cape's rejection, often under a different title (*Wrapped in Lemon Leaves*, e.g.) and with a pseudonym ("Tom Crampton"), was finally published in 1982. In 1985 *Crampton Hodnet*, written in 1939-40 and then put away, was revised by Holt on the basis of Pym's own changes and notebook entries and then published. *An Academic Question*, a novel Pym worked on in the early 1970s but put aside, followed in 1986. Finally, in late 1987 *Civil to Strangers and Other Writings* appeared. *Civil to Strangers* is a full-length novel written in 1936 when Pym was only twenty-three. The "other writings" are comprised of parts of three novels, four short stories, most of which were written before or during the war, and a radio talk entitled "Finding A Voice," recorded for BBC on February 8, 1978. Two of the short stories were previously published, one commissioned by the *Church Times* in 1977, entitled "The Christmas Visit," the other, "Across a Crowded Room," commissioned by *The New Yorker* in 1979. *Civil to Strangers* is the final new Pym publication.

None of the posthumously published novels (excluding *A Few Green Leaves*) is as good as any of the novels published while Pym was alive, but they all have their moments of exceptionally good comedy and sharp insights into character that have become legendary Pym wisdom. In terms of thematic focus, they are typical Pym. *An Unsuitable Attachment*, the first novel Hazel Holt edited for publication, has serious flaws in unity, focus, and credibility. There are too many characters given equal attention, producing a split focus which is never effectively resolved. The "unsuitable attachment" of the title is scarcely believable, even allowing for the belief in the 1950s which assumed that husbands must be older than their wives, not the other way around. With something like five years' difference in age and a slight class difference between the two principals involved in the attachment, it is difficult to work up the proper amount of concern for the mismatched couple. *Crampton Hodnet*, on the other hand, is typically Pym and probably her funniest work. It is the novel one is most likely to laugh out loud at, with the scene in which Mr. Latimer proposes to Jessie Morrow exquisite in humor. It also provides the first appearance of Miss Doggett and Jessie Morrow and introduces the subjects of spinsterhood and ill-advised matches which Pym returned to again and again in her other novels. Finally, it demonstrates Pym's growing skill as a novelist, for it is well crafted and, had Pym revised it as she did *Some Tame Gazelle*, for instance, has the potential to rank among her best. As it was, she was confident enough in the novel's characters and situations to rework many of them in *Jane and Prudence*.

An Academic Question, written after *The Sweet Dove Died* and before *Quartet in Autumn*, has neither the polish nor the brilliancy of either of those novels. Pym was trying to write in a different style--"a sort of Margaret Drabble effort" (**VPE** 263)--and consciously tried not to be "cozy." In trying to imitate someone else, however, attempting to "modernize" her work in an effort to become publishable again, she was not writing as herself. The result was disappointing, and in spite of two drafts, one in the first person, one in the third, Pym put the novel aside to work on what is generally regarded as her masterpiece, *Quartet in Autumn*. The last posthumously published full-length novel, *Civil to Strangers*, was written in 1936, after Pym had completed the first draft of *Some Tame Gazelle*. It lacks the mature style of the much-revised 1950 version of *Gazelle* but is a light, competently written exercise in imitation of Elizabeth von Arnim's *The Enchanted April*. As with *An Academic Question*, the attempt to imitate someone else's style produced disappointing results, but the novel also has a few purely Pym characters and scenes. Adam Marsh-Gibbon is a caricature of the male who becomes Archdeacon Henry Hoccleve, complete with his predilection for reading melancholy poetry in the churchyard among tombstones. Literary quotations abound, particularly as Adam Marsh-Gibbon is himself a writer and enjoys the same sort of strutting of his erudition as Hoccleve. The centrality of love and marriage is emphasized by the matching of three couples, one young, one middle-aged, and one old, and by the reaffirmation and strengthening of Cassandra and Adam Marsh-Gibbon's love for one another. Finally, women dote on men but essentially see them as children.

The other novels excerpted or "reduced," as Hazel Holt describes the process, in *Civil to Strangers and Other Writings* are interesting in terms of ideas and characters Pym used again or reworked in her more successful finished efforts. In the Finnish novel, *Gervase and Flora*, written in 1937-38 for her friends' amusement and based on letters Pym wrote to Henry Harvey in Finland, there are the usual entanglements of male-female relationships as well as the prototype of the elderly, domineering woman, Miss Emily Moberley. In the *Home Front Novel*, which Pym began in 1939 but never finished, Connie Aspinall and Edith Liversidge from *Some Tame Gazelle* appear as Connie Aspinall and Agnes Grote. Lady Wraye is a version of Lady Beddoes in *Crampton Hodnet* and Mrs. Lyall in *Jane and Prudence*. A remark Mrs. Lyall makes in that novel about the way breakfasts used to be such large meals when her husband was alive seems to refer directly to a breakfast scene in the *Home Front Novel* in which Lady Wraye looks disapprovingly on the large spread the cook has prepared for them. Further, the phrase "excellent women" is used for the first time to describe those ever-busy women bent on doing good for the village. Finally, *So Very Secret*, written in 1941 and the last fiction Pym wrote until after the war, is a delightful attempt at a spy novel.

8

The heroine, a typical excellent woman living quietly in her village, becomes entangled in a spy plot and manages to carry off the delivery of a secret document with resourcefulness and verve. The condensed version appearing in *Civil to Strangers* is an almost breathtaking series of conflicts. Reading it, one longs for the background details that Pym would have given had she worked on it seriously for publication.

What one notices about all of Pym's novels is the way she rarely presents anyone or any issue as purely good or purely bad, purely right or purely wrong. Characters and themes are treated with a complexity that adds richness and texture to the books. Pym's excellent women are not the totally selfless, charitably-spirited people the world would see them as. The church is a great comfort but its clergy are as pompous or silly or selfish as its congregation. Literature, a real consolation, can be painful as well, and education for women has mixed blessings. Married women, having achieved a socially approved and highly regarded position, seldom fit the stereotyped traditional notion of that role and often look enviously at unmarried women. The company of other women is ambiguously regarded sometimes as a comfort, sometimes as a burden. Romance and marriage seldom turn out to be anything like what the women and men who think they want them had been led to believe. Mothers seem to be the only parent and are variously revered or resented. Change is sometimes embraced, sometimes resisted. Pym recorded in her journal in October of 1943: "I am a wretched melancholy creature when I would like to be noble and strong and very intelligent. I lie in a hot bath brooding about G. (yes I still do in spite of putting him right out of my life) when I ought to be thinking about the Metaphysicals in a scholarly way or planning a great comic novel" (VPE 160). This entry exemplifies Pym's lifelong pull between thinking she ought to be intellectual at the same time she could not help being romantic. The result is that her characters fluctuate between the two opposite impulses as well, most of them adopting a detachment in self defense to avoid being too miserably swallowed up by their own romanticism.

Because of her own ambivalence, Pym does not "insist" on any viewpoint other than that characters and situations be seen with understanding. She is a comic writer, true enough, poking fun at the foibles and weaknesses of even the most staid and proper people, but hers is a gentle, loving, and forgiving humor.

In the *Times Literary Supplement* article naming Pym the most underrated writer of the century, both Philip Larkin and Lord David Cecil praised her ability to write with humor of the quotidian. Larkin lauded "the six novels published between 1950 and 1961 which give an unrivalled picture of a small section of middle-class postwar England," adding that "she has a unique eye and ear for the small poignancies and comedies of everyday life," while Cecil called her "unpretentious, subtle, accomplished novels, especially *Excellent Women* and *A Glass of Blessings*, ... the finest examples of high comedy to have appeared in England during the past seventy-five years" (66). It is her skill at describing the small sufferings and joys of ordinary people which makes her novels extraordinarily good reading. Pym wrote in one of her literary notebooks that she had little interest in theories about "the novel" because she was too occupied in trying to get published herself (**MS PYM** 88). This comment reflects Pym's absorption in the everyday realities of her own life: her very real concern for fourteen years was trying to get into print once again while wrestling with the perplexing problem of having once been a modestly successful writer who is no longer regarded as one by the publishing world. Despite her assertion that she does not have a "theory of the novel," however, many passages in her novels and literary notebooks indicate that she did indeed have well-formulated ideas about what worked and what did not work in the novel.

One clear statement of her "theory" is this journal entry: "To make *my* (literary) soup I don't need cream and egg, and rare shell fish, but just this old cod's head, the discarded outer leaves of a cabbage, water and seasoning" (**MS PYM** 56, fol. 3). Everyday events, ordinary people, and the trivialities of their lives are the ingredients of her novels, told in detail and fully realized. In her radio talk "Finding a Voice," reprinted in *Civil to Strangers*, Pym comments that she has been criticized for her use of detail but that it was a practice she developed early. She was annoyed and frustrated that she was faulted for that practice, writing in her journal, for example, on November 9, 1970, that the reading public was no longer interested in her kind of book: "What is wrong with being obsessed with trivia? Some have criticized *The Sweet Dove* for this. What are the minds of my critics filled with? What *nobler* and more worthwhile things?" (**VPE** 260). In a talk entitled "The Novelist's Use of Every-Day Life" that she gave in Barnes in the 1950s, Pym supported her own use of such details by quoting a Denton Welch journal entry in which he expressed his wish to hear the details of people's daily lives. "'I would like to hear the details of their house, their meals, and their possessions,'" he wrote, "' ... the tiny things of their lives that give them pleasure or fear or wonder'" (**MS PYM** 98). In this discussion of the craft of writing, Pym pointed out that everyday life is not enough by itself but needed something done to it before it could become a satisfactory novel. In her own novels, Pym took her observations of everyday life and successfully rendered them into scenes, characters, and dialogue that sparkle brilliantly. She depended on life around her to provide the ingredients which she turned into immensely readable fiction. Her love of trivia and her belief in the essential centrality of everyday events are the hallmarks of her fiction, along with her constant theme of the relationships between men and women and their various hopes and disappointments. Her thematic focus is summarized in *No Fond Return of Love*, when Dulcie Mainwaring says that "'People blame one for dwelling on trivialities, ... but life is made up of them. And if we've had one great sorrow or one great love, then who shall blame us if we only want the trivial things?'" (169).

Another characteristic of Pym's novels is that most of her central characters are struggling toward worldliness or at least toward a greater understanding of the world and, more importantly, of themselves. They are conscious of their shortcomings, sometimes too eager to forgive, perhaps too humble and self-effacing, but Pym makes a compelling argument for their dignity and worth as human beings. While her most immediate focus is on the individual, narrow life, her vision is not naive and limited. She writes of people who need to "connect," uneasy, reluctant participants in a drama they would rather watch passively from the audience than become actors in themselves. Many of them think at first that, like Alaric Lydgate (**LTA**), they would rather remain alone, hiding behind a mask, or like Dulcie Mainwaring (**NFRL**) or Mildred Lathbury (**EW**), observe other people's experiences than have any of their own. In the course of the novels, these characters begin to live and to understand themselves and others in a way they had never before done.

Barbara Pym has time and again been compared to Jane Austen, but she was embarrassed by that comparison, claiming it was too strong a compliment to pay her.[1] Yet there is no denying that Pym's style reminds one of Austen's command of the humorous scene and her wry detached observations. Pym's is a more gentle poking fun of just about everyone, particularly those who take themselves too seriously, most often men. Her male characters come close to being buffoons at times, but women are just as likely to be targets of Pym's humor. Her real talent lies in her ability to detect the amusing side of just about any situation: life is comic and sad and indefinite, as Catherine Oliphant says in *Less Than Angels*, and Pym implies that seeing the comic in things helps keep a balanced perspective on the sad and indefinite. When Mildred Lathbury actually questions the necessity of tea, she is making an observation that puzzles and distresses Miss Statham, as if it "had struck at something deep and fundamental. It was the kind of question that starts a landslide in the mind" (**EW** 227). This passage illustrates Pym's skill at indicating emotional turmoil in a way that is both comic and dramatic: because of the centrality of trivialities in everyday life, it suggests just how far Mildred has gone in her personal crisis if she is capable of questioning something as basic as tea. Pym's treatment of ordinary middle-class people argues for the dignity of their lives, suggesting that they are characterized by quiet desperation rather than tortured anguish or blissful joy. The events in their lives are so quiet that the novels almost seem to lack plots. But they do have plots, and in fact, Pym's novels are classically structured.[2] Furthermore, her central characters all undergo their own personal crises, often with the result that they learn something about themselves that they had not previously known.

Belinda Bede in *Some Tame Gazelle* faces the crisis of strangers threatening to disrupt her quiet life as well as the very alarming possibility that she has the potential to be a rival to Agatha Hoccleve. In *Excellent Women*, Mildred Lathbury acknowledges a sensual side of herself but in the end becomes resigned to a decidedly less than lively future as an excellent woman. In *Less Than Angels*, Catherine Oliphant's usually strong self-sufficiency is weakened, not by Tom Mallow's unfaithfulness but by his death. She discovers in herself a positive, healing dependency as she works through her grief. In *A Glass of Blessings*, Wilmet Forsythe's is probably the most pronounced discovery of self, for she undergoes a series of profound insights into herself and emerges a changed woman. In *No Fond Return of Love*, Dulcie Mainwaring's conflict is whether or not she should become more actively involved in other people's lives. Leonora Eyre's insight into self in *The Sweet Dove Died* takes the form of acknowledging her loneliness and deciding to face it with a dignified but grim stoicism. Letty Crowe in *Quartet in Autumn*, faces for a time what seems like no alternatives for her future, then suddenly realizes she has control over her life and that she has infinite possibilities. Finally, Emma Howick's conflict in *A Few Green Leaves* centers on whether she will continue to behave in the coldly objective manner of the anthropologist or turn to the infinitely more appealing freedom available to fiction writers. In the posthumously published novels, Jessie Morrow of *Crampton Hodnet* refuses a proposal of marriage which might have changed her life but retains her personal dignity; Caroline

13

Grimstone of *An Academic Question* withstands her husband's infidelity and finds meaning and purpose in her life; and in *Civil To Strangers*, Cassandra Swan weathers a crisis in her marriage and reaffirms her love. for her husband.

The exception to this pattern occurs in *Jane and Prudence*. While Jane Cleveland is aware of the uneventfulness of her life, she holds no illusion about ever changing it; and while Prudence Bates has a minor blow to her ego when Fabian Driver reveals his intention to marry Jessie Morrow, she recovers swiftly. Neither Jane nor Prudence experiences an emotional crisis anywhere near the proportion of Mildred Lathbury's or Wilmet Forsythe's, for instance. Neither learns anything new about herself. In the end, Jane will continue playing matchmaker and being delightfully wry and witty, while Prudence fully intends to continue becoming involved in relationships which are doomed from the beginning.

Recurring devices in Pym's fiction include references to seasons, nature and church events that provide a framework useful for moving the story forward. They also become metaphors for conditions of the heart. Thus, Belinda Bede's passion for Henry Hoccleve has "mellowed into a comfortable feeling, more like the cosiness of a winter evening by the fire than the uncertain rapture of a spring morning" (**STG** 17), and the same kinds of descriptions appear in *Crampton Hodnet* as well. In that novel, Jessie Morrow embraces a tree in genuine delight that she had not precipitately accepted Mr. Latimer's proposal of marriage. In her own diary, Pym wrote several years after *Crampton Hodnet*, on April 27, 1943: "The beech trees are out in tender green leaves--the spinster feels like going rushing into the garden and embracing them, crying Thank you. *Thank* you. You at least do what is expected of you and never fail" (**MS PYM** 108). Church events also provide a structure for many of the novels, so that attendance at midnight mass, the rituals surrounding Easter, even daily morning and evening services, are touchstones in the lives of some characters and are useful events for creating particular scenes. Many of the novels,

14

for instance, narrate the ways in which characters spend Christmas and Boxing days. Although none of the characters is so preoccupied with churches as Edwin Braithwaite in *Quartet in Autumn*, who at one point rattles off a catalogue of the church calendar much as one would recite a rosary, several are devoted church goers and govern their lives by "the soothing rhythm of the church's year" which Edwin would wish for Letty **(QA** 73). In *Crampton Hodnet*, Mr. Latimer's taking too long for a walk in the woods results in his missing evening service and leads to the complicated story about a fictional village that provides the name of the novel.

Other recurring devices include detailed descriptions of food, clothes, and color as those things reflect character. Both Harriet and Belinda Bede in *Some Tame Gazelle* are quite fussy about the meals they prepare for others, Harriet's interest being curates and Belinda's her sewing woman. Almost all of the novels contain a chapter in which someone entertains, and what to serve guests becomes supremely important. Entire menus are supplied, along with remarks about the scarcity or plentifulness of particular foods. In *Quartet in Autumn*, one's interest in food even reflects one's mental health. In contrast to Letty Crowe's pleasure in eating and her hearty appetite, Marcia Ivory completely disregards food, drinking a cup of weak tea daily and eating an occasional pilchard from a tin left over from when her cat was alive or crumbs of bread encrusted with green mold. While Letty's prospects for her future grow brighter in the course of the novel, Marcia literally starves herself to death.

The food one selects to serve at parties and to guests as well as what one eats alone also indicates a great deal about character. Thus, Miss Prior in *Some Tame Gazelle* praises the meals Belinda Bede serves in contrast to the very poor offerings of Agatha Hoccleve. Harriet, a robust woman who appreciates good food, is astonished and perplexed by the knowledge that Bishop Grote never eats anything with tea: "Now this was exceedingly awkward, for how can any real contact be established between two persons when one is eating and the other merely

15

watching?", she wonders (193). In *Excellent Women*, Mildred offers Rocky a lunch of lettuce dressed "with a little of my hoarded olive oil and some salt. I also had a Camembert cheese, a fresh loaf and a bowl of greengages for dessert" (156). In contrast, eating alone after the Napiers have moved away, Mildred eats a melancholy lunch: "A dried-up scrap of cheese, a few lettuce leaves for which I could not be bothered to make any dressing, a tomato and a piece of bread-and-butter, followed by a cup of coffee made with coffee essence. A real *woman's* meal" (174). In every novel, at least one dinner party occupies a chapter, with much discussion of what to serve in light of guests' preferences. Certain guests require certain foods, with a bird of some kind, usually chicken, always appropriate for the clergy. Pym was even given to describing her writing process in culinary terms. Explaining to Caroline Moorhead in a *Times* interview what she did with the material in her notebooks, she said she "'boiled it all up and reduced it, like making chutney'" (11).

In addition to food, one's dress is often commented on and achieves such importance that it plays a part in the opening sentence of *Some Tame Gazelle*: "The new curate seemed quite a nice young man, but what a pity it was that his combinations showed" (7). While such matters are seemingly superficial trivialities, they very often reflect character and indicate levels of self-esteem. Pym's attention to such details as clothes and food is consistent with her belief in the importance of small details. The personalities of Belinda and Harriet Bede are contrasted in the opening scene of *Some Tame Gazelle* by their dress, for instance. The quiet, self-effacing Belinda wears her customary blue marocain, "a rather dim dress," while the bubbly, vivacious Harriet appears "radiant in flowered voile. Tropical flowers rioted over her plump body. The background was the green of the jungle, the blossoms were crimson and mauve, of an unknown species" (11). One passage in *Crampton Hodnet* is riotously colorful as it seeks to explain the contrast between the impulse to buy bright, flowerlike colors to match the exuberant feelings spring

16

brings, and the reality of what customers end up buying once inside the store:

> Out would come the old fawn, mud, navy, dark brown, slate and clerical greys, all the colours they always had before and without which they would hardly have felt like them selves. It would probably be raining tomorrow, and grey, fawn or bottle green was suitable for all weathers, whereas daffodil yellow, leaf green, hyacinth blue or coral pink would look unsuitable and show the dirt. (67)

In *Excellent Women*, when Mildred first meets Helena Napier, Helena is wearing "corduroy trousers and a bright jersey" in contrast to Mildred's "shapeless overall and old fawn skirt" (7). Worse than wearing the kind of clothes Mildred selects, however, is Winifred Malory's practice of selecting the best of the jumble sale contributions for herself, usually ill-suited costumes which "swamp" individuality. Daphne Dagnall, another woman living with and looking after her brother, does the same in *A Few Green Leaves*. Jane Cleveland's nonchalance about both clothing and food earn the disapproval of her husband's parishioners and occasionally makes her feel derelict in her duty as a clergyman's wife. But her laxity in these matters that everyone else takes so seriously is overshadowed by her sparkling personality and is a refreshing contrast to the elegant, perfectly dressed, heavily made up Prudence Bates.

That "clothes make the woman" is repeatedly stressed in Pym's novels. In *An Academic Question*, Caroline Grimstone often feels that something is wrong with her because she cannot dress in the sophisticated way Coco and Kitty Jeffreys think she ought to, but when she attends the Clovis memorial service wearing a suit with the popular longer skirt, the outfit seems just right, perhaps "even a little too smart, and that gave [her] a feeling of well-being unusual these days" (93). Accessories such as hats and shoes are just as important. Calling on Margaret Cleveland in order to tell her that her husband has run off with Barbara Bird, Miss Doggett in *Crampton Hodnet* wears "a terrifyingly new hat trimmed with a whole covey of cyclamen-coloured birds," while Jessie Morrow is "her usual drably comforting self" (198). Mildred Lathbury at one point in *Excellent Women* remarks that Allegra Gray's fruit-trimmed hat is much smarter and more unusual than her own rather conventional flower-decorated hat. Mildred even becomes depressed about her underwear: "Just the kind of underclothes a person like me might wear, I thought dejectedly, so there is no need to describe them" (85). When Belinda Bede thinks, "If only one could clear out one's mind and heart as ruthlessly as one did one's wardrobe" (**STG** 220), the comparison is not surprising, given the importance Pym places on clothes.

Another aspect of Pym's novels is that they seem not to conclude definitely, ending as they do with the implication that something is just about the happen, but they do have conflicts and patterns. The novels reflect the way she saw real life, and she was immensely curious about what was going on around her. Dulcie Mainwaring in *No Fond Return of Love* reminds one of the young Pym at Oxford, devising means to identify the handsome young Henry Harvey and then following him to his lodgings, or the older Pym, keeping tabs on the comings and goings of neighbors. Dulcie performs some real detective work to discover the interests of Aylwin Forbes and then tracks down his brother and finally his mother. Dulcie also finds herself in the kind of comic situation Pym is fond of creating. In Mrs. Forbes' hotel at Tavistock, Dulcie is caught in a potentially awkward but advantageous situation when, crouching behind a screen in an effort to locate a book, she overhears Aylwin and Marjorie discussing the best way to terminate their marriage. Pym had used this idea of crouching behind something before in *Crampton Hodnet* when Francis Cleveland and Barbara Bird hide behind a bush in an effort to escape the notice of Michael and Gabriel. It is more successful and comic in *Some Tame Gazelle*, when Belinda Bede, having only moments before been waxing philosophical as she compares the ability of the human heart to mend with the wonderful way plants survive hardships, is forced to crouch behind a rhododendron bush to avoid being seen by Nathaniel Mold.

Lurking behind some convenient object allows one to eavesdrop, to overhear what goes on between people who think they are alone. A similar device is Pym's characters' habit of peering through people's windows. In *A Few Green Leaves*, Tom Dagnall, wandering around the village looking for something to occupy him, stares in through Emma Howick's cottage window. Suddenly, she appears with a mousse in her hands and the two exchange looks. The moment is fixed, like the mold Emma holds, solidified: the two are "involved in a confrontation" that neither has expected (30). There is nothing to do but smile and acknowledge one another. This is the sort of happenstance which brings many of Pym's characters together, the chance encounter that might lead to something, as it does eventually with Emma and Tom, or to nothing, as it does for Norman and Marcia in *Quartet in Autumn* when Norman finds himself standing across the street from Marcia's home and sees her coming out of her shed. For a moment, they stand staring at one another. But neither acknowledges the other and in a few moments Marcia is denying she even knows Norman. Other characters, like Jane Cleveland and Dulcie Mainwaring, peep into the windows of strangers, hoping to glimpse a bit of other people's lives. It is a device Pym was fond of, for she used it in *Civil to Strangers*, when Cassandra catches Stefan Tilos looking through her husband's study window; in the *Home Front Novel*, when both the curate Michael Randolph and Agnes Grote are in the habit of suddenly appearing in people's french windows, catching them off guard; and in *An Academic Question*, when Alan and Caroline Grimstone are startled by Rollo Gaunt's sudden appearance at the window in Alan's study at the back of the house. Like Pym, many of her characters are inordinately curious about what other people do behind their closed doors. One senses something of Barbara Pym herself in them, or in a character like Senhor MacBride-Pereira, who views the world from his window and wonders what, if anything, he has missed.

There is another pattern to the novels: usually new people arrive on the scene to temporarily alter the normal routine. It was a device Pym used in the very early novel, *Civil to Strangers*, when the Hungarian Stefan Tilos arrives to inhabit Holmwood. In *Some Tame Gazelle*, two men come to the village and threaten Belinda's happy stability by proposing marriage. In *Excellent Women*, the arrivals of the Napiers and Allegra Grey produce the conflict, while in *Jane and Prudence*, the Clevelands themselves move to a new community. In *Less Than Angels*, Tom Mallow's return after a long absence precipitates the novel's action; in *A Glass of Blessings*, the arrival of the new curate Father Ransome and Wilmet's meeting Piers Longridge again after a long time begin the novel. In *No Fond Return of Love*, Dulcie Mainwaring actively seeks a change in her life and new people by attending the learned conference at which she meets Viola Dace and Aylwin Forbes, while Rupert Stonebird has just moved into the neighborhood at the beginning of *An Unsuitable Attachment*. *The Sweet Dove Died* opens with Leonora Eyre meeting James and Humphrey Boyce. *Quartet in Autumn* differs from the formula, with new people only tangentially related to the conflict, but *A Few Green Leaves* returns to the old pattern, as Emma Howick, new to the village, looks forward to meeting its inhabitants.

Pym is able to find humor in just about every character and event. Her treatment of otherwise pathetic or sad situations is gentle, subtle and understated, seldom acrylic. She wrote to Paul De Angelis at Dutton, for instance, that "it is the comedy and irony of the situation of the four people in *Quartet in Autumn* that I had in mind when I was writing the book" (**MS PYM** 164, fol. 167). Thus, in *Less Than Angels* the description of the room at the Institute which has become a "general dumping-ground for unwanted anthropological specimens" might also apply to the people who gather there, former students who have "nowhere else to go, ... shabby hangers-on" (48-49). Occasionally a reader may laugh out loud when reading her novels, but more often she is smiling.

Pym is master of the short, vividly descriptive and funny scene, as in *Crampton Hodnet* when Barbara Bird, standing in the lobby of the hotel in Dover where she and Nicholas Cleveland have gone, looks around her:

> She saw that the room was decorated with stiff palms in brass pots and that, grouped in a corner, as if for artistic effect, were a number of old people reading the newspapers. They looked as if they had been left there many years ago and abandoned. Or perhaps they were people who at some time long past had intended to go abroad and had then either not wanted to or forgotten all about it, so that they had stayed here ever since, like fossils petrified in stone. (188)

Often these vignettes are brief, consisting of the sort of thing one would observe in passing but never be given an explanation for, as in *Less Than Angels*, when Alaric Lydgate and Catherine Oliphant run into Mortimer Jessop and his sister. As they are parting, Mortimer suddenly whispers to Alaric: "'By the way, who *was* that dwarf I saw you with on the road in '45?'" (158). Occasionally Pym cannot resist a line like that following Father Anstruther's wondering, in *An Unsuitable Attachment*, who used to make the delicious fairies for church bazaars: "'Why, Father, it was Mother,'" said Sister Dew oddly (66). Then there is the witnessing of the sort of bizarre thing that one feels simultaneously fascinated and repelled by, as in *No Fond Return of Love*, when Dulcie gets off a bus behind three elderly ladies, "one of whom, when she turned round, was seen to be startlingly bearded" (194).

Pym's central character heroines frequently have Pym's witty and wry sense of humor. Jessie Morrow in *Crampton Hodnet*, for instance, tells Stephen Latimer that "'there are no sick people in North Oxford. They are either dead or alive. It's sometimes difficult to tell the difference, that's all'" (32). Cassandra Swan, narrator of the spy novel *So Very Secret*, reflects on a young man with political ambitions who is rummaging through his aunt's closet that "this ruthlessness with other people's property was rather a good sign in a budding politician" (**CS** 305). *In Less Than Angels*, Catherine Oliphant replies to Mrs. Beddoes' complaint that girls seem to be getting so enormous: "'And to think that they grew up under the Labour Government and austerity'" (137).

Furthermore, Pym's delightful practice of having characters reappear in subsequent novels, besides giving a certain amount of pleasure to readers who have already met the characters, functions to establish a kind of fictional reality, in which the characters exist not just in the novel in which they first appear but before the novel opens and after it ends as well. In *Jane and Prudence*, Prudence and Geoffrey Manifold have dinner in a quiet restaurant in Soho. As they study the menu, they are suddenly embarrassed by a man from the next table who comes to offer them advice on what to order. The entire scene takes a scant half page and is wonderfully comic, but the humor is enriched when one knows that this strange, fussy man is William Caldicote from *Excellent Women* and that this is the same restaurant he and Mildred Lathbury dine at on their annual outing together.

But the most frequently recurring character is Esther Clovis, so that news of her death in *A Few Green Leaves* is met with the feeling that one has lost an old friend. It is comforting to attend her memorial service, for there one hears the remarks of Digby Fox, now a professor, and sees people one has not seen nor thought of for some time-- Deirdre Swan, Dr. Apfelbaum, and Gertrude Lydgate. Catherine Oliphant in *Less Than Angels* believes that each of us is alone in this world and that we can never truly know our fellow humans completely. We can be compassionate and understanding, however, seeking the fellowship of others as a kind of buffer against that loneliness. Pym's practice of having characters reappear, more than once, is reassuring: it establishes their continuity and implies a larger world populated by people who do not cease to exist at the end of the novel in which they are introduced. They marry and have children, or they remain single and childless; but they live and die

22

nonetheless, just as people in reality do. Their familiarity gives readers the sense of fellowship and camaraderie that makes opening any one of Barbara Pym's novels, peopled by old friends and comic new ones, a joy.

Another aspect of Pym's humor is her skill at comic juxtapositions. In *Less Than Angels*, for instance, at a dinner party given by Mabel Swan and Rhoda Wellcome, the topic of what people in Africa eat and the manner in which they prepare their food comes up. When Deirdre recounts a film she saw at an Anthropology Club meeting in which aborigines simply flung a kangaroo on the fire and cooked it without skinning it, Rhoda breaks in with, "'Now who would like some potato salad?'" (147). In *A Glass of Blessings*, Wilf Bason's tea with Wilmet and Rodney Forsythe is interrupted by news of the death of Ella Beamish. Wilf remarks that "'it was really rather upsetting though, hearing the news like that--one always wonders who will be the next to go. Now, Mrs. Forsythe, what did you think of my meringues?'" (114). These scenes are written for their comic element alone, but often Pym will use comic relief following an especially sober observation. When Jessie Morrow conjectures that Lady Beddoes appears to be the kind of woman who has not had all she expected out of life and has now given up hope, she falls to musing over what one could in general hope for, "if there *was* anything. But was there? And if there was anything, wasn't it often much less than people expected? Wasn't it moments, single hours and days, rather than months and years?" (**CH** 119). This serious observation--which is, in fact, a statement of the way in which many of Pym's characters have come to regard life--is followed by the information that Jessie is pondering it "with her mouth full of ham and beetroot and rather tough lettuce" and that by the time the cornflour blancmange has arrived, she has abandoned her search for a satisfactory answer (119). Hilary Walton, Barbara Pym's sister, has said that what she especially misses is her sister's sense of humor. She recalls laughing a good deal with Barbara, who always saw the comic side of every situation.[3]

laughing a good deal with Barbara, who always saw the comic side of every situation.[5]

Pym's novels are not unrelentingly comic, however, for she can be quite serious. In a letter to Philip Larkin, she refers to something as "a rich subject for fiction if one can look at it with a novelist's cruelly dispassionate eye, as I fear I sometimes can" (**VPE** 273). She apparently felt that at times her detachment became too severe, almost cruel, as it sometimes does when characters seem almost too removed from their experiences. Pym also, though rarely, can be vicious, as in this description in *Excellent Women* of women applying makeup in a department store Ladies Room:

> Inside it was a sobering sight indeed and one to put us all in mind of the futility of material things and of our own mortality. *All flesh is but as grass* ... I thought, watching the women working at their faces with savage concentration, opening their mouths wide, biting and licking their lips, stabbing at their noses and chins with powder-puffs. Some, who had abandoned the struggle to keep up, sat in chairs, their bodies slumped down, their hands resting on their parcels. One woman lay on a couch, her hat and shoes off, her eyes closed. I tiptoed past her with my penny in my hand. (131)

The language in this passage is loaded with violence: "savage," "biting," "stabbing." Furthermore, the chief image of the passage is death, from the "sobering sight" which reminds us of our mortality and the Biblical reference which might be used at a burial service, to the reference to placing pennies on the eyes of the dead. While Pym is frequently ironic and close to sarcastic at times, this sardonic quality darkens only the occasional scene. The effect is jarring because she uses it so sparingly.

Detailing further the lives of the "shabby hangers-on" who come to the Institute in *Less Than Angels*, the narrator tells us that "they lived in the meaner districts of London or in impossibly remote suburbs on grants which were

Dostoievsky to do justice to their dreadful lives" (49). And in *An Academic Question*, there is an uncharacteristically mean passage following the cremation of Mister Stillingfleet, when Caroline Grimstone, too aware of her own mortality and resenting the old people for reminding her of it, thinks, after a woman in the retirement home complains about contemporary plays: "But they're not meant for you, I wanted to say, you pathetic old creature with your too-bright lipstick and your raddled old face. Nothing's meant for you now" (53). There is an edge of something very dark indeed in these passages, the kind of nervous laughter that borders on hysteria, as in *Quartet in Autumn* when Norman and Edwin find themselves laughing uncontrollably at the pathos of Norman watching Marcia's house.

Pym has been accused by some readers and critics of writing about a world which no longer exists and of creating unworldly characters who are charming but lack heights and depths of emotions. Charles Burkhart in *The Pleasure of Miss Pym*, for example, calls her first novel, *Some Tame Gazelle*, "a fantasy, never-never novel" (22), and Eve Auchincloss, reviewing her last novel, *A Few Green Leaves*, for *The New York Times Book Review*, remarks that spinsterhood is "a condition little known in the modern world but a constant in Barbara Pym's novels" (9). This is not to say that Pym's reviewers and critics are unkind to her but simply to point out that some regard her subject matter, however well handled, as simply being irrelevant to the contemporary world or out of date. But *Some Tame Gazelle* is not fantasy. It is a touching account of the daily lives of vividly realized and true-to-life characters. The novel is more than a harmless idyllic fantasy of a world that never was. It introduces themes and character types who reappear again and again throughout Pym's canon, from the everyday concerns of the meek, excellent unmarried woman who wistfully loves from afar to the intricacies of social relationships, church activities, and personal responses to change. Even more to the point is the fact that the characters are all based on real people, albeit people projected some decades into the future, and are rooted in observed reality. Furthermore, "spinsterhood," perhaps not a word much in vogue among the young today, is a concept very much alive in many quarters, and certainly in the generation and society that Pym wrote about.

The prevailing image of spinsters for centuries in both British and American literature had been to denigrate them. Usually they were pitied, ridiculed, or despised, seldom admired and even less frequently emulated.[4] Pym does not follow that tradition but rather explores in detail the effects of the social attitudes of the 1950s about unmarried women on their lives, particularly on their sense of self. What she reveals is a complex, at times ambiguous and conflicting, set of emotions. Thus, while Belinda Bede might see herself as "dowdy and insignificant, one of the many thousand respectable middle-aged spinsters, the backbones or busybodies of countless parishes throughout the country" (STG 176) or even as a pathetic creature, she also good-humored thinks that simply recognizing pathos in oneself might mean that it did not actually exist. Although Pym's spinsters might appear on the surface to conform to certain stereotyped notions about them--their nosiness, their dullness, their settling for less than a full life--in the course of her novels she reveals that they have emotional depths and moral insights that belie those stereotyped assumptions. Jessie Morrow of *Crampton Hodnet* is a good case in point. Although Miss Doggett repeatedly tells her she can know nothing of life, she has moments of worldly insight which would never occur to Miss Doggett: "But of course Simon would never marry Anthea, [Jessie] realised. . . .He wanted to do things that people would remember, great things, and making a woman happy could hardly be called that" (115-16). The boisterous, bossy, self-important Miss Doggett is incapable of having such insights.

While they are regarded by many as defective because they lack husbands, far from feeling sorry for themselves, Pym's unmarried women quietly and sensibly accept the reality of their lives, like Belinda Bede, who had come to appreciate by the age of thirty the meaning of "calm of mind, all passion spent." In her chronicle following her breakup with Gordon Glover, Pym at one point wrote: "It is sometimes intolerable to be a woman and have no second bests or spares or anything. I struggled with this feeling" (**VPE** 119). The result of her struggle was the development of wisdom about life and relationships that carries over into her treatment of single women in her fiction. Her portrayal of the emotional life of spinsters gives attention to badly maligned human beings who had rarely been treated positively in either literature or life. Particularly in the early novels, Pym reveals the way the spinster is firmly regarded by society as an unfortunate person. As the women who do volunteer work, are often faithful churchgoers, and fuss over men, Pym's spinsters provide valuable support services; but as the odd women unable to secure husbands, they suffer reduced status in the social structure. The way the world sees spinsters in Pym's novels, especially in *Excellent Women*, is not much different from the view expressed one hundred years earlier, in 1853, by J.M. Ludlow in the *North British Review*. Ludlow wrote that unmarried women should not write novels. Instead, he noted, they should take upon themselves "'the daily working, the drudgery of all charitable institutions. ... Who does not know some one old maid who is the blessing of a whole circle?'"⁵ As a result of their particular position in society, Pym's central-character unmarried women are able to achieve insight into themselves and others that makes them a real source of strength and comfort. While spinsters have their faults and shortcomings like everyone else, as unmarried women they have the additional misfortune of belonging to the community of the incomplete, the odd, the put upon. It is a community they rather hope to leave, given the bleakness of the adjectives used to characterize their lives: nondescript, bland, anonymous. If leaving this community means shouldering a new responsibility, as it does for Mildred Lathbury of *Excellent Women*, then one does it "bravely and cheerfully." Pym does not ask for pity but rather for understanding and even admiration of these women.

27

Pym's novels of the 1970s give lipservice to the changed social attitude about unmarried women, but the older generations she portrays still cling to the earlier views that women were not complete until they had married. Pym had begun early in life to half-jokingly, half-seriously identify with the kind of dependable but dull, slightly odd excellent women she wrote about. In 1939, at age twenty-five, she referred to herself in a letter to Elsie Harvey as an old spinster "already rather queer in the head" (VPE 88), and she continued to make such references thereafter. But perhaps because of that identification with spinsters, Pym refused to continue the long-standing literary tradition of pitying and ridiculing them. If they appear ridiculous occasionally, it is only because everyone in her novels is seen to be just slightly dotty at times. The sensible, steadfast characters are, for the most part, Pym's unmarried central characters, while not one of the men they love is equal to them in strength of character, in intelligence, or in compassion for others. Pym treats her unmarried women with humor and irony, but there is an undercurrent of poignancy, an understatement of quiet desperation, about them nonetheless. Their resignation to the inevitable predictability of life is typical of Pym's spinsters, though it is a bemused resignation, a wistful acceptance of lost opportunity combined with a cheerful determination to "make do."

But it is not only Pym's spinsters who have resigned themselves to uneventful lives. A dominant theme throughout the canon is this idea that many people have missed something that would have made their lives fuller. Cassandra Marsh-Gibbon in *Civil To Strangers*, for instance, would seem to have a full life taking care of her handsome husband, but she is reminded by the rector that her life is missing a child. The novel concludes happily with the pregnant Cassandra anticipating life with her child-husband as well as an infant. While Belinda in *Some Tame Gazelle* seems to have all she needs in life with her beloved Henry and her greater English poets, in *Crampton Hodnet*, the idea of something missing recurs throughout. We are told, for instance, that Margaret Cleveland never even

28

stops to consider if she is missing anything in her life, implying that there may very well be something, and Jessie Morrow is sure that Mrs. Beddoes has missed something, though Jessie never can determine just what it is that makes one's life complete. Francis Cleveland certainly feels he is missing affection and attention in his marriage, which drives him to his liaison with Barbara Bird. Mildred Lathbury in *Excellent Women* becomes fully conscious of the voids in her emotional life. In *Jane and Prudence*, Prudence thinks that Jane seems to have missed something, particularly as her studies of obscure seventeenth-century poets have come to nothing. At the same time, while Prudence thinks her own life is rich and full of promise, Jane regards Prudence as needing a husband to bring fullness to her life. The question of what makes a full life recurs throughout Pym's novels, with no really satisfactory answer other than the obvious, that one settles for less than one might have and enjoys what compensations one can find.

It is not surprising that a recurring motif in the novels is the idea of spent passion, the way the fires of youthful love settle into a cozy fondness. While one hesitates to draw too much from the life of the writer when trying to understand her fiction, Barbara Pym's own experiences very much influenced her creative work. One sees how her early intense love affairs and their bitter endings become subjects of her fiction, for instance. Thus a diary entry following her affair with Gordon Glover in which she writes of the small compensations and spinsterish delights as the years pass by becomes more interesting in light of the frequent references in her novels to small sources of pleasure. Belinda Bede in *Some Tame Gazelle* for example, is moved to tears of joy when Miss Prior, whom she worries excessively about offending, takes the matter of a dead caterpillar in her cauliflower in her stride, complimenting Belinda on the quality of her meals in general: "Her heart like a singing bird, and all because Agatha didn't keep as good a table as she did and Miss Prior had forgiven her for the caterpillar, and the afternoon sun streaming in through the window over it all"

(52). One does not have to be unmarried to experience such elation over seemingly small matters. Jane Cleveland, immensely relieved to learn that Mr. Mortlake has come to tune her piano, not chide her for speaking out when she ought not to have, picks up his hat, places it on her head, pirouettes around the hall, sings a tune, and fairly frightens away a young man who calls at that moment.

Naming Pym's best work is far less difficult than choosing a favorite Pym novel. *Quartet in Autumn* is a masterpiece, perfectly conceived and brilliantly executed. It is a skillfully crafted work, chilling in effect: characters are fully realized, the plot moves effortlessly and inevitably to a wonderfully satisfying if nonetheless slightly unsettling conclusion, and it is a powerful rendering of the pathos and humor of aging people in an increasingly disturbing world. These are qualities which transcend the boundaries of the novel itself and touch something deep in the human heart. It is easy to see why that novel was short-listed for the Booker Prize. On the other hand, *Some Tame Gazelle* has an exuberance that never ages, a comedy as fresh after a dozen readings as after one, and a gentle and loving tone that makes it a comfort to read. Similarly, *Less Than Angels* is a rollicking good dig at anthropologists and has some uproariously funny scenes--the one in which Digby and Mark have lunch with Miss Clovis and Miss Lydgate is unmatchable. It also has one of Pym's most sensitive and self-sufficient female characters, Catherine Oliphant.

Perhaps more than anything else, the strength of Pym's novels resides in her female central characters, of whom Catherine Oliphant is eminently representative: she is a resourceful, competent, and independent woman who recognizes the need to love and be loved. For the skill which finally separates Barbara Pym from the mass of writers is her ability to elevate the most ordinary of human beings into compelling and poignant characters. Although she relies at times on stereotypes and caricatures, Pym takes those characters who might have been treated in a shallow manner by a lesser writer and turns them into intelligent, compassionate, vulnerable in some ways, and immensely likeable people. Jessie Morrow of *Crampton*

Hodnet, Belinda Bede, Mildred Lathbury, Catherine Oliphant, Jane Cleveland, Wilmet Forsythe, Dulcie Mainwaring, Letty Crowe and Emma Howick are vividly drawn individuals who possess admirable traits as well as typical human weaknesses. They want, perhaps, too much, like Flora Palfrey in the very early novel *Gervase and Flora*, who prays "that she might be good and kind and helpful and unselfish and self-controlled and brave. That was plenty, she thought with a sigh" (CS 214). Indeed, it is plenty, and Barbara Pym's central character heroines are blessed with just the qualities that Flora Palfrey prays for.

TWO

RIDICULOUS, REALLY, THE RELATIONSHIP

BETWEEN MEN AND WOMEN

The relationship between men and women is central to Barbara Pym's novels, the intricacies of plot and subplot revolving around potential matches and mismatches between any number of pairs of males and females. Although many her characters want very much to be loved and married, Pym's portrayal of such relationships makes one wonder why they bother. "Love" is a word Pym frequently uses to describe how men and women feel about one another, but it is a passionless emotion, seldom emerging in any of the characters as a genuinely felt experience. Marriages are often slightly antagonistic arrangements whereby each spouse has learned to tolerate the other's idiosyncrasies. Men are ineffectual, childish creatures who want women to be little more than domestic servants and clerical help, believing such services are their due and taking for granted that women should devote themselves exclusively to their needs. Women are defined in relationship to men and most have accepted the prevailing social belief that a woman is not fulfilled until she has married. According to a widely held notion, it is, as Mildred Lathbury of *Excellent Women* reflects, the wedding ring on the left hand that proves one's worth as a human being, no matter how dull the man one manages to marry. It becomes clear, then, why both men and women seek relationships: men are privileged by them and women are validated by them. Pym underscores the absurdity of this narrow view with wit and humor. Her image of relationships more often than not is like the observation of Beatrix Howick when she tells her daughter Emma, who has just described Graham Pettifer's spending the night in her cottage as "'ridiculous, really'": "'Well, in a way, that's what it is, isn't it, the relationship between men and women'" (**FGL** 98).

There are two kinds of women in Pym's novels, both of whom are defined by their connection to men: the married--including widowed--and the unmarried. Women like Prudence Bates who flit from romance to romance are not typical. As her friend Eleanor Hitchens puts it, one has to eventually settle down to being either spinster or wife. Both married and unmarried women alike can be irritatingly preoccupied with deferring to men, serving them, and inflating their already healthy egos, but the unmarried woman is Pym's special province. The spinster is a type seldom given such full treatment elsewhere in literature and is perfected in *Some Tame Gazelle* and *Excellent Women*, in the characters of Belinda Bede and Mildred Lathbury. Other women in subsequent novels, no matter how bright or well-educated, never quite rid themselves of the compulsion to serve men the way these spinsters do. Of Pym's thirteen novels, ten feature unmarried women. Only *Civil to Strangers*, *A Glass of Blessings*, and *An Academic Question* have married central characters. In *Jane and Prudence*, there are two central characters, one married and the other unmarried. The pervading image one retains of Pym's unmarried women is that of the self-sacrificing, self-denigrating, second class woman. It is an unfortunate picture, for most of the women display a courage and mettle that the stereotype belies.

One needs to remember that most of the novels published in Pym's lifetime were written during the 1950s, before the contemporary women's movement, and that although she makes passing references, largely negative, to

34

women's equality, her female characters belong to pre-liberation days. When she first began writing novels as a young woman, "spinster" was viewed by many as an almost dirty word. During the period in which she was growing up and attending Oxford University, there was a large imbalance in the sex ratio in England. According to a study by Jane Lewis of women in England between 1870 and 1950, English women who were not married by their late twenties would very likely never marry. Lewis discovered that "of those women who were single and in their late twenties in 1921, 50 percent were unmarried a decade later,"[1] a figure that is particularly striking "when compared with that for men, of whom only 30 percent failed to marry."[2] According to Lewis, because of the keen competition for husbands, spinsterhood was often called a "'failure in business' in middle class households."[3] Pym's novels proclaim this imbalance quite clearly: there are close to twice as many women as there are men. Furthermore, unmarried and widowed women outnumber married women by about five to one, while unmarried or widowed men outnumber married men by about three to one. Pym comically reflects this unequal distribution of men and women in her very early novel *Civil to Strangers*, when the English people Cassandra Marsh-Gibbon joins for safe-keeping from Stefan Tilos is a tour group composed of three clergymen, three clergymen's wives, three widows, and eight spinsters. When Flora points out to her mother in *Jane and Prudence* that, at Prudence's age, the supply of available men is not what it was when she was an undergraduate at Oxford, she is stating a reality of Pym's own life. Despite this imbalance in the numbers of women and men, the general assumption of the society Pym wrote about was that women ought to marry and were not complete human beings if they did not.

It is *Excellent Women* which fully illustrates the dubious benefits and certain drawbacks of being an "excellent woman," though *Crampton Hodnet* and *Some Tame Gazelle* anticipate its major theme and central character. Jessie Morrow, Belinda Bede, and Mildred Lathbury represent the larger group of excellent, unmarried women who populate the novels, women whose merits and private pains Pym treats with gentle humor and loving care. They may be emotionally isolated, but they have vivid inner lives which are ultimately more satisfying than reality. They make well-intentioned efforts to bring meaning and usefulness to their lives, usually by performing any number of trivial tasks for others. They see love relationships with men as beyond them now that they are over thirty, and all are astonished, a little flattered, but largely flustered when men actually pay attention to them. It is precisely because they are not threatening to men that these women are able to sustain comfortable relationships with them. For instance, Mr. Latimer, who does not mind women fussing over him as long as they do not expect to get anything in return, regards Jessie Morrow as if she were some comfortable, familiar inanimate object. He is prompted to propose marriage to her because he feels she might be some protection against the onslaught of women he is growing weary of.

All three women have characteristics in common. Belinda Bede is somewhat timid, wears sensible, sturdy shoes, and is not quite as clever nor nearly as striking in appearance as her sister Harriet. Jessie Morrow is described as "a thin, used-up- looking woman in her middle thirties" (**CH** 2) who is "a comforting neutral thing, without form or sex" (**CH** 160), while Mildred Lathbury tells us that she is mousy and plain and has long ago accepted the uneventfulness of her life. All three women are useful to others and are regarded as splendid, excellent, and highly esteemed, characteristics which they find less than flattering for what those words imply about their lack of sensuality and appeal. Belinda Bede, for example, thinks that the new curate's remark about her having done a lot of good work in the parish makes her sound "almost unpleasant" (**STG** 10). She becomes defensive when the Archdeacon makes fun of Father Plowman's parish being almost entirely composed of spinsters and reflects bitterly on the Archdeacon's words when he describes her to Bishop Grote as an excellent person.

The words "respect and esteem" take on such negative connotations that Pym uses them as the title of a hilarious chapter in *Crampton Hodnet* when Mr. Latimer proposes to and is rejected by Jessie Morrow. Her response to his proposal is to suggest that he is over-tired and needs some Ovaltine. When he presses the issue, declaring that he respects and esteems her, she points out that those feelings do not constitute love and that he would soon regret having married her. After he leaves the room, understandably deflated, Jessie has these thoughts about the proposal: "A man had asked her to marry him and she had refused. But did a trapped curate count as a man? ... 'I respect and esteem you very much.... I think we might be very happy together....' *Might*. Oh, no, it wouldn't do at all! Even Miss Morrow's standards were higher than that.... For she wanted love ... and she knew perfectly well that she would never get anything like that" (94). Jessie has the wisdom to appreciate the inappropriateness of Latimer's proposal: she knows both of them would be miserable were she to accept it. Furthermore, she wants far more than he is offering. She wants romance, the flushed exuberance and hope that spring brings:

It was only sometimes, when a spring day came in the middle of the winter, that one had a sudden feeling that nothing was really impossible. And then, how much more sensible it was to satisfy one's springlike impulses by buying a new dress in an unaccustomed and thoroughly unsuitable colour than by embarking on a marriage without love. For, after all, respect and esteem were cold, lifeless things--dry bones picked clean of flesh. There was nothing springlike about dry bones, nothing warm and romantic about respect and esteem. (94)

Like Jessie Morrow, Belinda Bede receives a totally unexpected proposal of marriage and turns it down. When Bishop Grote proposes to Belinda, she tells him quite frankly that she cannot marry him because she does not love him. Jessie and Belinda are not desperate women.

Both Bishop Grote and Mr. Latimer have selected these women because they want wives who will be useful, safe, serving, and self-sacrificing. Thus, when Belinda rejects Bishop Grote, his only thought is that he must hurry on in order to get his round of calls made. Later, he proposes to Connie Aspinall, who eagerly and happily accepts in order to escape her misery in Edith Liversidge's home. Mr. Latimer, on the other hand, at first seems really to feel dejected, but before long he has found a car to occupy himself. Pym repeats the image of dry bones for respect and esteem in *Excellent Women*, when Everard and Mildred are discussing the kind of person Everard would marry. When Everard says that he respects and esteems Esther Clovis, Mildred replies: "'Oh, respect and esteem-- such dry bones! I suppose one can really have such feelings for somebody but I should have thought one would almost dislike a person who inspired them'" (190). One suspects Pym of choosing Everard Bone's name precisely because of this "dry bones" image it evokes. Ordinarily "excellence," "respect" and "esteem" are desirable qualities, but for the men who use the words, they carry no emotional value. When they apply to an unmarried woman for whom romance seems unlikely, they are bitter reminders of her marked difference from the less-than-excellent but decidedly fortunate married women.

Some Tame Gazelle is populated with fictionalized versions of Barbara Pym herself, her sister Hilary and her circle of Oxford friends, projected some thirty years in the future. The novel was conceived for her friends' amusement when she was twenty-two, was revised extensively over the next fifteen years, and finally was published in 1950. Belinda and Harriet Bede are Barbara and Hilary Pym and Archdeacon Henry Hoccleve is Pym's adored Henry Harvey. Between the time of the novel's inception and its publication, Pym had experienced a brief but happy love affair with a young man several years her junior, Julian Amery, and then an intense but again brief love affair with Gordon Glover which left her so devastated when it ended that she joined the WRNS in order to help her get over the pain. Belinda Bede's quiet acceptance of her unrequited love for the Archdeacon and her preference for "the cosiness of a winter evening by the fire" versus the "uncertain rapture of a spring morning" (17) suggests that Pym's own experiences had resulted not in bitterness, but in a mellow wisdom about relationships: fierce passion in a one-sided relationship results in pain; better, then, to love quietly, without passion, and live in peace. Belinda would prefer to be a pillar of salt, without feeling, to the pain of loving deeply and actively again.

While both Jessie Morrow and Belinda Bede suggest the type, Mildred Lathbury is really the archetypal excellent woman, the spinster characterized by a self-deprecation and low self-esteem coupled with a self-sufficiency and competency in handling crises that make her a valuable, if secondary, addition to society. On the surface, Mildred's life is quiet and uneventful, which often seems to imply a limited inner life as well. Mildred does, in fact, at first seem to conform to all the stereotyped notions about spinsters--their nosiness, their dullness, their settling out of necessity for less than a full life--especially as she is a clergyman's daughter. But she dislikes this image of herself. The role of excellent woman is not at all pleasing to Mildred: she is dissatisfied with bearing the burden of "doing for" everyone else. The very image of Mildred with a tea pot in her hand in moments of crisis is as distressing to Mildred herself as it is comforting to those she pours for. However, it has been so deeply ingrained in her to serve others that when she finally refuses to do something she has been asked to do, it greatly troubles her. Toward the end of the novel when Everard invites her to dinner, Mildred makes up an excuse not to go because she thinks she will be asked to cook the meat and is depressed by that prospect. Later she feels so guilty that she finally goes to his home for dinner, fully expecting to cook it as well. Her surprise at not having to do so predisposes her to agree to proofread and index his book and ultimately, we learn in a later novel, to marry him. Thus, although under Rocky Napier's influence Mildred does manage to become more assertive, going so far as to shock her circle of friends with her changed appearance and her heretical question about the necessity of tea, by the end of the novel she seems destined to go on serving others selflessly.

Despite acknowledging that probably no man was worth all the trouble, Mildred has been conditioned too thoroughly to do otherwise. Her relationship with Everard has made it seem unlikely that she will ever marry him, for she actually dislikes him from the first and must force herself to try to think kindly of him. She does not regard him in the same romantic light as she does Rocky Napier, seeing him in a kind of asexual way, as when she signs her postcard to him "M. Lathbury" and thinks that it could have been either a man or a woman's signature. In *Jane and Prudence*, Miss Doggett passes on the news from Miss Bonner that Mildred has married Everard, and we are told that Mildred has learned to type so that she can type Everard's manuscripts for him. Miss Clovis in *Less Than Angels* remembers Mildred as the dull woman who was a great help to Everard in his work, and in the same novel, Mortimer Jessop and his sister are on their way to lunch with Mrs. Bone, who, Mortimer says, always serves a good meal. Finally, in *An Unsuitable Attachment*, Everard goes to a dinner party without Mildred, who is home with the flu, and seems to forget about her entirely until it is time to leave. These references to Mildred clearly indicate that selflessness continues to characterize Mildred's life after she has married, suggesting too, the aridity of that life.

Mildred is different in a significant way from all the other spinsters. Belinda Bede, for example, cherishes her spinsterish delights and the small compensations of her world. She resists change wholeheartedly, her most energetic actions taken in an effort to maintain life as it always has been. Her world is small, narrow, and limited, like Mildred's, but the crucial difference is that Mildred strongly desires to change her life. While outsiders are a threat to Belinda, they suggest possibilities for expansion to Mildred. Belinda's love for Henry, based on her idealization of him in her youth, lacks vitality and flame, but Mildred's strong infatuation for Rocky stirs in her a deep capacity to feel intensely, wonderfully represented by her brazen purchase of a lipstick in a bright red shade called "Hawaiian Fire." While virtually no male in any of the novels is worthy of the woman who loves him, Mildred's having to settle for being exactly as she was before falling in love with Rocky, especially if she marries Everard, is truly tragic. Mildred does what she can to change herself but in the end is doomed by the limitations of her world to eternal sameness. The cozy comfort of *Some Tame Gazelle* is replaced in *Excellent Women* by a frightening resignation to the static life.

In *Some Tame Gazelle*, there is a simply stunning chapter which illustrates what Belinda holds dear, in contrast to Mildred. Struggling to make ravioli, a process that takes thirty minutes of kneading and pounding to achieve a texture that should resemble the finest chamois leather, Belinda is exhausted after ten minutes of that hard labor. Just then Bishop Grote arrives to propose to her. Belinda is variously described in that brief interlude as "agitated," "alarmed," "miserable," "annoyed," and "horrified." She regards his marriage proposal as "fantastic" and "terrible" and is impatient for Harriet to come talk to her once he has gone. Returning to her ravioli, she is reminded of Keble's lines on "the trivial round, the common task," and wonders if he had "*really* understood.... Belinda imagined him writing the lines in a Gothic study, panelled in pitch-pine and well dusted that morning by an efficient servant. Not at all the same thing as standing at the sink with aching back and hands plunged into the washing-up water" (227). But a few minutes later, Harriet joins her, they discuss the recent turn of events, and the chapter ends with Belinda holding up the sheet of ravioli, beaming with pleasure, joyfully exclaiming that it is "'even finer than the finest chamois leather'" (229). Clearly the pleasure derived from accomplishing a perfect ravioli is more comfort to Belinda than the knowledge that she had been proposed to by a bishop. In contrast, Mildred Lathbury, considering proofreading and indexing for Everard, imagines that before long she would be standing over his sink, peeling potatoes: "Was any man worth this

41

burden? Probably not, but one shouldered it bravely and cheerfully and in the end it might turn out to be not so heavy after all" (**EW** 255). Mildred had earlier revealed that she has "never been very much given to falling in love" but regrets not having had the experience of marriage or "even [the] greater and more ennobling one of having loved and lost." While she has had "a curate or two" and "later a bank-clerk who read the Lessons," none of her feelings had been very deep (**EW** 44). With Rocky she gains the experience she regrets having missed, so that by the end of the novel she is prepared to make a match that is completely lacking in passion. In subsequent novels, the unmarried woman does not long to escape the way Mildred does. Prudence Bates, Catherine Oliphant, Dulcie Mainwaring, and Emma Howick are all reasonably content with their lives, willing to consider changing but not desperate to do so.

Belinda Bede's quiet, self-effacing manner and her deep devotion to the self-indulgent, comic Archdeacon in *Some Tame Gazelle* provides the pattern for love relationships in all the subsequent novels. Typically, Pym's female central characters fall in love with men who are childish, egocentric, and weak. If they are not in love with them, they at least feel an enormous responsibility for them. The Archdeacon is actually a tame version of Adam Marsh-Gibbon of *Civil to Strangers*, whose preening egoism is catered to by his devoted wife Cassandra. In *Crampton Hodnet*, Anthea Cleveland is infatuated with the politically ambitious and callous Simon Beddoes; in *Excellent Women*, Mildred Lathbury is smitten by the dazzling but shallow Rocky Napier, is linked romantically by her circle of friends with the ineffectual vicar Julian Malory, and finally is coupled with the good-looking and intelligent but far from warm Everard Bone. In *Jane and Prudence*, Prudence continues her series of doomed romances with the self-absorbed, handsome Fabian Driver, whose "affections" are finally won by the clever Jessie Morrow. Catherine Oliphant in *Less Than Angels* feels strong motherly impulses not only toward Tom Mallow and Alaric Lydgate but even toward anthropology students

42

Digby Fox and Mark Penfold. Tom Mallow is another attractive man, like Rocky and Fabian, who can give little emotionally to the women who love him, in this case not only Catherine but also Elaine and Deirdre. Wilmet Forsythe in *A Glass of Blessings*, making Piers Longridge her "project" for the fall, becomes infatuated with him and, after the blow of discovering that he is homosexual, feels an immediate affinity for his lover Keith. Dulcie Mainwaring in *No Fond Return of Love* falls in love with Aylwin Forbes, yet another wishy-washy male whose affectations and self-importance are his chief characteristics. The pattern continues with *An Unsuitable Attachment* with Ianthe Broome's engagement to the young, aimless John Challow. In this same novel, Rupert Stonebird, Basil Branche, and Mark Ainger are more variations of the weak, comic, befuddled male. James Boyce of *The Sweet Dove Died* is perhaps the most ambivalent and malleable of all of Pym's men: he is bisexual, impressionable, and extremely weak willed. Even so, the elegant, cool Leonora Eyre finds herself affected by him in a way no other man has touched her, despite the vast difference in their ages. Caroline Grimstone, attempting to be a contemporary woman in *An Academic Question*, is compelled to establish her worth by being of some use to her husband, who is similar in character to Aylwin Forbes. Even in *Quartet in Autumn*, the scenario is repeated in the subplot involving Father Lydell, a middle-aged village vicar devoted to his aging mother, who is the center of a struggle between two older women. Finally, in *A Few Green Leaves*, there are Tom Mallow, a confused, helpless vicar, and Graham Pettifer, a self-centered, self-important researcher. Emma Howick finds herself looking after Graham, making love to him when he wants to, and, once he is gone, turning to Tom, whom her mother can only describe as "ineffectual."

These women are aware of the comic or ridiculous nature of their attraction to these men, as *No Fond Return of Love* illustrates particularly well. When Dulcie begins her investigation of Aylwin Forbes, she is aware of how "ridiculous and impossible" such research is but how powerful an incentive is love (36). It seems barely plausible at this point that Dulcie could love Aylwin, but she has built up her image of him since the learned conference at which she met him to such a degree that she actually believes she may be in love with him. A short time later, having read in *Who's Who* that he has named "conversation and wine" as his recreations, Dulcie is scornful of his affectation: "And for you, she thought, a wife will go back to her mother, an unhappy woman will lie on the grass, wearing red canvas shoes and not caring about anything. And perhaps another--usually so 'sensible'--will begin to think she is falling in love ..." (46). While she can see the "ridiculous" side of relationships, Dulcie manages not to become too jaded. Although she thinks "Really, the ridiculousness of men!" when Bill Sedge quotes poetry to the fascinated Viola Dace, for example, she knows she would have the same look on her face if a man were quoting poetry to her (153). Even Viola Dace, falling in love with Bill Sedge, is aware that "all love had something of the ridiculous in it" (171), a line that Jessie Morrow uses almost word for word in *Crampton Hodnet* (127).

Dulcie has acquired her somewhat sour view of relationships as a result of Maurice Clive's breaking off their engagement. Although she has strength of character enough to recover sensibly--the delightful first line of *No Fond Return of Love* is: "There are various ways of mending a broken heart, but perhaps going to a learned conference is one of the more unusual"--Dulcie's view of her broken engagement is what one might expect, given the general view of themselves held by most of Pym's central character unmarried women. When she meets Maurice for the first time after their break up, she is understandably shaken, but her reaction is not to wonder how she could have loved him; rather, she wonders how he could have considered marrying her. Meeting him plunges her into "a sudden feeling of desolation" and of "sinking down again into that state of lowness that she had hoped never to experience again" (88). But by the time she sees him again, at her dinner party, she can treat lightly Maurice's sudden warmth and his suggesting it had been a mistake to break up. Dulcie's sarcastic thought when he comments that she is different now suggests her realistic view of him: "Yes, she thought, older and duller and with the added interest of being somebody to be won back again" (126).

Dulcie's initial feeling of inadequacy, wondering how Maurice could have loved her, is similar to Catherine Oliphant's feeling responsible for her failed relationship with Tom. Following his death, she feels a "selfish and personal sorrow at the failures in their relationship which had been her fault. How annoying she must sometimes have been with her wild fancies and her quotations!" (**LTA** 235-36). In the same manner, Emma Howick becomes involved with Graham Pettifer again when he comes to live in the village for the summer, though the relationship is nothing like the affair they had had years before and she is critical of his treatment of both her and his wife. Yet, while she jokes to her mother about him and never thinks positively of him, she can wonder at one point if he has decided to make love to her again--as if all that matters is what he wants--and she develops a rash presumably brought on by the stress of their uncertain relationship. Furthermore, when her sympathies go out to Tom Mallow, she reminds herself of what that sort of thing leads to, but then at the end of the novel, she anticipates embarking on a love affair with him. Dulcie, Catherine, and Emma all seem to have a sense that they are unworthy of men but that they should inevitably become involved with them. Almost paradoxically, they are emotionally distanced enough to engage in relationships with men with just the right amount of bemusement and worldliness to prevent there being the least bit of pathos about them.

The opinion that men's needs are superior to or more pressing than the needs of women is reiterated with the same sort of bemusement throughout the novels. Countless women perform domestic tasks and menial clerical labor for men. We see this attitude expressed in Belinda's devotion to Henry Hoccleve and Harriet's to young curates in *Some Tame Gazelle* and in Mildred's falling under Rocky's spell and then acting as drudge for him and Julian, not to mention Everard, in *Excellent Women*. Men are fussed over at meals, given larger portions, and granted special treatment. Mrs. Crampton, who runs an inn with Mrs. Mayhew, automatically gives Nicholas in *Jane and Prudence* two eggs and Jane one and then serves a roast chicken with full accompaniments to Mr. Oliver. The bemused Jane thinks, sarcastically, "Man needs bird.... Just the very best, that is what man needs" (52). Jane, comfortably married and enjoying perhaps the best relationship of any of the married couples in all the novels, repeatedly makes wry observations about the things women will do for men. When she meets Dr. Grampion, with whom Prudence is for the moment in love, she thinks with something like wonder of the splendid things women do for men: "Making them feel ... they were loved and admired and desired when they were worthy of none of these things--enabling them to preen themselves and puff out their plumage like birds and bask in the sunshine of love, real or imagined, it didn't matter which" (75). Judging by the way women fawn over men, this statement is only too accurate. When Digby Fox remarks that Catherine Oliphant is the kind of woman a man wants because she can "'cook *and* type,'" he is being absolutely serious (**LTA** 75).

Mark Penfold's description of what he assumes is the arrangement between Catherine and Tom, though said when he is slightly tipsy and perhaps meant to be tongue-in-cheek, is nonetheless an accurate account of what many men fantasize: "'It would be a reciprocal relationship--the woman giving the food and shelter and doing some typing for him and the man giving the priceless gift of himself.... It is commoner in our society than many people would suppose'" (**LTA** 76). Elsewhere in *Less Than Angels*, the narrator succinctly summarizes the role of women in relation to men when, describing the room at the Institute where former students with nowhere else to go congregate, the narrator tells us that:

> Some of them had been fortunate enough to
> win the love of devoted women--women who

might one day become their wives, but who, if they were thrown aside, would accept their fate cheerfully and without bitterness. They had learned early in life what it is to bear love's burdens, listening patiently to their men's troubles and ever ready at their typewriters, should a manuscript or even a short article get to the stage of being written down. (49)

This passage implies several things about male-female relationships: the control men have over women, the ineffectuality of men to actually produce any substantial work, and the readiness of women to give far more than they can expect to receive. This view is illustrated in Pym's novels in the way many men see their relationships with women: Stephen Latimer, Henry Hoccleve, Everard Bone, Rocky Napier, Fabian Driver, Tom Mallow, Piers Longridge, Aylwin Forbes, Rupert Stonebird, even Tom Dagnall and Graham Pettifer, all expect more of women than they are willing to give.

Men seem helpless because they have never had to do for themselves. In *A Glass of Blessings*, Father Thames pleads in his parish newsletter for someone to replace his housekeeper, for he and Father Bode need someone to cook for them desperately. Likewise, Tom Dagnall in *A Few Green Leaves*, whose sister Daphne had moved in with him when his wife died, wonders what he will do about meals once she has gone. In fact, Tom sees Daphne only for the services she performs: When Daphne comes for a New Year visit, feeling guilty for having left him, his first thought when he sees her arriving is relief that she will make the coffee. Daphne is like Mildred Lathbury in this respect, that while she longs to escape and complains to herself about the drudgery of cooking and cleaning for a man, she will do the work anyhow. Despite Emma's observation that men are not so helpless and cope much better than they used to, Tom is disappointed that people do not rush forward with dinner invitations after his plea for help in his parish newsletter. Even Emma, who thinks "it was a mistaken and old-fashioned concept, the helplessness of men" (145), arranges for Graham Pettifer to have groceries waiting for him when he arrives at the village and can be seen carrying a casserole to him. She sympathizes with Tom's plight, too, but feels she cannot be looking after both men at the same time.

In *Less Than Angels*, Tom Mallow, accustomed to having women look after him, awakens on his first morning at Digby and Mark's flat wishing they would bring him tea in bed, as he knows a woman would do for him. Deirdre Swan wades through his thesis as a mark of her love, and Catherine does his laundry before he leaves for Africa. Even a married clergyman, whose wife is recovering from an illness, presumes upon Rhoda Wellcome to wash his albs because he cannot manage the task himself. When her niece Deirdre scornfully says she would never do a man's wash for him, the narrator wisely points out that she is "forgetting or perhaps putting into a higher category the typing she had sometimes done for Tom" (174). Dulcie Mainwaring's Aunt Hermione, in *No Fond Return of Love*, becomes engaged to marry her vicar after his sister's death because he cannot manage on his own: as she anticipated it would, everything got into a muddle, Hermione tells Dulcie, because he did not know what his sister had done to get his surplices looking so white. Men *would* be able to do on their own, as Emma Howick observes, but with so many women around to do the work for them, why should they bother to learn?

For men are in general a spoiled lot. The pompous Henry Hoccleve, the dazzling but shallow Rocky Napier, and the narcissistic Fabian Driver, for example, are hardly heroic figures, yet all have women eager to serve them. In *Excellent Women* Mildred is flushed with pleasure by the attentions of Rocky Napier even though she constantly reminds herself of how superficial he is, and in *Some Tame Gazelle*, Archbishop Hoccleve has held the undying devotion of Belinda Bede for some three decades. While Belinda is too modest to risk revealing her love by knitting him a sweater, she can mend a hole in his sock, a gesture that earns the Archdeacon's praise and which pleases her immensely. Henry cannot help knowing Belinda's feelings for him, which must give him a sense of smugness, especially when he is so critical of his wife's "shortcomings." Even though Agatha is not as steadfastly devoted in her domestic services as Henry would like, Agatha has not weathered the years nearly as well as Henry has. While Henry has retained his youthful good looks and figure, Agatha has been fairly ravaged, presumably by a combination of passing time and the rigors of being married to such a man: "Her pointed face had lost the elfin charm which had delighted many and now looked drawn and harassed. She had rheumatism too, but Belinda realized that she would have to have something out of self-defence and perhaps with the passing of the years it had become a reality" (24-25). One explanation for why men fare so well with age is that they do not work very hard at anything. Like Nicholas Cleveland and Edward Lyall, for instance, Fabian Driver sighs about the exhausting nature of his work but actually works very little. Henry Hoccleve never takes the early service, preferring to sleep late, and in *An Academic Question*, Alan Grimstone and his colleagues regard their academic duties of perhaps eight to ten hours a week as "'a crushing teaching load'" (28). Taken all together, men seem a shiftless, lazy lot whose inactivity is abetted by the constant attentions of women.

But in terms of life-draining capabilities, nothing can match Fabian Driver in *Jane and Prudence*. Tall and good-looking, Fabian is spoiled and pampered by a variety of women. Pym introduces him in a comic scene whose sexual overtones are unmistakable. When Fabian comes to the church to offer a marrow for the Harvest Festival, the women exclaim it is magnificent, the largest they have had. Viewing this display, Jane feels "as if she were assisting at some primitive kind of ritual at whose significance she hardly dared to guess" (31). The marrow takes on ironic meaning in addition to its initial suggestion of phallic symbol in a kind of fertility rite, for another meaning of "marrow" is "vitality." Fabian Driver is anything but vital; indeed, he has been destructive, sapping the energy and identity of his late wife and passing his days in a mock pose of mourning that is incredibly self-indulgent. When Mrs. Glaze conjectures that Mrs. Arkright has prepared a casserole of hearts for Fabian, Jane, "thinking of [Constance's] grave and the infidelities," wonders: "Did he eat his victims, then?" (33). Fabian Driver does indeed seem to have consumed his poor Constance. His treatment of his now-dead wife is chilling even though this is a comic novel. We are told that she became "faded-looking" but had been pretty when she married Fabian. Older than he, gentle, and better off financially, Constance had loved him and tolerated over the years his series of infidelities. One can imagine the humiliation Constance must have felt, particularly when these mistresses came for the weekend and Constance had to entertain them. Even more self-centered than Henry Hoccleve and Rocky Napier, he has few redeeming qualities. Fabian has very little substance and is easy prey for Jessie Morrow, who, for some inexplicable reason, loves him.

One wonders why men like Fabian and Rocky and Henry are so attractive to women. Part of it is their good looks and charm, but there is more to it than that: women have been conditioned to see themselves as secondary to men, to believe that they must have husbands to give validity to their own existence. Within Pym's memory and the collective memory of all the women in her novels, this is the way women have always behaved toward men. Watching her daughter Flora look adoringly at her young man Paul, Jane thinks: "Oh the strange and wonderful things that men could make women do! ... She remembered how once, long ago, she herself had started to learn Swedish ... and when she had first met Nicholas, she had tried Greek. And now here was her own daughter caught up in the higher flights of Geography! He seemed a nice young man, but that was only the least one could say. Was it also the most?" (**JP** 158). Men's work and men's needs are always valued more highly than women's. In *Less Than Angels*, for instance, Minnie Foresight, attempting to listen politely to Miss Lydgate's description of her anthropological article, has an expression "of rather strained interest" on her face: "Women must so often listen to men with just this expression on their faces, but Mrs. Foresight was feminine enough to feel that it was a little hard that so much concentration should be called for when talking to a member of her own sex. It seemed, somehow, a waste of effort" (16). This is a brilliant summary of the way women are expected to view men's work, to appreciate this difference in their relative worth, and to respond accordingly. Catherine Oliphant's wry observation about "the general uselessness of women if they cannot understand or reverence a man's work, or even if they can" (105) is particularly appropriate for describing a basic tenet of the relationship between men and women. As Dulcie Mainwaring thinks, it is sad the way "women longed to be needed and useful and how seldom most of them really were" (**NFRL** 99).

Jane Cleveland looks at the phenomenon between women and men from the perspective of a comfortably married woman whose husband is congenial, mild, and even-tempered. He makes no demands of her, generally accepting her as she is with only an occasional misgiving. For Jane is inept at housekeeping and cooking; she can barely open tins and panics at the thought of fixing an entire meal. She is only slightly bothered by her failure to conform to the typical role of a clergyman's wife. She is affectionate, open-minded, and amused by the seriousness with which people treat trivialities. She puzzles over the unbalanced relationships between men and women and just what it is men want from them. When Miss Doggett tells Jane, "'We know that men are not like women.... Men are very passionate.... [Y]ou and I, Mrs. Cleveland--well, I am an old woman and you are married, so we can admit honestly what men are,'" Jane responds: 'You mean that they only want one thing?'" But then Jane goes on to name those things men really want: "'Typing a man's thesis, correcting proofs, putting sheets sides-to-middle, bringing up children, balancing the house-keeping budget'" (**JP** 127). When it comes down to it, the truth is that even Fabian Driver wants more than the "one thing" Miss Doggett hints at, as Jane realizes when, writing Prudence about Fabian's engagement to Jessie Morrow, she thinks of

51

the fact that Prudence did not really love Fabian and had, in fact, found him

> boring and irritating. But wasn't that what so many marriages were--finding a person boring and irritating and yet loving him? Who could imagine a man who was *never* boring or irritating? ... Prudence's pride would be seriously wounded when she realised that it was plain, mousy Jessie Morrow who had taken Fabian away from her. Perhaps this was after all what men like to come home to, someone restful and neutral, who had no thought of changing the curtains or wallpapers? (**JP** 192-93)

This is the sort of insight that comes with age, for the narrator observes that Jane, at forty-one, is at an age which has certain compensations not readily apparent when one is at that desperate, anxious age of twenty-nine and unmarried, like Prudence Bates.

Men may think they want women who are sexy, attractive, and bright, Pym suggests, but in reality, they want women who will cook for them and do the washing up, women who will not let the moths get into their clothes or let holes in their socks go without darning them. The women who will do this sort of work are the mousy, unassuming spinsters of the world. As Mildred Lathbury points out, the irony is that it is "not the excellent women who got married but people like Allegra Gray, who was no good at sewing, and Helena Napier, who left all the washing up" (**EW** 170). Not selected in the exuberant first round of marriages in their youth, "excellent women" may eventually be taken up by men, but only when the psychological damage of years of thinking themselves unworthy has had its effect.

Marriage is valued highly even by those who find it somewhat of a nuisance, with married women often viewed as superior to or more advantaged than unmarried women. One of the rare occasions on which women take precedence over men, Jane Cleveland tells us, is in school magazines or college newsletters of girls' and women's school, where the marriages of Old Students are announced, while at school reunions, interest centers on who and who has not married. Beatrix Howick in *A Few Green Leaves*, despite her own very satisfactory career as a don, feels that women ought to marry or have some sort of relationship with a man. Widowed for decades, she had early in life fulfilled her womanly role by having married and borne a child. Now she wants Emma to be fulfilled in that way as well. This viewpoint in Pym's last novel is not much different from that expressed by women in Pym's first novels. In *Excellent Women*, for example, Allegra Gray wonders aloud to Mildred, "'What do women do if they don't marry?'" (129). Helena Napier cannot imagine what Mildred will do once she and Rocky are gone. When Rocky points out that she had a full life before they came--"'Very much so--what is known as a full life, with clergymen and jumble sales and church services and good works'"--Helena responds, "'I thought that was the kind of life led by women who didn't have a full life in the accepted sense'" (238). Like many others, Helena equates the full life with the married life. Having failed to marry, Mildred has failed as a woman. Through some fault of her own, she is responsible for her singleness.

Occasionally someone will speak up for unmarried women, as in *Some Tame Gazelle*, when Belinda weakly attempts to defend spinsters by telling the Archdeacon not to mock them, saying, "'After all, it isn't always our fault...'" (27-28). But Belinda recognizes the higher status of married women: she is distressed when she imagines Agatha's being crushed and pathetic when it is she herself who has been proposed to by Bishop Grote. She is enormously relieved when Agatha is her old self again at the party celebrating the curate's engagement to Olivia Berridge: "Now she knew that there could never be anything pathetic about Agatha. Poised and well-dressed, used to drinking champagne, the daughter of a bishop and the wife of an archdeacon--that was Agatha Hoccleve" (248). Mildred Lathbury also defends unmarried women, telling Mrs. Morris, her cleaning woman, that many women live alone without husbands because they have no choice. However, Mrs. Morris expresses the more commonly held opinion when she scornfully laughs, "'No choice!'" and derisively places the blame squarely on women for not being clever enough to get husbands (**EW** 170). Similarly, Dulcie Mainwaring, wondering if she might become friends with Aylwin Forbes' estranged wife, "realized that Marjorie was in a superior position, for she had at least acquired a husband and been married to him for some years, whereas she herself had only got as far as a fiance" (**NFRL** 225). When Tom Mallow's aunt calls on Catherine Oliphant in *Less Than Angels*, she announces: "'I am Mrs. Beddoes. I live in Belgravia.'" Remembering that Tom's other aunt is a spinster who lives in South Kensington, Catherine thinks: "Clearly Mrs. Beddoes was the superior one--Belgravia and the married state had raised her up" (132). Because women have traditionally been defined through men and their power limited to the domestic realm, women without men have been relegated to a kind of wasteland where, having failed to establish their worth through marriage, they are expected to dwell meekly and anonymously.

The idea that men somehow validate women by their very attachment to them is reinforced in all the novels, often to ridiculous lengths, as illustrated by the comment in *The Sweet Dove Died* that "to be involved with a man's furniture, especially to have some of it in one's possession, even if only temporarily, adds considerably to one's prestige" (83). That this is true is demonstrated in the clash of wills between Phoebe and Leonora over James's furniture. We see the importance of attachments to men in the way widows and even ex-wives of rich or influential men are regarded with a veneration that would not be given unmarried women. Lady Beddoes in *Crampton Hodnet*, Lady Clara Boulding in *Some Tame Gazelle*, and Lady Selvedge in *An Unsuitable Attachment* are just such women. Lady Beddoes, widow of an ambassador, living in Belgravia, is pleased to be invited to perform an opening ceremony at a church garden party. Like Agatha Hoccleve, daughter of a bishop and wife of an archdeacon, Lady

Clara Boulding is doubly important as not only the widow of a former Member of Parliament but the daughter of an earl and is called on for such distinguished activities as performing the opening ceremony at the vicarage garden party. Finally, Lady Selvedge is the ex-wife of Sir Humphrey Selvedge, whose infidelities forced her to divorce him. She is "usually known as Lady (Muriel) Selvedge. The parentheses gave her a sense of not existing, un-being perhaps was not too strong a word" (UA 57). Even though she is an ex-wife, she has retained the title of "Lady" and therefore, like Lady Boulding, has the requisite prestige for performing opening ceremonies at social events.

Wilmet Forsythe of *A Glass of Blessings*, Prudence Bates of *Jane and Prudence*, and Leonora Eyre of *The Sweet Dove Died* are different in significant ways from the larger group of heroines in Pym's novels in their relationships with men. In contrast to Belinda Bede, Mildred Lathbury, Catherine Oliphant, Dulcie Mainwaring, and Emma Howick, they are physically attractive, elegant in manner, and stylishly dressed. But while men are attracted to them, men also perceive them as aloof, cold, and unloving. Pym implies that women who have physical beauty are cold, remote, and unloving, while those who lack physical beauty are compassionate, caring, and generous. Beautiful women, she suggests, lack sensitivity to others and certainly are not presumed upon to the degree their plainer sisters are. They are self-centered and take for granted the kinds of attentions other women only dream about.

Thus, Prudence Bates is beautiful and independent, dresses exceptionally well, has a lovely flat elegantly furnished, and likes her career as assistant to Dr. Grampian. She has a long history of love affairs and not much interest in marrying, though she conceives the notion that she ought to and actually plans in a detached way to marry Fabian Driver. At the Old Girls' Reunion in the opening scene of the novel, Prudence, perhaps feeling on the defensive after Jane's remark that she has at least had one child, is critical of the dowdy, frumpy women collected for dinner, thinking it strange that they had all married. At the same time, Jane is thinking how lovely Prudence looks and is wondering why it is that she has not yet married. This passage suggests the opposite of Mildred Lathbury's observation that it is not the excellent women who marry, for Prudence is thinking of these other women in exactly the terms one would describe Pym's excellent women. Indeed, it really is the excellent women who marry and make good wives, for women like Prudence will have nothing to do with the sorts of requirements men who want helpmeets have of their women--men like Bishop Grote, Everard Bone, and Tom Mallow. Prudence seems to be attempting to disprove her friend Eleanor Hitchens' belief that "one couldn't go on having romantic love affairs indefinitely" (**JP** 200). She will very likely go on having affairs, ending, perhaps, like Leonora Eyre, whom she resembles in her sophisticated remoteness and neat, ordered life. When, in *A Glass of Blessings*, Rodney Forsythe tells Wilmet that he has taken Prudence Bates to dinner twice, it is not surprising when he tells her that Prudence reminded him of her.

Wilmet, having married young and being possessed of that beauty and sophistication that Pym's unmarried heroines yearn wistfully for, does not have the kind of worries spinsters have. She has long ago established her worth by marrying, but when we meet her on her thirty-third birthday, we see that she is still in a narcissistic, almost adolescent stage of development, her growth presumably arrested when she married and moved into her mother-in-law's home with her husband. She seems remarkably inexperienced despite her years in Italy as a Wren. One of Wilmet's chief frustrations is that others regard her as unloving and unlovable. Piers wounds her considerably when he makes remarks about her aloofness. Because she is so self-centered and sure of herself, she projects a cool and detached image that even her husband Rodney comments on. Her relationship with Rodney has long ago lost the exuberance of their courtship days in Italy. Wilmet is more actively interested in her mother-in-law Sybil than she is in Rodney, and theirs seems to be one

56

of those classic situations in which the marriage stagnates and each goes searching elsewhere for what they vaguely feel is missing. Thus we have Wilmet's interest in Piers, her feeling flattered at Harry's attention, and even her response to Marius Lovejoy's good looks; and on Rodney's part, the confession that he had taken Prudence out to dinner not once but twice. Their relationship improves considerably by the end of the novel, however, with Sybil married to Professor Root and Rodney and Wilmet being forced to find their own home. Their marriage is also helped by Wilmet's insights into other people and her realization of just how seriously she has misjudged people, even dear old Rodney, who it had never occurred to her could be capable of interest in other women.

Wilmet is an illustration of the fact that a "full life" does not magically and immediately follow marriage. The status that Pym's plain, excellent women lack does not guarantee a sense of personal fulfillment. Although Wilmet seems to like her idle life, she is plagued by thoughts that hers is not as useful as other lives. She compares herself to other women: Mary Beamish reminds her of her uselessness, women with children of her barrenness, Sybil of her lack of commitment to social causes, and even Rowena of the idleness of her life. The activities she foresees for her "winter programme"— lunching with Harry in order to praise Rowena to him, reclaiming Piers from his debauchery, and donating blood— fill her with joy at what seems limitless possibilities for doing worthy deeds. That she might be responsible for finding a job for Wilf Bason and solving the domestic help crisis for Father Thames makes her feel proud, "'as if there were some justification for [her] life after all!'" (GB 32). But by the end of the novel, Wilmet is humbled, more understanding, and willing to take responsibility for herself and others. She has now achieved a degree of autonomy she never before had, as mistress of her own home; she even enjoys selecting colors and materials for carpet and draperies. She is pleased to be nearer the church and feels closer to Rodney than she has for a long time. Having discovered certain unpleasant truths about herself, Wilmet finally grows up.

In *The Sweet Dove Died*, Leonora Eyre, older and even more self-centered, is a recapitulation of Wilmet, a grotesque version of what might have become of her had she not been humanized by insights into herself nor humbled by her misconceptions. The coolness of Wilmet is carried to frozen extremes in Leonora. Her friend Meg tells her that she lacks feelings, or rather, that she is not upset or ruffled by things. Leonora is "not sure she that liked the picture of herself it suggested. Of course one wasn't like that at all, cold and fossilised. It was only that all one's relationships had to be perfect of their kind" (56-57). Leonora is very much this way, cold and fossilised, and her fascination for James is almost inexplicable. She certainly does not love him, finding the idea of love disturbing. Rather, he is one more man she can control, one more exquisite addition to her collection, and as perhaps the weakest of all of Pym's ineffectual men, he is easily molded--by anyone. Leonora's inability to manipulate him once he falls under Ned's control is a genuine source of frustration and dismay. Furthermore, the fact that James is bisexual and that Ned is a more powerful influence on him than Leonora adds to the truly distorted vision of male-female relationships in *The Sweet Dove Died*. None of the characters feels deeply for any other; they all operate on superficial levels and use others for their own needs.

In *An Unsuitable Attachment* Ianthe Broome gives the same impression as Wilmet Forsythe and Leonora Eyre, for although she identifies with an Elizabeth Bowen rather than an Austen heroine, Ianthe has an elegance of a bygone era. Furthermore, she expects courtesy from men and gets it: "It was as if they realised that she was not for the rough and tumble of this world, like the aggressive women with shaggy hair styles who pushed their way through life thrusting their hard shopping baskets at defenceless men" (26). This comic image of aggressive women is not surprising, given Pym's proclivity for making fun of just about everything. Women's liberation and the drive for sex equity are natural targets for Pym's sharp wit. In the comic world she creates, where men's supremacy over women is assumed, it is natural that men would fear and be suspicious of bright, aggressive women. Not only is Ianthe Broome representative of a standard of womanly behavior which contrasts favorably with the meanness of modern women, but even Penelope Grandison, who finds Ianthe's bedroom "chilling and virginal" and her own dress and hair style much more in vogue than Ianthe's, lays great stress on the formal acts of courtesy "that women in their emancipated state seemed to be in danger of losing" (41). Wilmet Forsythe also views with a certain amount of disdain the modern woman attempting to balance career and marriage, as she and Sybil joke about those "splendid and formidable women" (**GB** 11). When the homosexual Piers Longridge says that he finds the combination of beauty with brains "'unnatural and therefore rather repellant'" (**GB** 134), Pym seems to be suggesting that aggressiveness in women is in part responsible for homosexuality. As she was writing *A Glass of Blessings*, she made the following entry in her notebook in December, 1955: "On TV I thought that women have never been more terrifying than they are now . . . no wonder men turn to other men sometimes" (**VPE** 197). But when Piers tells Wilmet that "'women are so terrifying these days and seem to expect so much, really far more than one could possibly give,'" (**GB** 9), he is doing no more than echoing the cry of Pym's men throughout her novels.

Given men's egocentrism in Pym's novels, it is only natural that men would view aggressive women with some trepidation. Given Fabian Driver's treatment of Constance, readers must surely feel a sense that he has gotten no more than is coming to him when we are told that life with Jessie seems to him "a frightening prospect" and that he feels "as if a net had closed round him" (**JP** 199). This leitmotif of the all-consuming, aggressive woman is suggested in such observations as that of Jane Cleveland when, pointing out to Prudence Bates that women no longer have to wait for men to propose and that women can do almost everything men can these days, she adds: "And they are getting so much bigger and taller and men are getting smaller, haven't you noticed?'" (**JP** 161). No wonder such emphasis is laid on the height of men: Mrs. Beddoes tries to round up tall young men for her daughter's coming out party in *Less Than Angels*, for instance, and Miss Doggett remarks in *Jane and Prudence* that the main thing in the Lathbury-Bone marriage is that Everard is good looking and tall.

Marriages in Pym's novels are typically either antagonistic or boring relationships, disappointments indeed in light of all the energy expended in achieving that state. When Dulcie Mainwaring asks Viola Dace if Aylwin Forbes is married, Viola tells her that he is--"'in a sense, that is.'" Dulcie thinks: "People usually were married, and how often it *was* 'in a sense'" (**NFRL** 7). Although the context of Viola's particular observation is that Aylwin's wife has left him, making him indeed married "in a sense," an examination of some of the other marriages in Pym's novels reveals what Dulcie means in general. While it seems that everyone wants to be or thinks people should be married, the marriages themselves are not particularly comforting or loving. Husbands and wives are often sources of irritation to one another, some couples arguing frequently, others having coped by generally ignoring one another. In *Some Tame Gazelle*, for instance, Henry and Agatha Hoccleve argue loudly over her "failure" to prevent moths from getting into his gray suit and often seem antagonistic toward one another. Even passing references to marriages suggest that they are restrictive of women's liberties and largely serve men's interests and needs. When the President of the Learned Society dies in *Excellent Women*, his widow gives all his anthropology collection to the society. Mildred believes his widow must now be experiencing freedom and, when Helena says that she does not have church or good works to keep her busy, Mildred's first response is "'Oh, did he take even that from her? ... Oh, the wicked things men do, leaving her nothing for her old age, not even anthropology!'" (177). In *No Fond Return of Love* Dulcie Mainwaring's sister is delighted that Laurel wants to take a bed-sitting-room with a friend, having apparently long suppressed an unfulfilled desire to do the same:

> It was rather sad, Dulcie thought, that an apparently happily married woman should confess to a secret hankering for such a life. And yet, stealing a glance at her brother-in-law, ... she could appreciate that perhaps a desire for escape was not so surprising. Many wives must experience it from time to time, she thought, especially those whose husbands smoked old pipes that made peculiar noises, and were so preoccupied with their harmless hobbies that they would hardly have noticed if their wives had been there or not. (112-13)

In *An Unsuitable Attachment*, there is a brief but scathing portrayal of a truly horrid marriage between Ianthe's aunt and uncle, Randolph and Bertha Burdon. They have made a loveless marriage, as we are told that Bertha Burdon has never loved, had married because her parents thought the match a suitable one, and almost regrets not having had the experience of love. Their discord is apparent in subtle ways--in Bertha's irritation at her husband's delight over Sophia's quince jelly and Randolph's pointed remark about his wife being too weak to make his favorite jelly.

Mark and Sophia Ainger in *An Unsuitable Attachment* have their own particular problems, with Sophia's devotion to her cat Faustina seeming to have supplanted that which Mark feels ought rightly be his. In fact, when Sophia tells Ianthe that she and Mark are far apart, she compares her difficulty in reaching him with her difficulty in reaching Faustina, a comparison which Ianthe finds remarkable for its irreverence. Sophia even tells Mark at one point that Faustina is all she has, a statement that momentarily brings a distant look to his eyes. It is no wonder that Mark feels expansive and solicitous about the cat's well being once he has Sophia alone in Italy. Feeling romantic toward her, he thinks, pressing her hand, "at this moment she is all mine and without Faustina" (151). These two people seem to have little to offer one another.

Like Mark and Sophia, Alan and Caroline Grimstone in *An Academic Question* are "together yet apart, not exactly incompatible." Caroline sees Alan as "an adequate husband, an unenthusiastic lover, a dutiful father and a son who despised the family he had grown beyond." Add to that the fact that Caroline "had once been in love with him and in a way [she] still was," and the picture of their marriage is complete (28). Her marriage is similar to that of Rodney and Wilmet for most of *A Glass of Blessings*, for the two of them often have little to say to one another, sleep in separate beds, seldom exhibit tenderness toward one another, and find each other boringly predictable. At one point, during tea at Wilf Bason's when Wilf is called out of the room, Wilmet even feels uncomfortable alone with Rodney. Both the Grimstones and the Forsythes manage to work out their difficulties, but only after thoughts of infidelity on Rodney's part and actual infidelity on Alan's. Wilmet and Caroline handle the straying of their husbands in different ways, but both in the end forgive them.

The character of Caroline Grimstone in *An Academic Question* is interesting for what Pym was trying to do to make her a contemporary woman. She is educated, lives quite well on an inheritance from her grandmother, has a Swedish au pair girl to look after her child and will not do her husband's typing. But she is still sister to Pym's other heroines: she has a great deal of time on her hands, finds herself too educated for the trivial tasks that are open to her, has a husband who is preoccupied with his own career, and finds herself wanting to do something useful for him. She romanticizes men, having fallen in love with Alan while recovering from a broken relationship with a Byronic looking man who turned out to be a cad. In this novel, we finally have a woman with a Ph.D. and a position at the university, Iris Horniblow. It is not this successful, talented divorcee whom Alan goes to bed with, but rather Rollo Gaunt's assistant editor, "a jolly friendly girl who would go to bed with anyone and think nothing of it" (129). Pym's portrayal of male-female relationships in *An Academic Question* is finally not much different from the way it is portrayed in her earlier novels, with the woman wishing to be of use to a man and the man taking her for granted.

A most successful marriage is that of Jane and Nicholas Cleveland, but even they have occasional misgivings, and their relationship is characterized less by intimate sharing and joyous loving as it is by a kind of putting up with one another and having learned to adjust to each other's eccentricities. Nicholas, for example, at one point feeling less tolerant than usual of Jane's speaking out when she ought not, considers, not for the first time, that there may be something to be said for the celibacy of the clergy after all. On Jane's part, "Mild, kindly looks and spectacles... ; this is what it all came to in the end. The passion of those early days, the fragments of Donne and Marvell and Jane's obscurer senventeeth-century poets, the objects of her abortive research, all these faded away into mild, kindly looks and spectacles. There came a day when one didn't quote poetry to one's husband any more" (JP 48). But later in the novel, Pym describes them as "two essentially good people" sitting in front of their fire, comfortably occupied with their own activities and thoughts (JP 138). Jane is conscious of not quite living up to the image of a vicar's wife, but Nicholas himself is given to whims, as when he buys soap shaped like animals and decides to grow his own tobacco. But they do things together, such as putting up plums in the kitchen at the same time Nicholas is drying his tobacco leaves, which is what they are doing when Miss Doggett comes to them with her suspicion that Jessie Morrow is up to something deceitful with Fabian Driver. The general chaos of the scene, particularly the vicar's wearing a flowered apron, is distressing to Miss Doggett but perfectly natural to Jane and Nicholas. Jane and Nicholas are a married couple who understand and accept one another very well.

Pym had used virtually the same words, certainly the same idea, in *Crampton Hodnet* when describing the marriage of Margaret and Francis Cleveland as she does to describe the marriage of Jane and Nicholas Cleveland.

63

After thirty years, Margaret has long grown accustomed to taking for granted her husband, whom she had once loved deeply, and now, like Jane, never thinks of seventeenth-century love poems. Their marriage never achieves the warmth of the Clevelands as they are reincarnated in *Jane and Prudence*, however. For one, in *Crampton Hodnet*, Francis Cleveland makes repeated attempts to speak frankly and from the heart about his sojourn to Dover with Barbara Bird, but Margaret puts him off every time. She consistently ignores his attempts to talk, preoccupied with first her daughter's problems and then putting him to bed and taking his temperature. It was her desire to have him out of the way which drove Francis away in the first place. She treats Francis as she would a child, for that is how she sees him. As a result, they never truly communicate as married partners ought but seem destined to continue operating within their own separate worlds.

Another aspect of marriages in Pym's novels is that they are almost never fruitful. Agatha and Henry Hoccleve, Helena and Rocky Napier, Wilmet and Rodney Forsythe, Aylwin and Marjorie Forbes, and Sophia and Mark Ainger are all childless. Fabian Driver had no children by Constance and is not likely to have any with Jessie Morrow. Jane and Nicholas Cleveland have only one child, as do Caro and Alan Grimstone and Francis and Margaret Cleveland. Perhaps Pym did not feel comfortable writing about children, having none herself, but she could have written about them had she wanted to, just as she wrote of other character types--by observing those around her. More likely, the barrenness of these fictional marriages is one more indication of the egocentric and one-sided nature of the relationships between men and women. In many cases, it is the men who are like children, or at least are seen as such by a large number of women. In *Civil to Strangers*, for instance, Cassandra Marsh-Gibbon not only treats Adam as a child but thinks of him as one. In *No Fond Return of Love*, Dulcie Mainwaring, wondering what marriage to Maurice Clive would have been like, cannot picture herself as a mother, thinking that Maurice had been the child and that "theirs would have been one of those rather dreadful marriages, with the wife a little older and a little taller and a great deal more intelligent than the husband" (46). In the same novel, Dulcie's Aunt Hermione, and in *Excellent Women*, Winifred Malory, both observe that men are just children. Margaret Cleveland regards her husband Francis as being just like a restless, difficult child when he can find nothing to occupy himself. Catherine Oliphant, reflecting on the fact that she and Tom had been living together without being married, feels she would have liked children: "The fact that she tended to regard most men, and Tom in particular, as children wasn't quite the same thing" (**LTA** 27). This view of men as children runs throughout all of the novels.

Married women seem resigned to their restrictive roles, but it would seem that the "full life" of married women is not all that wonderful. This view is particularly clear in the case of widows, who enjoy the privilege of their attachment to men but no longer have to bother with them. In *Civil to Strangers*, for instance, Mrs. Gower's widowhood has been a relief from the pretense of interest in literature and she no longer regrets the death of her husband some eight years before. Cassandra Marsh-Gibbon day-dreams of being an old woman: "To have money and leisure to sit in a lovely garden, enjoying the sunshine and doing Jacobean embroidery; to be a comfortable widow, not recently bereaved, but one whose husband had been ten to twenty years in his grave and whose passing was no longer deeply mourned, would not this be a delightful existence?" (91-92). In *Crampton Hodnet*, Lady Beddoes tells Miss Doggett that she has gotten quite used to the absence of her late husband, Sir Lyall, and hints that he was not the great love of her life, much to Miss Doggett's dismay.

Furthermore, married women occasionally express envy of unmarried women. Rowena in *A Glass of Blessings*, married and the mother of three children, at one points tells Wilmet she envies spinsters because they still have their dreams: "'The despised spinster still has the chance of meeting somebody.... At least she's *free*!'" (149). Wilmet herself has told us a short time before that April this year was cruel in precisely the way Eliot meant it: "mingling memory and desire. The memory was of other springs, the desire unformulated, unrecognized almost, pushed away because there seemed to be no place for it in the life I had chosen for myself" (148). In *An Academic Question*, Iris Horniblow tells Caroline Grimstone that she envies the unattached their freedom from domestic responsibilities. Belinda Bede, a confirmed spinster, points out in Pym's first novel that one real advantage of being unmarried is the freedom to imagine what might have been or could possibly yet be, and this idea seems to be confirmed by many widowed and married women. Like the figures on Keats's Grecian urn, spinsters have before them the possibility for joy, while married women know full well the reality. Unlike the characters on the urn, however, neither married nor unmarried stay "forever panting and forever young."

Besides simply wanting more freedom, married women find themselves envying single women because they do not have to bother with childish or unfaithful husbands. This matter of husbands' infidelity comes up from time to time. In *Jane and Prudence*, Fabian Driver's affairs are common knowledge. The subject is broached in *No Fond Return of Love* with Aylwin Forbes's alleged involvement with another woman, which turns out to have been just an innocent kiss with Viola Dace. In *Crampton Hodnet*, Francis Cleveland has an inclination to be unfaithful and goes so far as Dover with his young lover, who abandons him there, much to his relief. His wife, feeling pressured by Miss Doggett to do something about Francis when she would rather just ignore him, finds herself thinking of the freedom of not being married. Sitting in a restaurant puzzling over her husband's presumed infidelity, she equates excellence in women with good sense. Observing a woman in a "sensible hat and costume," Margaret notices that she is not wearing a ring:

Then, presumably, she hadn't got a husband. She was a comfortable spinster with nobody but herself to consider. Living in a tidy house not far from London, making nice little supper dishes for one, a place for everything and everything in its place, no husband hanging resentfully round the sitting-room, no husband one moment topping and tailing gooseberries and the next declaring that he had fallen in love with a young woman. Mrs. Cleveland sighed a sigh of envy. No husband. (172)

Margaret's envying of unmarried women comes at a time of real strain on her relationship with her husband, of course, yet Margaret has for some time had the sense that Francis is largely someone who gets underfoot, more or less an inconvenience to put up with when he is around.

Only Alan Grimstone in *An Academic Question* actually goes to bed with another woman in the course of a novel, and he dismisses the incident as meaningless. When Caroline goes to confront this other woman, Cressida, she too dismisses the incident, for she understands how little the episode has meant to either Alan or Cressida. Before meeting Cressida, however, Caroline regards with envy two spinster sisters who have recently retired from their jobs and who are now occupied with interesting and satisfying activities. For Caroline has been uneasy and disappointed in her marriage, going so far at one point as to think of "the horrors of marriage into which we entered so glibly" (81). But even though Caroline observes that the ridiculous notion that simply being married no longer carries the status it once did, in the next moment she is wondering if it really is true. Much emphasis, even in the liberated 1960s, is placed on a woman's marital status. Most women in Pym's novels would agree that marriage is still the preferred state, with spinsters regarded as less than complete human beings, and perhaps widowhood being the best of both worlds.

Unmarried men in Pym's novels comprise the majority of males by far, and it is they who are objects of great interest to women. Sophia Ainger states it bluntly in *An Unsuitable Attachment* when she tells Rupert Stonebird: "'A single man probably inspires wider and wilder speculation than a single woman.... His unmarried state is in itself more interesting than a woman's unmarriedness, if you see what I mean'" (248). Some men have purposely avoided getting married, some just have not had the time nor opportunity, and others are widowers or divorced. Men in this last group have had less-than-fulfilling relationships with their wives, who seem not to have made much of an impression on them. Tom Dagnall can scarcely remember his dead wife, hardly thinks of her now, and is not even sure what color her eyes had been. One need not assume from this that his wife was nondescript, for Tom is fairly oblivious to the qualities of all women. He takes Daphne for granted, gives little attention to her interests or needs, and at times hardly thinks of her as a human being. Edwin Braithwaite, looking at the naked breasts of women displayed on magazine covers, "suppose[s] that his wife Phyllis had once had breasts" (**QA** 45), but presumably is not sure. Aylwin Forbes' wife divorces him because of his interest in other women. Fabian Driver woefully mistreated his poor dead wife and thinks only of himself. It is Fabian's photograph which adorns her grave, and Jessie Morrow's sardonic comment that "'her death came as a great shock to him--he had almost forgotten her existence'" (**JP** 28) indicates the degree of his self-absorption. In *An Unsuitable Attachment*, Edwin Pettigrew's wife had left him years before because he could not give as much attention to his marriage as he wanted to give to his animals.

A few men do find wives in the course of the novels, often as arrangements of convenience for the man. The wedding of Edgar Donne and Olivia Berridge ends *Some Tame Gazelle*, while Bishop Grote and Connie Aspinall are making arrangements for theirs. Belinda's assessment of Olivia is that she seems perfectly equipped to be a clergyman's wife, taking care of him, protecting him, and perhaps even helping write his sermons for him: "A helpmeet indeed" (235). This thought is a reference to the scene in which Theodore had proposed to her, assuring her that she is quite equal to being his helpmeet, or, as Belinda more realistically puts it: "A man needs a woman to help him into his grave" (224). Belinda is not surprised when

Connie tells her that Theodore has assured her that she is equal to being a bishop's wife, for Belinda knows exactly what he means. In *Jane and Prudence*, when Jessie Morrow and Fabian Driver become engaged, he tells Jane that Prudence would have wanted too much, something that the shrewd Jessie has realized all along and used to her advantage. When Marius Lovejoy discusses his impending marriage to Mary Beamish with Wilmet in *A Glass of Blessings*, he tells Jane that Mary will be able to do so much for him. As the rector Mr. Wilmot says in *Civil to Strangers*, every man ought to have a wife if for no other reason than for safety. Stefan Tilos marries the woman his parents have selected for him not only because he needs a housekeeper but because she will be protection against Angela Gay. Stephen Latimer proposes to Jessie Morrow in *Crampton Hodnet* because he believes he could do worse, and marriage to her would protect him from the scourge of unmarried women who will not leave him alone.

Pym treats the self-centeredness of men with wonderful humor and irony, pointing out the absurdity of this preferential treatment in the way men's importance affects even the most intelligent and admirable of women. Pym seldom treats the relationships between women and men with heaviness or anger. Mildred's implied fate at the end of *Excellent Women* has a sense of doom to it, and Fabian Driver's vampirism in *Jane and Prudence* is strongly suggested, but in general all the men are treated so mockingly, often as caricatures, that, like the women who love them, one can only smile good humoredly at their pomposities and self-indulgences. For Pym's women, compelled as they are to form attachments with these men, also look at them with wisdom and themselves with a kind of self-mockery. When Prudence Bates, for example, says scornfully that she has no need of a husband, Jane Cleveland immediately thinks of how useful her husband Nicholas is for such things as telling silly jokes to, carrying luggage, and much more, and when Mrs. Glaze tells her that the previous curate was already married when he came to them, Jane thinks: "Oh, but that was bad! Bad of the Bishop to send them a curate already engaged. It was a wonder the ladies of the parish hadn't torn him to pieces" (**JP** 19). Jane's humorous approach to the silliness of men and the way women flutter about them is refreshing and delightful.

While men are portrayed as ineffectual, lazy, seemingly involved with women almost helplessly, they are not all to blame for the problems with relationships, as Pym makes clear in her comic portrayal of women's emotional needs. Women do seem to be overbearing at times, as Catherine Oliphant realizes when she thinks about it: "Men appeared to be so unsubtle, but perhaps it was only by contrast with the tortuous delicacy of women, who smothered their men under a cloud of sentimental associations--*our* song, *our* poem, *our* restaurant--till they struggled to break free" (**LTA** 110). Women often desire love and marriage so much that they are grateful there are still a few available men left, some even stooping to manipulation in order to marry. Jessie Morrow coolly sets out to seduce Fabian Driver, who is not nearly as eager for the ceremony as Jessie is and feels the sensation of being trapped in the very way Catherine describes it.

The differing viewpoint between men and women that Catherine points out is illustrated elsewhere in *Less Than Angels*, when Catherine tells Alaric Lydgate about a story she is writing about a big game hunter just back from Africa, sitting in his hotel room thinking wistfully of his adventures in Africa. When Alaric inquires what happens in the story, Catherine tells him that he meets the niece of one of the elderly women sitting in the hotel lounge and goes for a walk in the rain with her. Alaric wants to know what happened then, a question which surprises Catherine until she realizes that he would not be a reader of romance fiction. But the point is clear: for a woman, the end of the story occurs when man meets woman and walks off in the rain, while such an event appears to a man as something incidental on the way to the real drama of the story.

In *Some Tame Gazelle*, Pym sets forth the idea that one only needs something to love in order to be content. The rest of her novels illustrate this tenet in one form or another, with men espousing the belief almost as much as women. Certainly the majority of her characters embrace this view, for most of them actively seek involvements with members of the opposite sex. There are few exceptions, though two of the central character unmarried women have never experienced love and are quite frankly not much interested in it. Letty Crowe finds it a mystery she has never experienced: "As a young woman she had wanted to love, had felt that she ought to, but it had not come about" (**QA** 54). Similarly, despite her many involvements with men, Leonora Eyre has not truly loved. Listening to her friend Liz's complaints about her ex-husband and all that wasted love, Leonora thinks: "She had never been badly treated or rejected by a man--perhaps she had never loved another person with enough intensity for such a thing to be possible" (**SDD** 58). By and large, however, most of Pym's characters, male or female, want love and marriage. Pym's particular comic stance points out the often ridiculous lengths men and women go to in order to attain those things by portraying the tremendous burden social attitudes and expectations surrounding romance and marriage place on women in a society where there are far too many women for the number of available men. With supreme irony, she also demonstrates how that social attitude toward women results in wonderful perquisites for men. Thus, when Beatrix Howick tells her daughter in Pym's final novel that the relationship between men and women is ridiculous, she is voicing a sentiment that Pym has illustrated throughout her canon.

THREE

THE COMPANY OF WOMEN

Almost by necessity, women in Barbara Pym's novels depend on one another for companionship and understanding, but while the company of women is often seen as a comfort, it is almost as frequently denigrated and belittled. Unmarried women find themselves competing for the same man, while married and widowed women feel superior to unmarried women. Women's friendships are often, as Mildred Lathbury describes them, "dull, solid friendships without charm" (**EW** 226), yet they can be, as Wilmet Forsythe exclaims, "splendid and wonderful" (**GB** 137). These ambiguous feelings about women's friendship are not surprising given Pym's portrayal of male-female relationships. If one's identity depends on being attached to a male, if men are ultimately more important than women, then women will not value one another as much as they value men and their relationships will be fraught with suspicion and rivalry. On the other hand, in a world where the number of women is far greater than the number of men and where relationships between the sexes are not particularly intimate, then women understandably turn to each other for support and companionship.

One aspect of the lopsided world in which men are elevated to a higher status than women is that men also affect relationships between women. Mildred Lathbury points out the difference men can make in women's relationships with one another when, shopping one afternoon with her old friend Dora Caldicote, she is able to forget for a while the complications the Napiers have brought to her life: "I was back in those happier days when the company of women friends had seemed enough" (**EW** 102). Women's friendship is something one must settle for: if it now is something that had once "seemed enough," then something else--in Mildred's case, the excitement of Rocky Napier--is more desirable. Indeed, just a moment later Mildred is thinking nastily of Dora's appearance when Dora wants to choose the same color dress she has always worn for every day. Similarly, when Emma Howick's mother Beatrix and her mother's friend Isobel visit Emma at Christmas, Emma resigns herself "to a quiet female celebration of the festival... There seemed little prospect of any other form of entertainment" (**FGL** 235). The "other form of entertainment," it is implied, is spending the day in the company of a man. Prudence Bates at one point thinks of how husbands always take women friends away and considers herself fortunate that her friend Jane Cleveland has remained fairly independent despite her marriage.

Certainly Letty Crowe's relationship with her longtime friend Marjorie in *Quartet in Autumn* suggests that relationships with men supersede women's friendships. While Marjorie had married, Letty had not. But as a widow, Marjorie has gone on several package tours abroad with Letty, and Letty is planning to share Marjorie's cottage once she retires. On Letty's two-week visit with Marjorie during her summer vacation, however, Letty is once again reminded of her secondary role when Marjorie becomes involved with a man, for David Lydell, the new vicar, gets much more attention than Letty does during that visit. Later, when Marjorie and David become engaged, Marjorie wants Letty to consider retiring to an old people's home, it being impossible now for her to live with Marjorie. Yet not long after, when her engagement is broken, Marjorie naturally assumes that Letty will once again change her plans and move in with her. Marjorie's behavior reminds one of the often tenuous nature of female friendships, at least their instability when men come into the picture. Marjorie's readiness to abandon her friend for marriage is understandable, but her behavior with David Lydell before their engagement, during Letty's visit, reminds one of the common arrangement among high school girls that a date with a boy, even one made at the last minute, is reason enough to cancel plans with a female friend. Women who were taught to value men more highly than women may very well behave exactly as Pym depicts Marjorie.

Related to this aspect of men's effect on women's relationships is that there is a good deal of rivalry for men's attention. Part of the subplot involving Marjorie in *Quartet in Autumn* is the competition Marjorie has with Beth Doughty, both women attempting to woo David Lydell with food and wine and solicitous concern about his gastric troubles. In the end, Beth seems to have won David away from Marjorie even though David and Marjorie are engaged. This contention of women with one another for the attentions of men is a recurring motif in Pym's novels. *Some Tame Gazelle* treats it lightly in Belinda Bede's relationship with Henry Hoccleve after Agatha goes on holiday alone. Often, one of the women in contention for a man's favors is not even aware that the other is after him. In the very early novel *Civil to Strangers*, for example, Angela Gay hates Cassandra Marsh-Gibbon, having once imagined herself in love with Cassandra's husband Adam, but Cassandra seems blithely ignorant of Angela's animosity toward her. Nor does Prudence Bates in *Jane and Prudence* know that Jessie Morrow is determined to seduce Fabian Driver away from her. One of the conflicts in *An Unsuitable Attachment* involves the rivalry Penelope Grandison feels with Ianthe Broome over Rupert Stonebird, even though Ianthe has absolutely no interest in Rupert as a lover. Penelope's initial response to Ianthe Broome, before she actually meets her but only hears her voice, is that Ianthe is "perhaps in some way a kind of 'rival' for the affections of a man [Rupert Stonebird] she had not yet seen," though she is immediately conscious of the ludicrousness of her thought (38).

Women are often quick to dismiss other women or to value them less than they value men. Miss Prideaux, herself a single woman living in a bed-sitting room, surprises Wilmet Forsythe by the strength and violence of her language when she suggests that Father Ransome could stay in the spare flat in Julian and Winifred Malory's Pimlico vicarage: "'I believe there's a deaconess in it at the moment, but I've no doubt she could be got rid of'" (**GB** 122). The deaconess to whom she is referring is Sister Blatt, whom readers first met, along with Julian and Winifred Malory, in *Excellent Women*. In that novel, the renting of the flat in question produces a good deal of stress when the woman to whom it is rented, Mrs. Gray, becomes engaged to Julian. Mrs. Gray's first thought is that she must have Winifred removed from the vicarage. She approaches Mildred with the idea, but Mildred is strongly opposed to it. Although she likes Winifred very much, she knows that if Winifred were ever to move in with her, whatever chances she might have of marrying would be gone forever.

An extreme example of dismissing or devaluing other women occurs in *The Sweet Dove Died*. Leonora Eyre has "little use for the 'cosiness' of women friends, but regarded them as a foil for herself, particularly if, as usually happened, they were less attractive and elegant than she was" (53). This attitude toward other women is in keeping with Leonora's icy personality and her need to collect and control men. She does have two "close" friends: Meg, whose relationship with the homosexual Colin gives Leonora an opportunity to treat her with contemptuous pity but becomes an object lesson when her own relationship with James turns out to parallel Meg's; and Liz, whose bitter experience with a broken marriage again provides a contrast to Leonora's customary success with men. Liz and Leonora have a strange relationship: when the two have supper together one evening, each is equally bored by the other's conversation. Liz would go on and on about her unhappy marriage, we are told, and Leonora would eventually get around to her reminiscences of her girlhood and romantic adventures. Nevertheless, "at the end of the evening each woman would feel a kind of satisfaction, as if more than just drink and food had been offered and accepted" (58). Their friendship lacks the genuine concern friends ought to have for one another and instead seems self-serving and false. They provide company for one another, but each is too involved in herself to offer much else.

The prospect of women's company can be depressing, as Mildred Lathbury puts it. Indeed, part of Mildred's new awareness of the circumscribed nature of her life is a profound deepening of her disgust for women just like herself, whom she describes as nondescript, anonymous, and mediocre. Repeatedly she comments on the gatherings of women just like her, women who, taken together, form an odd lot. She describes Miss Statham and Miss Embers as birdlike women she tends to confuse, and their voices along with Sister Blatt's sound like a lamentation to her. Sister Blatt and Miss Clovis are gruff and have a blunt, no-nonsense manner about them. Winifred Malory, the vicar's dependent sister, is awkward and gaunt, dressed in other people's jumble sale contributions. Others in this group of friends or potential friends are Dora Caldicote, Mildred's former roommate, who wears unimaginative clothes and has an irritating habit of hanging dripping laundry in the kitchen; Miss Jessop, a timid, bland friend of Mrs. Bone; and Mrs. Bone herself, a strange, eccentric woman preoccupied with eradicating wormwood and eating as many birds as she can to stave off their attacks on the human race. While the Napiers seem to have darkened Mildred's attitude toward her predictable and dull friends, she has never been very charitable toward women. When they first meet, for instance, Mildred instinctively dislikes Helena Napier; but she feels an immediate affinity for Rocky before she meets him, leaping mentally to his defense, as it were, when Helena describes her own slovenly ways. She has "an inexplicable distrust of widows" (**EW** 45) and therefore is not at all friendly to Allegra Gray, though in all fairness to Mildred, Allegra's superior air does not make her particularly lovable. Having lived with Dora Caldicote once, the prospect of living with her

77

again in twenty or thirty years, bickering over trifles, is "a depressing picture" (**EW** 105). She is in a panic about the possibility of Winifred's living with her, and at the end of the novel, she is not looking forward to the company of the two women who are moving into the flat vacated by the Napiers, even though they are exactly the sort of people one would like to share a house with.

Mildred's low opinion of herself and other women is what comes from living in a society where one's importance hinges on one's attachment to a man: it not only reduces one's sense of self-worth but distorts and embitters one's views of other women. We see this phenomenon in *An Academic Question*, for instance, when Caroline Grimstone feels inferior to Iris Horniblow and Cressida, particularly when she suspects that these women have won her husband's affection. On her way to see Cressida, she feels "a deep sense of inferiority" (127). Certainly Belinda Bede's sense that Agatha Hoccleve is a stronger woman than she stems in part from her having lost out to Agatha in her bid for Henry's attentions when they were all at university together.

Back-biting, cattiness and distrust among woman are concomitant characteristics of the rivalry between them. When Letty wonders how Beth Doughty could have stolen David out from under Marjorie's nose, with all the other problems David was having, Marjorie responds: "'You can't know what a woman is up to.... It's something that can never be expected or explained'" (**QA** 207-08). Wilmet Forsythe's reaction when Mary Beamish announces her engagement is "the perhaps typically feminine one of astonishment that such a good looking man as Marius Ransome should want to marry anyone so dim and mousy as Mary Beamish" (**GB** 228), while Viola Dace in *No Fond Return of Love* is amazed that Dulcie was once engaged to Maurice Clive because she thinks he is too good looking for Dulcie. Laurel's roommate Marian resents the attention Laurel is getting from Aylwin Forbes and Paul Beltane: "It was annoying that Laurel, the country mouse whom she had initiated into the sophistications of London life, should have two such good-looking admirers while she herself had only the constant and boring devotion of the young bank clerk who lived on the top floor" (**NFRL** 165).

Caroline Grimstone in *An Academic Question* takes an almost immediate dislike to Iris Horniblow, an accomplished colleague of her husband and thus a perceived threat to Caroline. After Iris's lecture, Caroline compliments her on both her talk and her dress, relieved that the rose which Caroline had imagined her husband placing in Iris's cleavage is actually artificial and thus not likely to have been a gift from Alan. Because such a gesture seems unusual to him, Alan thanks Caroline for being kind to Iris. When Caroline remarks that praise from other women is particularly pleasing, Alan conjectures that this is so because women are usually so bitchy to one another. Caroline can only conclude that, given her own recent thoughts about Iris, he is at least in this instance very likely right. Elsewhere, in *Less Than Angels*, Tom Mallow's aunt, Mrs. Beddoes, calls on Catherine Oliphant the very day Tom has moved out. When Mrs. Beddoes tells Catherine that it was very wrong of her to have lived with Tom without being married, Catherine smiles and suggests that she is thinking the very worst. When Mrs. Beddoes agrees that one does usually think that, Catherine observes: "'Yes, of course women do think the worst of each other, perhaps because only they can know what they are capable of'" (135). Catherine is one of Pym's most reliable observers of human behavior, and her wry comment is borne out in the behavior of many other women in Pym's novels.

Women's cattiness extends to their remarks on other women's appearances, the clothes they wear, including hats and shoes, and the food they serve. Both overdressing and underdressing bring the scorn of other women. Thus, when Belinda Bede is reassured that Agatha is her old self again at the end of *Some Tame Gazelle*, she feels "a glow of warm friendliness" toward Agatha's niece, Olivia Berridge, who is plain and wears ordinary clothes, nothing pretentious like Agatha's wardrobe (236). For Belinda thinks that Agatha's wardrobe is too sophisticated for even an Archdeacon's wife, while Mildred Lathbury believes

79

that Allegra Gray dresses rather *too* nicely for a clergyman's widow. On the other hand, Emma Howick looks with amusement at her friend Ianthe Potts, with her "lugubrious tone and appearance--she was tall and droopy, with mousey hair hanging in curtains round her pale face" (**FGL** 123). Part of Wilmet Forsythe's initial disdain for Mary Beamish derives from the fact that Mary is so plain. Early in *A Glass of Blessings*, when Mary offers her friendship, Wilmet is horrified lest she becomes friends with this person so totally unlike herself. Wilmet is self-assured, beautiful, and complacent next to Mary's plain, almost mousy appearance and demeanor.

Women who dress in drab, nondescript clothes also wear sensible, low-heeled, solid shoes. In *No Fond Return of Love*, for instance, Viola Dace's first impression of Dulcie Mainwaring, who is wearing a tweed suit and heavy brogued shoes, is that she is "already half way to being a dim English spinster" (2-3), while Dulcie is later struck by the oddity of Viola's wearing red canvas shoes. As for food, in keeping with Belinda Bede's opinion that Agatha Hoccleve is not a very conscientious wife or hostess, Belinda and Harriet are both disgusted at the meal Agatha serves them. The unsavory meal served by Edith Liversidge when she invites Belinda to take potluck with her one evening is one thing: beans, bread and coffee, a meal made all the more "interesting" when an ash from Edith's cigarette drops into the beans. A formal meal served to company is quite another. Furthermore, entertaining one's woman friend is an entirely different matter from entertaining a group of both men and women. Thus Dulcie Mainwaring is genuinely surprised by the delicious meal of exotic salads and croissants Viola Dace serves her, for she had anticipated the most distasteful foods: "Tripe, liver, brains, figs and semolina" (**NFRL** 34).

Women seem only too ready to question other women, to feel a smugness when they are humiliated or hurt, particularly where men are concerned. In *The Sweet Dove Died* Phoebe's friend Jennifer doubts Phoebe's description of her relationship with James and has to suppress a smile when they are going through his things at the furniture depository. It is almost as if, by discrediting her friend, particularly on the point of the actual degree of a man's affection for her, she has gained some sort of superiority over her. In *An Academic Question*, one can understand Caroline Grimstone's attitude toward Iris Horniblow, given her jealousy of her, when Iris introduces Caroline to a very young new instructor who is obviously her lover: thinking of Iris as a cradle-snatcher gives her a feeling of satisfaction as she pities her and foresees the end of her affair. In *Jane and Prudence*, when Miss Doggett is telling Jane Cleveland about Mildred Lathbury's marriage to Everard Bone, she describes the way Mildred has helped Everard in his work. Jessie Morrow's sharp comment is, "'Oh, then he had to marry her.... That kind of devotion is worse than blackmail--a man has no escape from that'" (126). Elsewhere in the novel, Miss Doggett is most unkind about other women. Snooping through Jessie's things, for example, she runs across a photograph of Jessie's mother, Miss Doggett's cousin Ella: "She had married late and had made an unfortunate marriage--Miss Doggett's thoughts lingered with satisfaction on this theme for a few minutes, for Aubrey Morrow had left his wife and child after a few years" (179). Furthermore, when she considers whom to tell her suspicions about Jessie and Fabian, Miss Doggett runs over a list of possible confidantes: most of the women she knows are "married women too busy with their children and household cares; Mrs. Crampton and Mrs. Mayhew were stupid fluttering creatures; widows, she thought scornfully, with a silly, sentimental view of life" (181). Only Mrs. Cleveland, the vicar's wife, seems suitable to confide in.

Miss Doggett's incarnation in *Crampton Hodnet* is no less unkind to other women: "I've never liked Margaret, thought Miss Doggett suddenly and surprisingly.... Margaret was a bad wife and mother" (83). It is, in fact, Miss Doggett's interference which precipitates the crisis in the Cleveland marriage. Perhaps because she dislikes Margaret, Miss Doggett does her best to hurt her. She saves up her knowledge about Francis's declaring his love to Barbara Bird in the British Museum, for example, only to be greatly disappointed when Margaret dismisses it. But her insistence that something ought to be done about Francis--in combination with Margaret's taking the news so calmly and treating Francis as if he were a child--forces Francis to declare that he does indeed love Miss Bird. Miss Doggett takes a perverse pleasure in the trials of Margaret and Francis Cleveland. As an aging spinster who believes-- like her reincarnation in *Jane and Prudence*--that she knows what men desire and the monstrous things they are capable of, Miss Doggett is ready at every moment to accuse her nephew of grievous crimes against the sanctity of his marriage. Knowing her feelings about Margaret, however, one suspects that her motivation comes more from maliciousness toward Margaret than any kinder source.

Miss Doggett believes that her advanced age puts her in the same category as married women, whose experience and worldliness place them in a class above lowly unmarried women. Miss Doggett constantly reminds Jessie Morrow of her lack of experience and consequent inability to draw any kind of sensible conclusions from the behavior of others. There is even a sense that unmarried women are not privy to certain knowledge and experiences shared by married women, an opinion rooted in long-held social attitudes. Mildred Lathbury seems to hold this view as well, exemplified by her remark about "the inadequacy that an unmarried and inexperienced woman must always feel" (**EW** 25). Letty, in *Quartet in Autumn*, goes away from a weekend visit to her widowed cousin feeling that she has failed in a way she had not realized before. Although she had long before gotten used to being without a man and not having children, now she is struck by the knowledge that she has no grandchildren to comfort her in her old age. In contrast to her friend Marjorie, Letty has never had romance in her life. She feels keenly aware of her shortcoming when, over dinner, she knows that Marjorie is keeping her exuberance over her engagement in check in order not to "emphasise the contrast between her own enviable position, that of being a helpmate to a man, and Letty's state of useless retirement" (124). Letty has always felt this contrast, from early on at school when Marjorie had found a husband and Letty had not, to the picnic she goes on with Marjorie and David Lydell, where at one point she feels "in some way belittled or diminished" as Marjorie and David sit on canvas chairs and she on the ground (44). She even defers to Mrs. Pope's opinion at one point when she knows full well that Mrs. Pope is wrong: "A married woman--and she must not forget that Mrs. Pope was that--might very well be able to detect subtle shades of meaning in a relationship which would be lost on the inexperienced Letty" (170). The irony is that Letty's instinct, in this case about the possibility of any special affection between Edwin and Marcia, is correct. It seems more likely to her that there is something between Marcia and Norman, but Mrs. Pope's certainty in her position as a married woman, albeit a widow, causes Letty to feel thoroughly confused about her own judgment.

Seldom do we get the kind of magnanimous attitude among women as that which Belinda Bede has toward Agatha Hoccleve in *Some Tame Gazelle* when she feels that Henry might actually prefer her. Generous in thought and kind in deed to almost all women, Belinda is most uncomfortable thinking of herself as Agatha's rival--she sees it as unbecoming to a spinster of her age and unworthy of her, finally. Having long before accepted Agatha's victory, Belinda finds some comfort now by thinking that Agatha had probably proposed to Henry. She cannot stand the thought of Agatha's being pathetic, as she fleetingly does after the Bishop proposes to her. At one point the Bishop had told Belinda that Agatha had made him a pair of socks which were not quite long enough in the foot. Belinda, realizing that she has rejected something that Agatha wants, feels

> that she could almost love Agatha as a sister now. The pullover that she might have made for the Archdeacon would surely have been wrong somewhere, but as it had never even been started, it lacked the pathos of the socks not quite long enough in the foot. To think of Agatha as pathetic

was something so new that Belinda had to sit down on a chair in the hall, quite overcome by the sensation. (226)

By the end of the novel, Belinda is genuinely relieved to find that Agatha is by no means pathetic but is, in fact, very much her old confident self, making sharp, critical remarks.

It seems almost at times as if Belinda thinks of herself as secretly sharing Henry with Agatha, but there are two men in Pym's novels whose women openly share them, with as much graciousness and lack of ill will as Belinda Bede. In *Jane and Prudence*, we are told that Constance Driver used to invited her husband's lovers to their home for the weekend, sitting with them under the tree in the garden while he stayed inside, imagining they were having long conversations about him: "In reality they may have been talking of other things--life in general, cooking or knitting, for the loves always brought knitting or tapestry work with them as if to show Contance how nice they really were. But they would be talking a little awkwardly, as two women sharing the same man generally do" (57). The perverseness of this scene is not repeated in *Less Than Angels*, but the idea of women sharing one man is, when Tom Mallow's three girlfriends gather with his sister for a kind of memorial luncheon after his death. Recalling Tom fondly, his childhood sweetheart Elaine tells Catherine that Tom had told her that Catherine wrote short stories and had been a very good cook. Hoping that is all Tom had told her about their relationship, Catherine feels certain that even with full knowledge of all that had been between them, Elaine would understand and forgive her.

A number of women live together in Pym's novels, with varying degrees of success. Many are unhappy arrangements, as in *Some Tame Gazelle*, with Connie Aspinall berated and harassed by the gruff, commanding Edith Liversidge, who has given her a home. The same Connie Aspinall appears under identical circumstances in Pym's *Home Front Novel* with her relative, Agnes Grote, who is the same character as Edith Liversidge. She always has a cigarette hanging out of her mouth, speaks in a barking, commanding voice, and traces her name in the dusty surface of the Palfreys'dresser, just as she is said to have done on the Bedes' piano. In the *Home Front Novel*, Connie is long-suffering, resentful, and bitter, but the discord between Connie and Agnes is lessened by Connie's rebellious nature. Whereas Connie in *Some Tame Gazelle* marries Bishop Grote to escape Edith, Connie in the *Home Front Novel* finds refuge in the friendship of another woman, Lady Nollard. They are kindred spirits, both suffering indignities in the homes of their relatives. Lady Nollard considers her sister-in-law Amanda Wraye a fool, while Amanda Wraye cannot tolerate Lady Nollard. Lady Nollard's friendship has the salutory effect on Connie of increasing her tolerance of Agnes as well as her rebelliousness. Arriving at a wool shop too late to buy the wool Agnes has sent her to get, Connie thinks: "Agnes ought to have got it herself.... I don't care--I don't give a *damn*! she told herself defiantly" (**CS** 262). The novel ends with Connie and Lady Nollard sitting together at a party, "isolated in another world where little courtesies were observed and relations were careful for one's digestion" (**CS** 269).

In *Some Tame Gazelle*, Belinda Bede at one point considers her options if her sister Harriet were to marry Bishop Grote with the thought: "Who was there apart from the forbidden Archdeacon? One's women friends, of course, people like Edith Liversidge and Connie Aspinall, but they were a cold comfort" (160). Jessie Morrow in *Jane and Prudence* is live-in companion to the imperious Miss Doggett, whom Jessie describes to Jane as more in need of a sparring partner than a companion. This same couple of women appear in the early novel *Crampton Hodnet*, where Jessie is even more verbally abused than she is in this novel. In *Crampton Hodnet*, Miss Doggett continually declares that Miss Morrow knows nothing of the world, cannot possibly have an opinion that counts, makes no impact on any gathering whatsoever, and, in short, has no more importance than a piece of furniture or some other blank, anonymous thing. In *A Few Green Leaves*, Miss

Flavia Grundy is bossed by her housemate Miss Olive Lee and harbors quiet resentments over small affronts like Miss Lee's offering a mirror that belongs to both of them as a prize in the "bring and buy" sale without asking her permission.

Daphne Dagnall is woefully disillusioned when sharing a home with her long-time friend Heather Blekinsopp turns out to be less pleasant than she had imagined, Heather having become bossier in her old age than she had ever been. Daphne's disappointment is more keenly felt because she very much enjoys the company of women. Dulcie Mainwaring in *No Fond Return of Love* is not particularly happy with her decision to share her house, large as it is, with other women. As she is discussing arrangements with Viola Dace, Dulcie remarks that, with her niece Laurel also living in her house, "'We shall be quite a houseful of women. Like some dreadful novel,' she said quickly, fearing that it really might be like that" (57). On the first night of Viola's stay, Dulcie wonders what on earth they are going to do with one another all of the time: "Was the companionship of this rather odd woman what she really wanted?" she asks herself (68-69). Later she acknowledges that Viola is a disappointment. Women put up with other women this way often because they have known their friends so long they do not want to let them down, as with Daphne and Heather, or perhaps it is simply that women are used to putting up with situations they would rather not, as with Dulcie and Viola. Mildred's friendship with Dora Caldicote in *Excellent Women* seems to be founded largely on school girl loyalty, for Mildred is quite critical of Dora's personal habits and preferences. The same holds true in *A Few Green Leaves*, when Emma invites her old school friend Ianthe Potts to visit her in the summer, more out of guilt and pity than anything else: "She always felt guilty about Ianthe, who had doggedly kept up with her since school days when Emma would have let their acquaintance drop" (122). Women often share homes with other women, but such arrangements frequently turn out to be disappointing and anxiety-laden.

Women's friendship is not always marked by antagonism or rivalry, for often it is genuinely appreciated, as in *A Glass of Blessings*, when Wilmet Forsythe laughs with her friend Rowena about Rowena's husband Harry paying a bit too much attention to Wilmet. Wilmet reflects that "it could surely be said that Rowena and I were fortunate in each other" (137). Elsewhere, Wilmet imagines a hypothetical office scene in which she is cosily bonding with the other women office workers against their male boss. She especially appreciates her mother-in-law, with whom she gets on very well. When Sybil prepares all of Wilmet's favorite dishes for her birthday, Wilmet tells us that "the men would not of course have realized that they had been chosen especially for me, looking on the whole meal as no more than was due to them" (13). But she knows that Sybil has been generous and gracious enough to take extra care for this special occasion. Women even find themselves bonding together for a common cause when they are not particular friends. In *Jane and Prudence*, Prudence shares an office with four women, two of whom are "of an indeterminate age" but hovering around fifty--Miss Trapnell and Miss Clothier--and two of whom are very young. Prudence, Miss Trapnell, and Miss Clothier find themselves in "a kind of neutral relationship" in which "they banded together against the inconsiderateness of their employer and the follies and carelessness of the two young typists" (35).

The friendship of women has the potential to be--and often is--nurturant. In *Less Than Angels*, for example, after discovering Tom and Deirdre together, Catherine wishes she had some female friend to confide in, thinking regretfully of those she has not kept in touch with and "rather shamefacedly of others whom she had rejected as being dull" (108). Later, after Tom leaves for Africa, she feels the lack "of that cosy woman friend with whom she might spend an afternoon at a matinee, or shopping with a pleasant gossipy tea afterwards. She seemed to know more men than women and, delightful though their company was, she imagined that they were somehow less comforting than a woman would have been" (154). But Catherine discovers the real comforts of women friends when, grieving over the death of Tom, she goes to Mabel Swan and Rhoda Wellcome, is asked to tea and then dinner, and stays on for two weeks.

Women friends are very good at providing solace and comfort. For instance, when Fabian Driver announces his intention to marry Jessie Morrow, Prudence is grateful for the friendship of both Jane Cleveland and Eleanor Hitchins to help her through her distress: "What would one do without the sympathy of other women?" (**JP** 200). Ianthe Broome in *An Unsuitable Attachment* feels a strong desire to confide in another woman about her feelings for John Challow when she is in Rome. Often one simply welcomes other women because they are comfortable to be around. Ianthe would have preferred a woman her own age and background when John Challow is hired to replace Miss Grimes at the library: "She did not like men very much, except for the clergy, and found younger women rather alarming" (28). In *A Few Green Leaves*, sorting through items for a jumble sale, Daphne Dagnall is pleased when Emma Howick drops by: "Daphne was glad to be interrupted and always enjoyed the company of another woman, aware that there was a comfortable feeling about it that the company of men did not provide" (47).

As an "excellent woman," Mildred Lathbury finds that both men and women come to her for help with distressing frequency, with the result that she feels her allegiance split. As she tells Helena: "'I suppose there must be times when men band together against women and women against men. You and Miss Clovis against Julian and Rocky, and I like the umpire in a tennis match'" (**EW** 179). But Mildred feels more in league with women, as when she and her cleaning woman Mrs. Morris gossip and laugh, "a couple of women against the whole race of men" (**EW** 23-24). Such camaraderie between employee and domestic help is not uncommon in Pym's novels. In fact, cleaning women, sewing women, maids, and cooks are not only good sounding boards for ideas but excellent sources of information about other households in the community as well. They listen to the women who employ them, offer suggestions about dress and relationships, and generally behave in a manner more typical of equals than of subordinates.

In *No Fond Return of Love*, Dulcie Mainwaring listens good-naturedly to the details of the meals Miss Lord, her cleaning woman, has eaten and seems to enjoy her company. Mrs. Glaze in *Jane and Prudence* is a valuable source of information about the members of the parish the Clevelands have just moved to. Jane is delighted to be filled in on people she will soon meet. Likewise, in *Some Tame Gazelle*, Harriet tells Belinda that the Hoccleves' Florrie told their Emily "that she and cook aren't looking forward to managing the Archdeacon by themselves," leaving them to deduce that Agatha is going to Karlsbad by herself (20). Neville Forbes' housekeeper is quite eager to tell Dulcie all about Neville's troubles with Miss Spicer and later shares with her the intricacies of handling lunch when Father Forbes returned suddenly. Her willingness to confide the Father's romantic entanglements to a woman she barely knows might seem unlikely, but in the context of Pym's novels, it is perfectly normal. The entire group of domestic help in the novels might on the one hand conform to the stereotype of the gossiping, nosey servant class, but on the other hand, they function as a vast network of women who pass on news about other people, make important connections between households, and provide a solid support system for one another.

Frequently domestic employees are critical of their employers, too, and are not shy about speaking their minds. Thus, Miss Lord scoffs at Dulcie's reading so much and suggests that she could make herself a bit more glamorous if only she would try. Dulcie Mainwaring makes a point of having a word with Mrs. Sedge about the meal she has prepared for her Aunt Hermione and Uncle Bertram, thinking that Mrs. Sedge would expect it "and take it out on Aunt Hermione afterwards if I did not go. She was something of a tyrant without having acquired the qualities of a 'treasure'" (**NFRL** 97-98). In Some Tame Gazelle, Belinda, believing her cook Emily is critical of her

89

when she works in the kitchen when Emily is present, feels a real sense of freedom when she has her kitchen all to herself. Belinda is timid about so many relationships that it is not surprising she senses scorn and criticism when Emily watches her cook. It is even worse with her sewing woman, Miss Prior, whose needs Belinda is quite solicitous of. Miss Prior, who considers herself a step above Emily but not quite on a par with Belinda and Harriet, is outspoken and sensitive enough to produce in Belinda a mixture of pity and fear toward her. Mealtime is particularly stressful for Belinda, who wants to serve Miss Prior a suitable meal. She is mortified on the day that Miss Prior leaves her cauliflower cheese uneaten because there is a dead caterpillar in it, revealing that Emily had not carefully washed the cauliflower before she had cooked it. But Miss Prior is generous about the incident, telling her how nice her meals are in comparison to those served by Mrs. Hoccleve: "'*Very* poor meals there.' She lowered her voice, 'Between ourselves, Miss Bede, Mrs. Hoccleve doesn't keep a good table'" (51). Belinda is moved to tears by the surge of joy she feels. This passage illustrates again the way in which domestic help pass on information about the other families they work for. It also reveals much about Belinda's character, her solicitiousness and her fear of offending anyone, for instance. Most importantly, it demonstrates the genuine concern that at least some of Pym's women--the best ones, finally--have for other women.

The best relationships are between women who have no cause to feel jealousy or rivalry over a man. Thus sisters or married women have the best chances for successful female friendships, and these relationships often become more satisfactory than those they have with men, husbands included. The solid friendship of sisters in Pym's novels is nowhere illustrated more happily than in the relationship between Belinda and Harriet Bede, who are wonderfully good friends and companions. They share interests and clothes--Harriet benefitting from Belinda's closet more often than the other way around--but more importantly, they know one another thoroughly. Despite their own particular weaknesses and idiosyncracies, they accept and love one another openly. Harriet knows of Belinda's longtime love for Henry and anticipates hearing all about the pleasures of her evening alone with him. She knows the depth of Belinda's regard for the Archdeacon so well that, acquiver with excitement herself, she suggests a hot milky drink to calm Belinda down: "'Don't try to talk till you've finished. There'll be plenty of time for you to tell me all about it,'" she says (**STG** 155). Indeed, a few moments later, the Ovaltine having successfully loosened her tongue, Belinda is moved to confidentiality. The only time Belinda ever thinks anything negative about Archdeacon Hoccleve is when Ricardo Bianco tells her that the Archdeacon has said that Harriet is going to marry Bishop Grote: "The wicked *liar*, thought Belinda angrily. An archdeacon making mischief and spreading false rumours, that was what it amounted to" (**STG** 212). This uncharacteristic display of fierce disloyalty to her beloved Henry indicates that she cherishes her sister Harriet above all others. The prospect of living without her if Harriet marries and moves away from their home is almost more than she can bear to contemplate. Belinda is so relieved to hear that Harriet has turned down Nicholas Mold's proposal that she "kissed her impulsively and suggested that they should have some meringues for tea, as Harriet was so fond of them" (**STG** 142). Their relationship is ideal, for they are sympathetic to one another, share one another's joys and disappointments, and in all provide the best kind of comfortable and nurturing relationship one could hope for.

There are many other sisters in Pym's novels, but none are quite so fortunate as Harriet and Belinda Bede, probably because they are based on Barbara Pym and her own sister Hilary. Penelope Grandison and Sophia Ainger in *An Unsuitable Attachment*, get along well enough. Like Jane Cleveland, Sophia wants to play matchmaker, and in the process acts most uncharitably toward Ianthe Broome, who she mistakenly assumes is her sister's rival. Rhoda Wellcome and Mabel Swan in *Less Than Angels* have worked out a comfortable living arrangement very much like that of Harriet and Belinda Bede. While each does things which the other finds irksome, in general they live harmoniously and are splendid companions for one another. On the other hand, Margaret Cleveland's sister in *Crampton Hodnet* is not much comfort to her, and Caroline Grimstone's sister in *An Academic Question* provides little real solace, although Caroline's first thought after Alan confesses that he has slept with another woman is that if he had told her earlier, she could have discussed it with Susan, whom she has just visited in London.

Instead of discussing her husband's infidelity with her sister, Caroline goes to her friend Dolly, but Dolly is too preoccupied with her own misery--the death of her favorite hedgehog--and for the first time lets Caroline down. Caroline turns, then, to Coco Jeffreys. Coco is one of Pym's many males who are either homosexual or of indeterminate sexuality. These are the only men with whom women can feel as comfortable as they do with other women, and many good friendships between women and men result precisely because the men lack obvious masculine characteristics. Caroline lets her mother think that Coco is a girlfriend when he telephones her, and an even more blatant confusion of Coco's sexual identity occurs when Alan suggests that Coco is like a sister to Caroline. There is never any question of behaving with this group of men as one must with those with whom one flirts or has romantic inclinations toward. At one point Coco and Caroline are sitting under a tree, discussing Alan's infidelity, when Caroline sees him bending over her: "There was concern in his dark eyes and his face had come close to mine. I waited in surprise and embarrassment, for I realized that in this kind of situation Coco meant nothing to me" (**AQ** 111). But Coco is only bending over her to remove a bug which has crawled onto her blouse, not making a pass, much to Caroline's relief. Indeed, Coco would be horrified to know that Caroline was thinking him capable of such an act.

Mildred Lathbury has a similar friendship with William Caldicote in *Excellent Women*. Their relationship is a "comfortable dull thing" like the relationship she has with her women friends (66). On her way to her annual lunch with him one splendid spring day, she wishes she were meeting someone romantic, not William, with his preoccupations with food and his health and "his spiteful old-maidish delight in gossip" (66). This inclusion of one's asexual male friends with one's women friends occurs from time to time in Pym's novels. When Francis Cleveland is thinking of all the gossiping North Oxford women likely to spread rumors about him, he thinks of "Aunt Maude, Mrs. Fremantle, old Mrs. Killigrew, Edward Killigrew. You could lump him in with the women and never notice the difference" (CH 194). In *A Glass of Blessings*, Wilmet Forsythe grows quite fond of Keith, with his chattering on about the most trivial of things, boring her at times, but amusing her as well. Cozy and comfortable to be with, Keith becomes a valued friend to Wilmet.

It is possible for women to have successful, satisfiying long-term friendships with women other than sisters. Jane and Prudence are excellent friends, Jane adopting a kind of motherly, matchmaking role with Prudence but appreciating her as an equal at the same time. Beatrix Howick and Isobel Mound, in *A Few Green Leaves*, have been friends from their college days and now spend holidays together and visit Emma in the village where she is living in her mother's cottage. One might almost judge a woman's character by the success she has with female friendships. For example, one measure of Wilmet Forsythe's growth to maturity in *A Glass of Blessings* is her acceptance of Mary Beamish's friendship. Early on, Mary's selfless devotion to church, social services, and her mother is repugnant to Wilmet, largely because Wilmet feels inadequate or less useful in comparison. By the end of the novel, however, Wilmet comes to cherish Mary's friendship and humbly and sincerely compares her own life to that of Mary, with her "glass of blessings." Like Emma Woodhouse, "having too much her own way and thinking too well of herself," Wilmet must go through a series of humiliating discoveries about herself before she can appreciate the real value of Mary's friendship. But *A Glass of Blessings* has no Mr. Knightly. Instead, the model for superior behavior is a woman, Mary Beamish. Sybil also provides an excellent model, but Wilmet has never had to measure herself against Sybil as she eventually does with Mary. Wilmet's self-absorption had blinded her to the reality of others and shaped her perceptions according to her own fancy; warmly accepting Mary's friendship is a strong indication of the degree to which Wilmet grows by the end of the novel. In contrast, Leonora Eyre of *The Sweet Dove Died*, who uses women as foils for herself, is the least likable woman in all of Pym's fiction. She never grows out of her self-absorption as Wilmet does but remains frozen in her inability to establish meaningful emotional ties with others, female or male.

The truly likable women in Pym's novels are sensitive and sympathetic to women as well as men. They are not without faults nor above making an occasionally too sharp comment, but Jessie Morrow of *Crampton Hodnet*, Belinda and Harriet Bede, Jane Cleveland, Dulcie Mainwaring, and Catherine Oliphant, for instance, are mature women, generous in spirit and deed, whose wry and witty observations on human behavior endear them to the hearts of readers as well as to their fictional friends. They do not derive pleasure from the misfortunes of their women friends nor do they disparage the company of women. Indeed, they are very likely the women one would choose for one's own friends.

FOUR

EVERYONE HAS A MOTHER

At one point in *A Glass of Blessings*, Wilmet Forsythe remarks to her husband Rodney and her mother-in-law Sybil as they discuss Wilf Bason and what to expect when they have tea with him: "'He strikes one as the kind of person who would have a mother.'" Sybil points out: "'Well, everybody has or had a mother.... But I see just what you mean'" (98). Just what Wilmet means becomes clear when one examines Barbara Pym's treatment of mothers: while it is true that everyone has one and that Pym portrays mothers of various ages and personalities, the kind of mother Wilmet is talking about includes those who never let their children function as mature, independent adults but continue practicing those protective, fussing activities associated with the mothering of young children. They are fairly harmless nuisances. Much worse are the elderly women in the care of single sons or daughters, women who dominate and severely limit the lives of their children. They live well into very old age, exerting undue influence over their children, who find themselves in the middle of their own lives, still involved in a curious dependency relationship with their mothers. Their sons appear to be of questionable sexuality, and their daughters are nondescript and weak. Rather than nurture, these mothers stunt growth. Not all of Pym's mothers conform to either the overly fussy or outright domineering type, but mothers are problematic for a large number of Pym's characters.

Mothers who exert such control over their children that their children virtually give up their own lives appear from the first in Pym's novels. She uses this character type in her *Home Front Novel*, for instance, with Beatrice Wyatt's mother, who, despite her energy and good health, had taken to her bed after her husband's death some ten years before because she believed she had no more reason to get out of bed. Beatrice, despite having a personality in her own right and being over thirty years of age, has nevertheless "drifted into a sort of subjugation to her strong-minded mother" (**CS** 222). As the only child of elderly parents, Beatrice feels duty-bound to care for her mother, an obligation that very nearly prevents her marrying the curate. Their happy union is made possible by the sudden "cure" of Beatrice's mother, a miracle brought about by the brisk, firm woman evacuee living with them, Miss Stoat. Miss Stoat had cared for her own bedridden mother for ten years and now seems fully prepared to read inspirational verse, bore Mrs. Wyatt with tedious monologues, and in general, take over for the duration in a way that Mrs. Wyatt finds intolerable. Mrs. Wyatt is a comic character whose "invalidism" provides the conflict whose resolution brings about a happy ending for the novel. But Mrs. Wyatt's type takes on darker, more serious tones in subsequent novels.

In *A Glass of Blessings*, Wilmet Forsythe describes Mary Beamish's mother particularly effectively: "I imagined old Mrs. Beamish crouching greedily over a great steak or taking up a chop bone in her fingers, all to give her strength to batten on her daughter with her tiresome demands" (20-21). This image of her seems justified when Sybil comments, after Mary has rushed home to feed her mother, that Ella Beamish is rich enough to have a paid companion, suggesting that Mrs. Beamish prefers running her own child ragged. Mrs. Beamish's domination takes many forms. Not only must Mary oversee her meals but she must also have permission to go out. When she meets

Wilmet to go to the blood donor's center, for instance, Mary explains that she almost did not get to come because her mother was restless and Mary had had to call on Miss Prideaux to sit with her. Later, they go shopping for a new dress for Mary because her mother had said she needed one. When Wilmet suggests she buy a black dress, Mary says her mother does not approve of black for girls; when Wilmet observes that she might benefit from wearing some makeup, Mary says, "'I don't know what mother would say'" (81). All of this would not be worthy of notice had Mary been a girl of fifteen or so, but she is Wilmet's own age, well into adulthood. To her credit, Mary does buy the black dress, but it is clear that Mary's mother dominates her to an unusual degree. When it becomes evident that Mrs. Beamish is mortally ill, Sybil, Rodney, and Wilmet try to imagine what Mary will do with her new-found freedom, conjecturing that she might travel, for surely a woman with money and freedom would want to travel. But Mary chooses to go to a convent, a decision which is not surprising given her training in obedience and self-sacrifice.

Even brief references to mothers suggest the oppressive restrictions elderly women impose on their children. Both Miss Jenner and Miss Prior in *Some Tame Gazelle* lead limited lives, in large part because of living with their mothers. Miss Jenner, the local wool shop owner who is getting on in years herself, lives over her shop with her old mother. Belinda Bede finds Miss Jenner's behavior with travelling salesmen silly and embarrassing, but she is quite sympathetic about her plight. She imagines that the dullness of Miss Jenner's life, exacerbated by having to live with her mother, is relieved only by her outrageous flirtations with the travellers. Miss Prior, Belinda's sewing woman, a dried-up little woman of uncertain age, also lives with her mother and can be seen attending local village functions with her. Belinda is especially kind to Miss Prior, not only because her manner is such that she is easily offended but also, according to Belinda, because "'one feels that perhaps Miss Prior's whole life is just a putting up with second best all the time'" (46). At least Miss

Jenner and Miss Prior have their own businesses and do not have always to be tending their mothers. The unfortunate Miss Spicer in *No Fond Return of Love* is burdened by an aged mother who keeps falling out of bed and cannot be left alone. While readers never meet Miss Spicer nor her mother directly, we hear about them from Neville Forbes's housekeeper, who tells Dulcie about the embarrassing scene in which Miss Spicer had declared her love to Neville. Miss Spicer's infatuation with Neville Forbes drives him from his church to the refuge of his own mother's hotel. By the novel's end, Neville Forbes's problem is solved by the removal of both Miss and Mrs. Spicer to a home they have bought in Eastbourne, but one can only wonder about the fate of poor Miss Spicer.

It is not only women like Miss Spicer, Miss Jenner, and Mary Beamish, but single men as well who live with their aging mothers. Edward Killigrew in *Crampton Hodnet*, Edward Lyall of *Jane and Prudence*, Mervyn Cantrell in *An Unsuitable Attachment*, and Coco Jeffreys in *An Academic Question* all are grown men who live at home with their widowed mothers. Edward Killigrew's mother, described as having always lived in Oxford, "first as a domineering wife and mother and then as a mother only" (**CH** 121), does not like Edward to be late for tea. Edward himself is described as being fussy, petulant and spiteful, enjoying gossip about his colleagues with the same degree of pleasure as his mother. Always conscious of his mother, he does nothing without wondering how she would react, what she would do, or what she will say. At the same time, Edward and Mrs. Killigrew have the kind of antagonism between them that characterizes some of Pym's married couples who have been together for years and find much to complain about each other. Like Margaret Cleveland with Francis, Mrs. Killigrew is given to treating Edward as if he were still a child, and he behaves accordingly. Edward's mother is sometimes too much for him, as indicated when Francis Cleveland inquires after her health. Edward replies that she is as full of beans as ever, the narrator adding that Edward wishes she were not quite so full of beans. Later, when Miss Doggett remarks on Mrs.

Killigrew's good health, Edward says that she is likely to see them all into their graves: "But behind his joviality there lurked a fear that it might be true. Of course Mother was his whole life and he would be quite lost without her, but he occasionally wondered if it might not be rather pleasant to be quite lost" (**CH** 121). Such an observation indicates that life with mother is not really so wonderful after all and that it has fostered as much malice as fondness in her son.

A similar thought might have occurred to Mervyn Cantrell, whose "disagreeable old mother," as Ianthe Broome pictures her (**UA** 27), does not like her son to be late for the evening meal. When his mother goes away for a few days, he takes advantage of her absence by inviting Ianthe out to dinner. It turns out that Mervyn has brought Ianthe to dinner with a purpose in mind: if his mother dies, he wants to know, would she marry him? Ianthe refuses his offer, and Mervyn's mother does not die. Indeed, she returns from her visit with friends with renewed spirits and will probably live for years. Interestingly, during their meal, a man comes to their table to tell Mervyn how sorry he is to hear about Mervyn's mum passing on, knowing his devotion to her. It is not, of course, Mervyn's mum who has not passed on, but, we learn later, Wilf Bason's mother. Pym conveys in this scene an impression one has of other mother-son relationships in her novels: the mention of Wilf Bason links Mervyn Cantrell to the group of middle-aged unmarried men whose fussiness and interests in such "effeminate" things as cleanliness, fine furniture, cooking, and the like hint at their dubious sexuality. The scene also points to the tediousness of living with one's querulous, demanding mother and the potential freedom that lies ahead once she dies.

Edward Lyall and his mother, "a gentle-looking person with a rather long, melancholy face" (**JP** 89), go everywhere together. Mrs. Lyall's concern for her son's success, health, and welfare presumably accounts for her appearance. When first seen, for instance, she seems anxious, then worried, and finally sad, as she speaks with Jane of the demands placed on her son in his position as

99

Member of Parliament. Mrs. Lyall's energies are focused solely on her son, who is the chief topic of her conversation at all times. She regales his admirers with details of his eating habits at the whist drive and later, at Fabian Driver's tea party, goes on about the exhausting nature of his work. Coco and Kitty Jeffreys of *An Academic Question* are another mother-son pair who have a close relationship and attend social functions as a couple. At forty-two, Coco and his sixty-two-year-old mother make "a handsome and interesting pair" (1). Both are meticulous about dress and appearance, dislike any talk of aging and death, and need to rest before social occasions. Coco has "long, useless fingers," a "tall, elegant figure" with a "thin, rather swarthy face" and combs his dark, curly hair forward in a manner which gives him an "air of a Regency dandy" (11). He fusses about Caroline's dress and hair, seems "prissy" and effeminate, and acts in such a way as to cause Iris Horniblow to ask Caroline frankly what his sexual leanings are.

Coco has several of those unmistakable stereotyped homosexual characteristics that Pym gives to male characters of questionable sexuality. Michael and Gabriel in her first novel, *Crampton Hodnet*, for instance, are beautiful young men who go everywhere and do everything together, often speaking--or gushing--in unison. They prance in the woods and dance "prettily in the path" (71). Pym repeated these mannerisms in such characters as Wilf Bason and Keith in *A Glass of Blessings*. Wilf Bason has a "fluty, enthusiastic voice" (55), likes chintz, fusses about meals, and takes Father Thames's Fabergé egg because he wants to have the exquisite creation in his possession. Keith is a neat-featured young man who occasionally models and has mannerisms and interests which suggest his homosexuality.

For one aspect of an old-fashioned and stereotyped picture of homosexual--or decidedly "effeminate"--males that Pym exploits for comic effect is that they have close relationships with their mothers, relationships which continue to be strong even after they have reached adulthood. Rodney and Wilmet discover that Wilf Bason does indeed have a mother: her picture in a silver frame sits on the mantelpiece, and she has made the chintz covers and lace tablecloth which contribute to the "charm" of his room. Implicit in the description of this room is its feminine quality, and Pym strongly implies that his mother has had a great influence on her son. In addition to Wilf Bason, there is another strongly feminine homosexual in *A Glass of Blessings*, Keith, Piers Longridge's lover. Keith is accomplished at things domestic and has a ready supply of helpful household hints. He is an exceptionally well drawn character, a funny and warm man whose fussiness about cleanliness is endearing and amusing. This stereotype about the strong attachment of homosexual males to their mothers is repeated in *The Sweet Dove Died*, when Meg goes to a play one evening with her young homosexual friend Colin, Colin's lover Harold, and Harold's mother. This is a perverted sort of double date, with two homosexual lovers and their mother and mother-substitute.

The bisexual James Boyce in *The Sweet Dove Died* also has had a very close relationship with his mother, who has only recently died. His father having been killed in the war and his being an only child, James had spent much of his time with his mother and finds older women much easier to talk to than younger ones. As a result, James has turned out to be sexually ambivalent and confused about women. On first meeting Leonora, he is struck by her old-fashioned elegance, perhaps reminded of his mother as a young woman. Leonora essentially becomes a mother substitute for James. Perhaps not entirely unconsciously, Leonora attempts to control James's life by curtailing his freedom of choice, shaping his tastes, and even "confining" him to a flat at the top of her own home, a room which, ironically, had once been a nursery and which still has bars on its windows. James is, not surprisingly, startled to see the bars, feeling quite rightly that he is being imprisoned by her, or at least being placed where he can be closely supervised, as one would a child. James's lover Ned emphasizes Leonora's role as mother substitute rather than lover by exclaiming how very much his own mother would like the way Leonora has decorated her room and by drawing attention to her fatiguing easily, just as his mother does.

Yet there are sexual overtones to the relationship between James and Leonora, and Leonora sees herself as a rival to his casual sex partner, Phoebe Sharpe. This becomes clear when Humphrey and she go to collect James's few pieces of furniture at Phoebe's cottage and Leonora feels triumphant over this "girl she now regarded as her vanquished rival" (**SDD** 126). At the same time, Phoebe is drawing the parallel between Leonora and James's mother. We have already been told that Leonora dislikes the photograph of James's mother as a beautiful young woman with the hair style and makeup fashionable in the early fifties because she looks fresh and young in contrast to Leonora's increasingly worn look. Although James's mother would be at least Leonora's own age, she is captured forever young in this photograph. When Phoebe sees it, she mistakenly assumes that James's mother had died young and even comments that it is sad that she never lived to see James grown up. James does not correct that impression. Now that Phoebe has seen Leonora and knows that she is not the kindly, white-haired mother figure she had imagined her to be, Phoebe scornfully classifies Leonora as a mother figure replacing his dead mother: "what the girl in the photograph might have become if she had lived" (**SDD** 126). Leonora would find Phoebe's connecting her with the picture of the young woman flattering, but the suggestion that she is a mother figure loathsome. Leonora's own mother had once had a young Italian lover, so Leonora's fancies about James would not seem entirely unreasonable to her. But the suggestion that Leonora is a kind of surrogate mother is reinforced when, near the conclusion of the novel, as James is on his way to see Leonora, he thinks of her as "some familiar landmark, like one's mother, even" (**SDD** 205).

In addition to the single men who live with their widowed mothers, other single men maintain close relationships with widowed mothers or at least visit often. In addition to Wilf Bason, there are Simon Beddoes in *Crampton Hodnet*, Everard Bone of *Excellent Women*,

Neville Forbes of *No Fond Return of Love*, and David Lydell of *Quartet in Autumn*. Mrs. Beddoes is a garrulous, voluble woman, rather vague but dressed smartly, her saving grace. Simon's fears that she will not know what to say and that she will talk too long are confirmed, but her gracious and elegant appearance occupies people's attention so thoroughly that they scarcely notice her speech. Simon acts almost like her caretaker; at the very least, he seems embarrassed by her open and frank way of revealing her entire history to strangers: "Simon was always saying how unwise it was to let his mother travel anywhere alone" **(CH** 112). Her unabashed manner and her son's discomfort about her topics of conversation remind one in a way of Everard Bone's mother, though Mrs. Bone is older and much more odd than Mrs. Beddoes. Mrs. Bone is a peculiar woman who speaks of Jesuits and wormwood and the "Dominion of the Birds." When Mildred tells Helena Napier that she had met Everard Bone's odd mother, Helena comments: "'Yes, she is odd, but then people's mothers usually are, don't you think?'"**(EW** 181). Another odd one is Aylwin and Neville Forbes's mother. Mrs. Forbes is rather a character: tight with her money, she serves coffee boiled with used grounds and inelegant meals to the few guests who come to her hotel, and she tends to live in the past. Mrs. Forbes's common background is apparently the cause of her husband's having been disinherited, and it would seem as if the Forbes sons are destined to make unsuitable matches as well.

Another only child whose aged mother is still living, is the handsome Father Lydell in *Quartet in Autumn*, to whom Letty's friend Marjorie is briefly engaged. His mother is ninety years old, living in a religious community, and seems in some way responsible for his breaking off his engagement with Marjorie. Although Beth Doughty is mentioned in the garbled story Letty gets from Marjorie over the telephone, the story she tells Letty in person begins: "'His gastric trouble, and then there was his mother being over ninety... ,'" for these are the reasons he had given for being reluctant to name a wedding date (207).

Their wedding had already been postponed once because of his mother's illness.

Thus, whether they live with their mothers or not, single men who are still close to their mothers have problems with women. Some clearly want nothing to do with women in a sexual or romantic way--Wilf, Edward, Mervyn, and Coco, for instance. Most of these men still live with their mothers. The others--James, Simon, Everard, Neville, and David, for instance--expect a good deal from women and have difficulty in relationships with them. The implication is that mothers, especially when fathers have long been dead, are in part responsible for the troubled relationships betwen men and women.

Mothers are not all negative forces in Pym's novels, for they may represent standards or guidelines of behavior. Their children, no matter how old or how mature, are reminded of them when they contemplate doing things their mothers would not approve of. A single exception occurs in the very early work *So Very Secret*, in which the central character heroine, Cassandra Swan, is a typical excellent woman, daughter of a vicar, who had cared for her parents until their deaths and now lives in the family home. Commenting on the fact that her father would not have liked the popish tendencies of the new village vicar, she tells us that she still thinks of what her father would have said, even though he has been dead for five years. After this novel, characters are almost always conscious of what their mothers would have thought, not their fathers. Mildred Lathbury, well over thirty years old, for example, thinks of her mother's pursed lips pronouncing that brandy is only for medicinal purposes as she contemplates opening her own "emergency" bottle. Dulcie Mainwaring, sceptically regarding her cheerless hotel room at Tavistock, is seized with an anxiety "inherited from her mother: was it certain that the beds would be properly aired? *A damp bed* ... she could hear again the horrified tone in which these words were pronounced" (**NFRL** 184). Ianthe Broome is not surprised that the image of her mother rises up before her after John Challow has kissed her in public, for one does not do such things.

One does not like to disappoint one's mother. Emma Howick is conscious of having let her mother down when she attends an old students' reunion at her college: "Emma always had the feeling at these college gatherings that her mother would have been happier if she could have presented her in a more favourable light, a daughter to be proud of--married, and the mother of fine children, or even not married, but still the mother of fine children" (FGL 126). Similarly, Prudence Bates is reluctant to visit her mother after learning of Fabian's engagement to Jessie because, while returning to her childhood home would be pleasant, her mother's unasked questions would be too much to face: "Why didn't she come and see her mother more often? ... Why wasn't she married yet?" (JP 202). When Digby Fox and Mark Penfold drop by Catherine Oliphant's flat hoping to be fed, they catch a glimpse of her with a mop in her hand. Both find it odd that she is cleaning in the evening, but Digby says, with a disapproving tone: "'I don't know what my mother would say'" (LTA 28). In a more serious context, Caroline Grimstone's response to her sister Susan's announcement that she has had an abortion is "'Whatever would Mother have said?'" (AQ 70). Susan assures her she has not told their mother. What one's mother would say has varying degrees of importance for people, but a significant number of Pym's characters govern their behavior by it.

In contrast to the men and women who are tied to aged parents, Pym's central character heroines are independent. But several have paid their filial dues. Mildred Lathbury, for instance, had looked after her parents until their deaths, as did Ianthe Broome, an only child born late in her parents' life. Dulcie Mainwaring lives on in the family home in which she had cared for her parents. The deaths of their parents opened up possibilities for choices their children had longed to make. Mildred Lathbury's parents' death had freed her to go to a High Church of her preference, for instance, but not without some misgivings: "I could imagine my mother, her lips pursed, shaking her head and breathing in a frightened whisper, 'Incense'" (EW 11). We are told that Dulcie

Mainwaring had begun doing her indexing jobs at home while her mother needed attention during the day, but "now she was free," she prefers to continue doing her work there (**NFRL** 22). In *An Unsuitable Attachment*, Ianthe Broome had lived with her mother, and now that her mother is gone, Ianthe is "free to choose" the church she would like, fix the sort of meal and read the kind of thing her mother would have disapproved of (31). There is a brief scene in *Less Than Angels* in which two women at the table next to Catherine's in a restaurant ask, because she is wearing a black dress, if she is in mourning. One of these women has just lost her mother, Catherine is told, and now she is free to go to the church of her choice. This is not a young woman, either, for Catherine has wondered how one who looked as old as she could possibly have had a mother recently living. The implication of these passages is than any child who has to take care of her aged parents pays with her freedom.

Another aspect of mothers in Pym's novels, particularly mothers who are still relatively young, is that they are understandably interested in who their daughters date and marry, more often disapproving than not, wanting the kind of happiness and success that they find missing in their own lives. In *Crampton Hodnet*, for instance, Margaret Cleveland wishes Anthea would not see so much of Simon Beddoes but more of the safe and dull young men destined to be Oxford dons, any one of whom could occupy himself in research at the Bodleian Library rather than stay around the house, getting in the way. Most of all, however, Margaret does not want her daughter to be hurt, and at nineteen and in love with an ambitious young man like Simon Beddoes, she is sure to be hurt. Mrs. Cleveland's solicitousness for her daughter's well being far outweighs her concern for her husband. Her role as mother not only to Anthea but also to Oxford undergraduates is more important to her than her role as wife: after thirty years of marriage, she takes her husband for granted and never thinks of poetry now, but only of her house, her daughter and the undergraduates, who sometimes need her as a friend and "even as a mother"

106

(15). Mrs. Williton's suspicion that Aylwin Forbes is "a man of loose moral character" is confirmed when she calls on him as he is entertaining Laurel, proof, she thinks, "of his degeneracy" (**NFRL** 136).

Sophia Ainger's mother, Mrs. Grandison, believes that Sophia has married beneath her and wishes that Mark's church were in a better district. Sophia is fond of recalling the more gracious surroundings of her childhood home and tries "to recapture the atmosphere of her mother's house with bowls of quinces, the fragrance of well polished furniture, and the special Earl Grey tea, but she often realized how different it really was" (**UA** 21). Caroline Grimstone's mother wishes that Caroline had married David, the politician with a promising future, instead of her university professor husband, and she disapproves of Susan's living with a man she has not married. Caroline's mother's disappointment in her daughters is heightened by the fact that she was unhappy in her own marriage. When she tells Caroline that she was in love with another man when she married her father, Caroline understands the implication: "She might have been the wife of a television personality, I of a Member of Parliament. As it was, she was the widow of a bank manager and I the wife of a lecturer in a provincial university" (**AQ** 117). Caroline's mother believes they have settled for second best and wishes more for her own daughters.

This is precisely what motivates Mrs. Wilmot in the much earlier novel *Civil to Strangers*. Mrs. Wilmot is immensely pleased with her daughter's match with the curate Mr. Paladin because of her own disappointing life as a rector's wife. Having had visions of herself as a Bishop's or at least an Archdeacon's wife, she is filled with hope that perhaps in her daughter Janie she can enjoy such happiness vicariously. Emma Howick's mother, on the other hand, simply wishes that Emma would marry-- anyone will do. To that end, Beatrix feels it "her duty to 'do' something for Emma, since she seemed to be incapable of doing anything for herself" and sets about to try to bring Emma together with Tom Dagnall, whom she had earlier dismissed as "ineffectual" (**FGL** 247). Jane

Cleveland, in *Jane and Prudence*, wonders if she is failing her duty by not having higher aspirations for her daughter Flora, thinking that the role of wife of a Member of Parliament is more suited to Prudence than someone like Flora. Jane is probably the least interfering mother of all, yet even she worries that Flora might make the wrong match or become too involved with a man at such a young age. Similarly, Rhoda Wellcome's concern for her niece in *Less Than Angels* is not that Deirdre will marry the wrong man but that she will not marry in time to prevent her going off to Africa to study the natives. Rhoda hopes Deirdre will find someone soon and settle comfortably in a house nearby.

Because mothers have this tendency not only to want the best for their children but to quite openly speak their minds, visits from and to mothers and mothers-in-law can be dreaded events. In *An Academic Question*, Alan Grimstone does not get on well with his mother and manages to be out of the way as much as possible when she visits. Although Alan is an only child whose father died in the war, he has grown away from his mother, which is unusual for a Pym male. Alan's mother can be a nuisance, Caroline tells us, and tends to be interfering with advice on what to feed Alan and how to rear her child. On the other hand, Caroline finds her agreeable enough and even joins forces with her against Alan on the matter of smoking. At the same time, Caroline resists visiting her own mother, whom she finds irritating. Pym used this idea of the son disapproving of smoking in *A Few Green Leaves*, where Martin Shrubsole, a doctor who specializes in geriatrics, conscientiously admonishes his mother-in-law Magdalen Raven not to smoke and to cut sugar out of her diet. He admits to wondering whether he actually wants to preserve her all that well, for her removal would leave more room in their already cramped quarters, where she permanently resides. His protectiveness on the matters of her smoking, eating rich foods, and hanging about the churchyard examining gravestones comes from the guilt he has about entertaining such thoughts. Martin is not overly fond of his mother-in-law and considers even speaking to her a waste of time. He can never think of her as "Mummy," which is what his wife calls her, nor can he "bring himself to call her 'Magdalen', as she would have preferred. When he addressed her by name, other than just saying 'you', he called her 'mother', but that didn't seem quite right either, for she was not and never could be 'mother' to him" (55).

Visits to mothers can become ways to avoid action for some people, as when Neville Forbes abandons his clerical duties and goes to his mother's hotel in order to escape the embarrassment of Miss Spicer. Neville, like his brother Aylwin, and like most of Pym's men, seems incapable of acting in a mature manner toward women. Mrs. Forbes is nothing like Dulcie's imagined picture of her--"a rather conventional kind of mother, elderly, of course, with white hair, and lace at her throat" (**NFRL** 127)--but instead, is "a gaunt-looking woman with a large nose and piercing eyes," whose frugality borders on stinginess (**NFRL** 158). Still, Neville finds that visiting his mother has exactly the calming and soothing effect he had hoped it would. Aylwin's wife Marjorie's return to her mother has the opposite effect. At first it was pleasant enough, but then it became just as it always had been before she was married, with Marjorie being pressed into service around the house and at church. Rather than the adventure and excitement she had anticipated, Marjorie found only boredom. In the end, Marjorie finds the romance she seeks on the dining car of a train, under circumstances very similar to those in which she met Aylwin. Her mother is useful to Marjorie in several ways, however: because Mrs. Williton distrusts Aylwin and is assured that he is a libertine, she presses Marjorie to sue for divorce; and because she does not take lunch on the train, probably because she does not want to spend the money, Marjorie is free to find the romance she is looking for.

In her notes for *Quartet in Autumn*, Pym wrote in 1973: "Mothers--Each character once had a mother. Four people in their sixties faced with the approach of old age" (**MS PYM** 72). In the novel itself, this observation is made early on. As Mother's Day is approaching, the four have been discussing the increase in the price of flowers: "Yet it

109

could hardly affect people too old to have a mother still alive. Indeed, it was sometimes strange to reflect that each of them had once had a mother" (7). Then follows a brief history of the fates of each mother and the age at which she died. Norman had not known his mother, Letty's had died after the war, Edwin's had died at seventy-five, and Marcia's had died just a few years before at the age of eighty-nine. That it seems odd that these four aging people had once had mothers echoes Dulcie Mainwaring's similar thought in *No Fond Return of Love* when she thinks of Christmas as a time when people "seemed to lose their status as individuals in their own right and became, as it were, diminished in stature, mere units in families, when for the rest of the year they were bold and original and often the kind of people it is impossible to imagine having such ordinary everyday things as parents" (106). This passage is a key to understanding why parents, particularly mothers, are problematic: they represent one's not having matured enough to function as complete individuals, "bold and original," but rather one's being in need of looking after.

That Pym makes a point of mentioning the mothers of the four aging people in *Quartet in Autumn* indicates the importance she attaches to mothers, to their fates, and particularly to how long they lived and therefore how much influence they had on their children's lives. Could it be, for instance, that Norman's never having known his mother might in some small way account for his general state of anger? Certainly Marcia's mother seems to have been of enormous influence in her life. The least stable of the four characters, Marcia ends her days having gone quite mad. That she and her mother lived alone in their big home with only the cat Snowy as Marcia grew into adulthood and then into her own old age cannot help but have in some way contributed to Marcia's unbalanced perspective, especially in light of Pym's portrayal of the influence of old mothers on their grown children. Thus we have a reference to Marcia's having been "one of those women, encouraged by her mother, who had sworn that she would never let the surgeon's knife touch her body, a woman's body being such a private thing" (18), and we are told that after her mother's death, Marcia stopped cleaning her house, wanting to preserve things as they always had been when her mother was alive. There is still an old fur ball from her old cat Snowy on her mother's bed.

Occasionally there are "motherless" children--grown ups who lost their parents early in life. If they are men, they are doted upon by women who feel great sympathy for them. Prudence Bates, for instance, thinks more kindly of Geoffrey Manifold after she learns that his parents died when he was eighteen. For Catherine Oliphant, on the other hand, having been without a family for much of her life has produced in her an almost compulsive desire to "mother." Thus, Digby and Mark call on her whenever they lack food or funds to feed themselves and Tom relies on her in the way a child might. Indeed, Catherine views most men as children, recognizing Tom's weakness as that of a child and feeling responsible for Alaric Lydgate, whose rough exterior hides what Catherine believes is a cowering "small boy, uncertain of himself" in need of a woman stronger than he (**LTA** 242). Much more common than a person like Catherine being left without relatives when parents die is the situation in which single siblings are left and sisters move in with their brothers to keep house and look after them. In such cases, sisters often become mother-substitutes for their brothers.

It is such a common arrangement that Rhoda Wellcome, who had kept house for her parents, lived alone for a time after their death, and now lives with her widowed sister, wonders why Alaric Lydgate's sister, Gertrude, does not live with him. Indeed, Gertrude Lydgate, fifteen years her brother's senior, tells Esther Clovis that she has always felt a sense of responsibility for Alaric: "'Mother always used to say that he was weak'" (**LTA** 227). Dulcie Mainwaring's Aunt Hermione and Uncle Bertram also live together, but Bertram looks forward to his move to a guest house in a community of monks, with "'good food, central heating, no women ... '" (**NFRL** 94). This remark, in combination with Bertram's later statement that the vicar whose sister had died "'has turned to Hermione at last, or rather she has indicated the direction he should take. I suppose women always do that, really'" (**NFRL** 243), implies that Bertram believes his sister has been too much in control in his own life. While in *Excellent Women*, Winifred Malory keeps house cheerfully and adoringly for her brother Julian and the two get along admirably, in *A Few Green Leaves*, Tom and Daphne Dagnall endure a strained and unhappy relationship. Daphne had rushed in out of duty to care for her brother the moment his young wife died and now seems stuck forever as his keeper. Tom has long regarded his sister as almost a non-person, someone who resents his interest in history and intrudes on his privacy, but at the same time he relies on her efficiency for cooking his meals, preparing tea, and running the vicarage for him. On her part, Daphne awakens each morning with the thought that some day she will escape this village, a wish she finally acts on when she moves in with her friend Heather Blekinsopp. When that arrangement turns out disappointingly, Daphne begins to wonder if perhaps she has made a mistake by abandoning her brother. In this way, Daphne imagines sisterly duty as a convenient escape from an undesirable situation.

Pym's mothers and mother-substitutes are all the more noticeable because of Pym's striking lack of fathers. Time and again there are references to fathers having died many years before. James Boyce's, Emma Howick's, and Alan Grimstone's fathers had all been killed in the war, for instance. Many of them seem to have died in their prime, a circumstance which takes on greater meaning in light of Pym's particularly unbalanced world. One wonders if perhaps for some of them their wives had simply been too much. The domineering Mrs. Killigrew in *Crampton Hodnet* tells Margaret Cleveland that she has seen two husbands go to their graves. In general, references to late husbands seem to indicate that their widows have adjusted quite well to life without them. In *Crampton Hodnet*, Mrs. Beddoes tells Miss Doggett that she loved someone else when she married Simon's father, for instance, and does not particularly miss him now that he is gone. Mrs. Lyall, in *Jane and Prudence*, apparently does not miss her late husband, expressing relief, for instance, that breakfasts are no longer the huge meals her husband demanded. Instead, her son has supplanted his father as the center of her life. The only references to the late husband of Mabel Swan in *Less Than Angels* are that when he was alive, Mabel had been expected to prepare a hot meal in the evenings year round, while now she is free to prepare salads for supper in warm weather. Furthermore, she thinks of her son Malcolm as "a good solid young man, very much like his father, reliable and, although of course she never admitted it, a little dull" (35). She regards her daughter Deirdre as more like herself when she was Deirdre's age, "before marriage to a good dull man and life in a suburb had steadied her" (35). Rhoda admits to having occasionally wished for "'the experience of marriage'" but not with "poor Gregory Swan" (36). The late Mr. Swan, then, must have been like so many Pym men: "exhausted" after a day in the City, in control at home, his needs attended to, and crushingly boring.

There are wonderful exceptions to the negative portrayal of mothers. Mabel Swan is a jolly, comforting mother whose two children are fairly independent even though they still live at home. In *No Fond Return of Love*, Mrs. Beltane also has two children who live at home but her fussy doting is focused on her dog, not her children. The fact that her son is a nice young man, quite lovable, who works in a flower shop while her daughter is "rather gauche and unfeminine" and teaches botany at London University probably suggested to readers in the 1950s that Mrs. Beltane's guidance as a mother is not all that it should have been. On the other hand, to readers in the 1980s, it suggests that her children have had more freedom than others to express themselves as they wish. Another mother who might come under scrutiny for laxity in that role is Jane Cleveland, for it is almost as if she has reversed roles with her daughter Flora. Flora is much more conscientious about the appearance of their house, the preparation of meals, and the necessity for proper behavior than is her mother Jane. Still, Jane is a delightful, loving woman who gives Flora all the freedom she needs. One cannot imagine her turning into a Mrs. Beamish, for instance.

Finally, perhaps the best example of good mothering is Sybil Forsythe. She is just the opposite of Mrs. Beamish; she is not intrusive, domineering, or dependent. Rather, she is a social worker with enough commitment to her causes that, despite her agnosticism, she answers pleas for clothing donations from local parishes. She is a good friend to both her son Rodney and her daughter-in-law Wilmet, with whom she shares her home. Wilmet especially values Sybil's friendship, but she has come to rely on Sybil so much that Sybil's engagement to Professor Root comes as a real shock to her:

> I can hardly describe how I felt on hearing this news. My first feeling was that I must have heard wrongly, my second that it was some outrageous joke. Sybil to be Professor Root's wife! But she was Rodney's mother and my mother-in-law--how could she ever be anything else? (**GB** 221)

It is to Sybil's credit that she marries Professor Root without feeling guilty about turning Rodney and Wilmet out nor excluding them from their planned trip to Greece. Sybil's independence and her refusal either to control or be controlled are refreshing: far too many mothers lack her wisdom. In the event, Sybil's marriage is one of the best things to happen to Wilmet and Rodney, for they are forced to become responsible adults. Wilmet discovers that she actually enjoys making choices for their new home and acting independently, and Rodney apparently does as well. In the process, their marriage is strengthened, for Wilmet is no longer almost like a sibling to Rodney. They begin to behave like husband and wife. With Sybil and Professor Root as models, they can hardly go wrong.

FIVE

ISOLATION AND LONELINESS

Many of Barbara Pym's characters live alone, but far worse than living alone is the failure to "connect" with other humans and the spiritual or emotional isolation that results. Marcia Ivory of *Quartet In Autumn* and Leonora Eyre of *The Sweet Dove Died* are surely the fullest explorations of such a failure. Both *Quartet In Autumn* and *The Sweet Dove Died* examine at length the issues of aging, loneliness, and isolation. They were written during the period when Pym was feeling her own alienation, at least from the publishing world, and at the same time getting older, watching favorite restaurants being closed and familiar buildings replaced by modern concrete structures, suffering from a terminal illness, and retiring from the International African Institute. For a writer whose works so closely reflect her observations of life around her, these changes could not help but become subjects of her fiction. Well before these disappointments and personal disasters, however, Pym was addressing the problem of the individual's isolation from her or his fellow human beings.

Given the nature of society as Pym depicts it, it is not surprising that her characters feel a sense of displacement or isolation. They are often trying to "cling to reality" or have sensations of "unreality." They dwell in a world that is rapidly losing its vitality: its men are ineffectual and vapid at the same time they feign world-weariness and drain the

115

energies of women; and its women are often depicted as marginal, bland, and useless except for performing trivial tasks. This enervating environment is made all the worse by the fact that characters cannot rely on their observations of reality, for what they think they see often turns out to be illusion, like the furniture depository Wilmet romanticizes in *A Glass Of Blessings*. The crippled beggar that Dulcie Mainwaring sees on the street early in *No Fond Return Of Love* turns out to be perfectly healthy. This sort of mistaking one thing for another occurs frequently. Caroline Grimstone in *An Academic Question* thinks she is looking at a violet and an unidentified flower, only to discover they are a purple chocolate wrapper and a piece of pink paper tissue. Pym liked the image of the chocolate wrapper being mistaken for a violet so well that she used it again in *A Few Green Leaves*. Things often are simply not what they seem.

One result of living in this uncertain world is that people feel a sense of isolation and loneliness. Pym's heroines, especially, are conscious of their distance from others, feeling displaced, not firmly tied to another human being. Most live alone and occupy themselves with thoughts of establishing relationships which will give some sort of meaning to their lives. None of them wants to be considered useless, unloved, or unlovable. All around them are signs of disturbing changes in postwar England which reinforce the sense of isolation and fragmentation. The church which Mildred Lathbury attends for Lenten services in *Excellent Women*, for instance, has been so badly bombed that only half of it is usable. Conditions never get better: by *Quartet In Autumn* the London landscape is defaced by filth and obscenities and madness, and in *A Few Green Leaves*, village life as it once was is being eradicated.

It is no wonder that Pym's heroines often experience a keen sense of being lost, as illustrated by virtually identical scenes in *Excellent Women* and *Less Than Angels*. Mildred Lathbury, lunching with Allegra Gray, suddenly feels "trapped" when Allegra urges her to take Winifred Malory into her flat, reminding her that she has no other ties.

Desperate to escape, Mildred almost runs from the restaurant and tries to lose herself by blindly following a crowd that surges into a large department store. She feels "bewildered and aimless" (**EW** 129). Like Mildred, Catherine Oliphant seeks to avoid confronting her own dark thoughts by wandering into a large restaurant, where the foyer is filled with a crowd of "bewildered, rudderless" people just like herself (**LTA** 194). Neither woman finds the solace she seeks in large crowds. Mildred's momentary surge of bravado when she buys an unsuitable shade of lipstick is followed by the sobering sight of exhausted and spent women in the Ladies' Room, while Catherine's brief few minutes of peace in a church is disturbed by the sounds of women's voices.

One critic, commenting on the displacement of Pym's heroines, goes so far as to suggest that their isolation is irremediable, that they are almost non-persons, and that they have "no sense of themselves" (Long 205). But Pym's heroines have a very real sense of themselves. Even the central characters in the early novels, who are considered by others and may even see themselves as being on the periphery of things, have a significant measure of self-confidence and a real sense of their own needs, possibilities, and limitations. Jessie Morrow of *Crampton Hodnet* may think of herself as something nondescript, a "thin, used up looking woman in her middle thirties" (2) who, if she "were suddenly *taken*, ... a substitute could easily be found. A dim, obedient woman" (214-15), but she is also "highly imaginative" (26) and is described very early in *Crampton Hodnet* as "a woman of definite personality, who was able to look upon herself and her surroundings with detachment" (2). Like Belinda Bede and Mildred Lathbury, Jessie Morrow is resigned to the fact that her life will never be different or more exciting than it is now, but such an acceptance of reality does not imply that she has no sense of herself. She has a decidedly realistic sense of herself and an eminently laudable practicality. Were she less secure or sure of herself, she could not have refused the proposal of Mr. Latimer with such wry and sensible behavior. The same holds true for Belinda Bede, whose refusal of Bishop Grote's proposal and her fear that Harriet might leave her are consistent with Belinda's strong belief that she has all she needs to keep herself content.

Pym suggests that the characters with real emotional depths and insights into others are precisely those women who superficially appear nondescript, self-effacing, and ill-equipped for life in modern England. One discovers strength and sensitivity beneath their surface. In the same way that Pym's characters often find that what things seem are not always what they are, so Pym's heroines turn out to be different from the initial impressions they make. Mildred Lathbury, for instance, is an emotionally strong woman, which makes her personal resignation to a lesser life than she would aspire to all the more poignant. She is keenly aware of the plight of lonely people, telling Rocky that not everyone has someone to comfort him in stressful times, "thinking of the many rejected ones who lived in lonely bed-sitting- rooms with nobody to talk to them or prepare meals for them" (**EW** 157). Her strength arises from her ability to cope with life's stock situations and great moments as well as from her solid sensibility. While she make disparaging comments about her own levelheadedness, it is that very quality that everyone depends on in moments of crisis. Despite the often fragmented nature of spinsters' lives, suggested by the bed-sitting-rooms, the corner in someone's home, or the flat with a shared bathroom, women such as Mildred can be counted on to do the unglamorous tasks no one else wants to do. When Allegra Gray asks Mildred what women do if they do not marry, Mildred's reply suggests the variety of ways in which they are valuable: "Oh, they stay at home with an aged parent and do the flowers, or they used to, but now perhaps they have jobs and careers.... And then of course they become indispensable in the parish and some of them even go into religious communities" (**EW** 129). In addition to her dependability, Mildred has enough sense of herself to want to preserve her freedom by resisting the efforts of others to move in with her. While she may be doomed to domestic servitude with Everard Bone,

Mildred's valiant effort to change her life indicates a very real understanding of her own needs.

One sees even greater self-confidence in Catherine Oliphant, Dulcie Mainwaring, and Emma Howick. The narrator of *Less Than Angels* tells us that Catherine Oliphant, in response to Tom's long absences, had turned in "upon herself and her own resources which had always been considerable" (104), while Tom thinks of her as being "too much of a personality in her own right" (152). Catherine's genuine appreciation of life's trivial pleasures, her detached manner, and her refusal ever to surrender to self-pity produce a truly admirable strength of character. Although both Catherine Oliphant and Emma Howick, intelligent and levelheaded as they are, find themselves inexplicably drawn to men who have not treated them well, they nevertheless retain their sense of personal dignity and have minds of their own. Catherine's feelings for Tom Mallow run much deeper than she would admit to herself. She handles his moving out of her flat rather better than he does himself, but her aimless wandering and sense of emptiness after he leaves for Africa and, more to the point, her profound grief over his death are evidence of her attachment to him. Self-reliant and resourceful though she is, something in her wants to nurture: Digby and Mark know they can rely upon Catherine to fix them a meal, she takes as much pleasure in cooking and cleaning as she does in writing, and she is so touched by the loneliness of Alaric Lydgate that she develops a genuine interest in as well as a sense of responsibility for him. But Catherine is able to successfully balance an effusive zeal to subordinate self with a well-developed sense of her own worth. She has enough self-confidence not to worry about what others think of her.

This culturally-shaped inclination in women to subordinate themselves is particularly strong in spinsterish women who feel compassion for others and who particularly desire a good relationship with a man. The problem in Pym's world is that there are no good men and relationships with other women are often unsatisfactory, facts which Pym's heroines have learned to adjust to. Thus,

Pym's best women have an ambiguous set of characteristics: they have developed a detached air as a kind of protective shield from the inevitable pain of relationships and at the same time they feel almost a compulsion to give of themselves. In *No Fond Return Of Love*, Dulcie Mainwaring goes to a learned conference to get over her broken engagement and is drawn immediately to both Viola Dace and Aylwin Forbes. Her chief experience in the novel is learning to reconcile her desire to become involved in life when she has previously thought of herself as being only an observer, watching other people's lives with detachment. Sensitive to the plight of the lonely and unfortunate, Dulcie has often been troubled by "beggars, distressed gentlefolk, lonely African students having doors shut in their faces, people being wrongfully detained in mental homes ..." (12). As a result, finding herself alone in her big house after the death of her parents, she offers a room to her niece Laurel and then to Viola Dace. Yet once Laurel and Viola actually move in, she becomes anxious about her privacy, anticipating the pleasantness of each of them all staying in their rooms, keeping to themselves.

For a time Dulcie is occupied in the lives of Laurel and Viola, and then she becomes increasingly involved in Aylwin and Neville Forbes' lives. At last she feels that, rather than sitting in an audience watching others perform, she is becoming an active participant in the drama of life. However, at the end of the novel, her feeling of loneliness returns, with Laurel having moved out to share a flat with a friend and Viola's having gone off to make wedding preparations. Dulcie realizes that she is faced with absolute isolation; she has cut all ties with other people: "[S]he had rejected Maurice's offer of friendship, and even the comfort of Father Benger and his church. It only remained now for her to turn away from the life than Neville Forbes had seemed to offer her" (259). Consoling herself with the prospect of her work, perhaps letting rooms to students, and even going to another learned conference, Dulcie is not absolutely without hope for the future. The novel ends with the possibility of Dulcie's becoming involved in another relationship, as she opens her door to receive Aylwin Forbes, coming to declare his love. That she also loves him suggests that she will receive him positively, thereby forestalling her lonely future. But the important point is that, faced with real loneliness, Dulcie immediately entertains ways of remedying the problem.

Emma Howick has a similar response to loneliness in *A Few Green Leaves*. She, too, appears to be taken advantage of by a man but also exhibits a strong sense of self. While it might seem as if her involvement with Graham Pettifer is one-sided, for instance, Emma Howick remains as detached from him as he from her. She has a sense of control in the matter, wondering, for example, after his second visit, if she really wants to see him again: she looks for something in his letter that might help her clarify her feelings for him, "for she was not sure whether she wanted him or not" (120). She has already regretted her impulsively-written letter to him when she finally meets him again at her cottage, but when he comes to the village for the summer, she cooks for him, looks after him at times, and even makes love with him. This latter event occurs when she visits him wearing a new, colorful dress. Having decided that she cannot always be carrying food to him, Emma has determined that "he would have to be content with her company only, her conversation, and whatever else he might be prepared to ask and she to give" (146). Once again, female assertiveness is accompanied by an ironic acknowledgement of the way male-female relationships operate. And when Graham finally begins to kiss and fondle her, he does it in "a rather abstracted way," while she is reminded of Miss Lickerish and the ruined cottage (148). He is, as it were, the only game in town for the summer, and Emma is human enough and woman enough to want some romance in her life, no matter how brief or inconsequential the encounter, no matter how self-centered and boorish the man. Later, she is irritated, not upset, that there has been no repetition of this amorous dalliance on the grass.

121

While Tom Dagnall seems the obvious match for Emma Howick, she must rid herself of any feelings she might have for Graham Petiffer before embarking on a more satisfactory relationship with another man. Once Graham is gone, she returns to the cottage and is reminded of his selfishness when she discovers that Graham has picked all of the tomatoes, even the green ones, that she had planted in pots in front of his cottage. Upstairs, she finds another reminder of Graham's unsuitability, a book of poetry he has borrowed from Tom. The book falls open, not to a love poem, but to a Richard Crashaw poem entitled: "Upon Two Green Apricots Sent to Cowley by Sir Crashaw," which she suspects "might have kind a of bitter relevance to her relationship with Graham" (**FGL** 192). Completely disabused of any lingering doubts about a relationship with Graham, she turns immediately to the future: "The only practical thing that occurred to her was to do something that had been on her conscience for some time, to ask Tom to supper.... After all, they were two lonely people now, and as such should get together" (**FGL** 193). Like Dulcie Mainwaring, Emma Howick is never for a moment pathetic or hopeless.

One other measure of how Pym's strongest female characters have a sense of their worth is the way they treat the suggestions from others that they change themselves. As a result of the importance placed on being married, women who do not have husbands are always being encouraged by others to do something to themselves in order to get them, and Pym's self-assured characters resist such suggestions. Whereas Mildred Lathbury's attempts to change her appearance are reflections of her strong desire to change her life, women in other novels are satisfied with what they have. As might be expected, Mildred's efforts do not gain her anything. She tries a different hair style, more makeup, and a new black dress, with unfavorable results: Miss Statham says her hair "'looks sort of scraped back as if you were going to have a bath'" (**EW** 250) and William Caldicote tells her that she has a sadder look than usual. When she asks him if he thinks that is an improvement, he asks: "'You mean an improvement on the way you usually look? But how do you usually look? One scarcely remembers'" (**EW** 251). Apprehensive after these reactions, Mildred waits for Everard to make a comment, but, of course, he does not even notice. In contrast, when Miss Lord, in an enthusiastic burst of good intentions, tells Dulcie Mainwaring that she would make a good wife and that she could make more of herself if she only would, Dulcie handles her advice with aplomb. By "making more of herself," Miss Lord means that Dulcie should try a different hair style and use more eye makeup. When Dulcie points out that marriages must be based on more than outward appearances, Miss Lord insists that a man has to notice her first before he can appreciate her inner qualities.

In the context of Pym's world, Miss Lord's remark does have some truth to it. For instance, in *Crampton Hodnet* Jessie Morrow's experiment with makeup and her hasty attempts to scrub it off produces a very high color, which Mr. Latimer notices at once. Jessie Morrow of *Jane and Prudence* deliberately and carefully applies foundation, rouge, powder, eye shadow, and lipstick as she prepares to seduce Fabian Driver. Her attempt to transform herself is so successful that Fabian does not at first recognize her, and before long, Jessie succeeds in capturing him. But Dulcie Mainwaring is too much her own person to change her appearance, and by the end of *No Fond Return Of Love*, she has succeeded in winning Aylwin's affection without altering her appearance. Likewise, Catherine Oliphant does not dress to please others. Aware that something is always wrong with the way she looks, even when she makes an effort, she is "too much aware of herself as a personality to make much effort to change" (**LTA** 69). At the gathering of women who have loved Tom Mallow arranged by his sister, Deirdre Swan wears her usually loose and flowing hair pulled back tightly and darkens her eyebrows, producing a severe look she apparently thinks is appropriate for one in mourning. Catherine, on the other hand, is "just herself" (**LTA** 251). Nor is Emma Howick much affected by her mother's wish that she would make herself more attractive by wearing a prettier dress or arranging her hair in a different style. Her one attempt at wearing a new dress results in the encounter on the grass with Graham Pettifer-- unfortunately bearing out Miss Lord's pronouncement on the importance of appearance in attracting a man--but that event is more unsettling than it is satisfactory. Pym's central character heroines are not irremediably isolated, nor do they deserve to be called nonpersons. They actively seek ways to combat loneliness. Often the only successful way to do so is to give generously of themselves, but such giving does not constitute weakness. Rather, it is proof that they value themselves enough to do what they must, given the transitory, uncertain, and fragmented natures of their lives.

While the central character heroines are able to cope with loneliness by seeking the company of others and giving of themselves, other characters in various stages of isolation find different ways of adjusting. A number of them have replaced their interest in humans with keen devotion to animals. In each of the three novels Pym wrote between 1961 and 1971, she reworked this idea. In *An Unsuitable Attachment*, Pym created two characters whose attention to animals has replaced their interest in humans: the veterinarian Edwin Pettigrew, whose relationship with animals was so consuming that his wife left him, and Sophia Ainger, whose love for her cat Faustina is a genuine source of jealousy and pain to her husband Mark. Love for cats as substitute for human love recurs in *The Sweet Dove Died* in the character of Liz, "whose husband had 'behaved so appallingly' that she now loved cats more than people" (26). Finally, Dolly Arborfield in *An Academic Question* has grown away from humans and now is inordinately preoccupied with hedgehogs to the point where she no longer leaves her home except for the briefest of periods because she cannot trust her neighbors to feed them. Dolly's interest in animals robs her of her ability to care for humans as she ought, for when Caroline goes to her on the morning following her husband's confession of infidelity, Dolly is so upset by her favorite hedgehog's death that she cannot comfort Caroline. It is a brief but telling scene, indicating the pathos of Dolly's turning away from human beings and letting her friend down when she truly needs her.

Senhor MacBride-Pereira has found compensations for loneliness by becoming a confirmed observer of others' lives, watching the small dramas of his neighborhood and the comings and goings of people from the window of his upstairs room in Mrs. Beltane's home. He has his private pleasure, eating almonds, and his secret indulgence, wearing a kilt of the MacBride tartan in private. At the conclusion of *No Fond Return of Love*, he hears the taxi but does not see Aylwin get out, and the novel ends with his "wondering what, if anything, he had missed" (261). This conclusion suggests that Senhor MacBride-Pereira has missed something of importance, at least in the lives of Dulcie and Aylwin. It also leaves readers thinking about Senhor MacBride-Pereira, a very minor character who takes on more importance at the conclusion of the novel than he has anywhere else in it. The implications of the closing scene go beyond Dulcie and Aylwin's future together by reminding readers of the masses of people living alone, just like MacBride-Pereira, and the ways in which they accommodate themselves to such isolation. At one point it occurs to MacBride-Pereira to propose marriage to Mrs. Beltane, when she has written him about the delicate matter of his flat rent. The idea of marriage never actually becomes full blown, however, because he dismisses it before it even has a chance to develop: "Marriage was not for him, and he had now become too set in his ways to consider even the marriage of true minds.... She would not be content with the quiet life he liked to lead, and she might mock at the way he liked to sit wearing his kilt in the evenings" (208-09). He is content to pass his days looking from his window, reading his favorite authors, eating almonds, occasionally keeping company with Mrs. Beltane, and recalling his past in Brazil.

Part of the explanation for the widespread sense of personal alienation among Pym's characters lies in the nature of modern life, with its new contraptions, its computers, and its televisions. Such progress has had the side effect of isolating people from one another and dulling their lives. Adam Prince, in A *Few Green Leaves*, is most struck by "the chilling lack of human contact" in the impersonal surroundings of a motel he has eaten at, with:

> no charming elderly lady ... knitting in the lounge after dinner; no cordial *'Buon giorno, signore'* from a smiling young waiter, bearing his breakfast on a tray high on his shoulder, as nostalgically recalled in some Roman *pensione* not too far from the Spanish Steps. Adam's plastic 'continental' breakfast appeared early and mysteriously outside his door as if brought by computer, which it may well have been.... But his desire for human contact, wasn't that the most disquieting thing of all? Could it be that he was getting old? (179-180)

This displacement of the warm, human touch with the impersonal efficiency of modern technology is suggested in the many references to television and its numbing effect on those who watch. Tom Dagnall, who does not own a television set, simply does not know what to say when Terry Skate tells him that his loss of faith is a result of watching television talk shows. When there is a power outage one evening in the village, those most seriously affected by it are the young, for whom television viewing has become a chief occupation of their time. In *Less Than Angels*, Tom Mallow's uncle sits in a semi-dark room, watching the television set "which had the central position in the room like a kind of altar" (180). Tom is saddened by his uncle's ties to television, feeling he is "a kind of prisoner, or a sacrifice laid before the altar of the television set" (181). David Lydell, in *Quartet In Autumn*, finds himself watching television programs when he visits his parishioners because they do not turn off their sets when he calls.

Holidays, especially Christmas, are particularly problematic for people who live alone. Their friends, neighbors, and relatives feel obligated to invite them to their homes, while the single person feels all the more her isolation for having to be "taken in." For example, Dulcie Mainwaring goes to her sister's home for the holiday but feels that such visits reduce her in status to nothing more than a spinster aunt. Viola Dace reluctantly travels to her parents' home out of duty, but, the narrator tells us, her parents would actually prefer to be by themselves. Dulcie feels that "Christmas put people in their places, sent them back to the nursery or cradle, almost" (NFRL 106). She prefers to get through the holiday as quickly as possible. Leonora Eyre passes Christmas Day "in the rather mysterious way that the Christmas Days of middle-aged people without young families usually do pass" (SDD 27), in this case, by entertaining her friend Liz with an elegant dinner that goes largely unappreciated because of Liz's preoccupation with her cats. In *Quartet In Autumn*, Norman is invited to share dinner with his dead sister's husband and his girlfriend and Edwin has his son's family to visit. Marcia, whose neighbors charitably invite her to join them for Christmas dinner, is so odd in her behavior that she makes the meal uncomfortable for them. Only Letty is left at first without the prospect of any companionship on Christmas day. Her friend Marjorie's usual Christmas invitation not forthcoming, she determines to face the holiday alone. But when Mrs. Pope's plans change at the last minute, the two of them share a meal for the first time. It is not a particularly pleasant meal, however, and Letty begins to wonder if she did the right thing in moving from the vitality and warmth of the Olatundes to the bleak, silent house and droning complaints of Mrs. Pope. In *A Few Green Leaves*, Daphne Dagnall, in her new home, feels guilty for leaving her brother Tom on his own, "especially at a time like Christmas" (240). Christmas brings increased attention to old people in Mark Ainger's parish in *An Unsuitable Attachment*, and Ianthe feels it her Christian obligation to call on Miss Grimes, who has recently retired from the library. Although Ianthe lives alone herself, she owns her own home while Miss Grimes resides in a large house with flats let to many people. Feeling uncomfortable as she thinks of all those people living alone, Ianthe in one wild moment even wonders if she ought to give Miss Grimes a room in her own home.

Pym examines in some detail the subject of personal alienation in *Less Than Angels*. Alaric Lydgate is a brilliant example of this disconnectedness, sitting in his study, wearing his African mask, and thinking:

> what a good thing it would be if the wearing of masks or animals' heads could become customary for persons over a certain age. How restful social intercourse would be if the face did not have to assume any expression--the strained look of interest, the simulated delight or surprise, the anxious concern one didn't really feel. Alaric often avoided looking into people's eyes when he spoke to them, fearful of what he might see there, for life was very terrible whatever sort of front we might put on it, and only the eyes of the very young or the very old and wise could look out on it with a clear untroubled gaze. (57)

Others notice Alaric's loneliness, especially his neighbors Rhoda Wellcome and Mabel Swan. When Rhoda tells Catherine one day at tea about Alaric's practice of wearing an African mask, Catherine remarks that loneliness in men is especially sad. Although Tom points out that women are lonely too, Catherine responds that such loneliness is not so bad, somehow, for "'loneliness can often be a kind of strength in women, possibly in men too, of course, but it doesn't seem to show itself so much'" (90-91). This idea that men are more lonely creatures than women is a myth that is probably best explained as simply being one more part of the picture of men as helpless and spoiled. While people say that women can occupy themselves more than men can, that men feel loneliness more keenly than women, the truth is that both sexes feel it equally intensely.

Despite her self-sufficiency, Catherine Oliphant herself experiences a keen sense of loneliness when Tom moves out of her apartment. She is more shaken than she would like to admit. Sitting in a cafeteria, she eavesdrops on the conversation of two women next to her who are discussing the impossibility of figuring out the filing system of someone who has left their office. One of them says that there will be no problem in finding things when she leaves, but Catherine thinks:

> Ah, but there will.... Understanding somebody else's filing system is just about as easy as really getting to know another human being. Just when you think you know everything about them, there's the impossible happening, the M for Miscellaneous when you naturally assumed it would be under something else. (**LTA** 109)

Although Catherine is fully autonomous and able to live alone comfortably, she is shocked to realize that she has misjudged Tom. This realization, coupled with her having no close family ties or any intimate friends, leaves her feeling vulnerable to a degree she had never thought possible. Tom's leaving for Africa produces an emotional crisis, brought on by her very real loneliness. This feeling is brought to peak intensity when she learns of Tom's death. Running from Digby and Mark, who have ineffectually tried to console her, Catherine gets on a bus, distracted, and rides it to the London district where Mabel Swan and Rhoda Wellcome live.

The scenes Catherine imagines in the suburban homes she passes are reassuring images of homey, safe comforts, of cozy fires and warm buttered toast and children happily amusing themselves. It is an idyllic image which warms her and leads her to the doorstep of Rhoda and Mabel, where she is welcomed with open arms and genuine concern for her well being. One truly wonderful event of the novel is Catherine's "adoption" by Mabel and Rhoda when she is grief-stricken over Tom's death. Finally Catherine has a family of sorts and even begins to feel the restrictions of that family in the same way Deirde does. She begins to long for "her odd solitary life" and the comforts of her own flat (**LTA** 248). She also feels limited in her relationship with Alaric. Having had to turn down an invitation to go to a pub with him because she would be expected shortly for lunch, Catherine worries that he will misconstrue her excuse, for she very much wants to go with him: "She felt she could re-establish the right sort of contact only if she were free and living by herself" (**LTA** 249). Obviously Catherine has enjoyed the comforts of feeling herself part of Rhoda's and Mabel's family, but she just as obviously needs to be by herself once again. The implication is that she can only truly be free living alone. The delightful thing is that part of that freedom includes strengthening her contact with Alaric Lydgate.

For another remarkable event of the novel is Catherine's bringing Alaric Lydgate out of his lonely shell. Having taken the "bold step" of inviting Alaric out for Sunday supper, knowing how depressing this particular meal is for people who live alone, Catherine makes the earth-shaking suggestion that he not write up his African notes. The oppressiveness of those notes, taken eleven years before, has soured his outlook on life, made him bitter at his failure, and turned him into a social hermit. The impact of her suggestion, at first seeming outrageous, is to immediately soften his manner: "[S]uddenly the sun broke through on the grim surface of the carved rock and he smiled" (**LTA** 224). Burning his notes releases him from his sense of failure and opens him to other possibilities. In turn, Catherine has developed a sense of responsibility for him, and the two establish a friendship that promises to blossom into something more. The last lines of the novel are the thoughts of Rhoda Wellcome, herself an unmarried woman who has made her home with her widowed sister and who has had to make her own adjustments to living in someone else's house. Rhoda thinks what a "difficult and peculiar couple" Alaric and Catherine would make were they to marry, thus planting the suggestion that they might be headed for marriage but also indicating that even the most unlikely sorts of people can find consolation in one another's company (**LTA** 256).

Jane Cleveland might seem the least likely sort of person to experience loneliness and isolation, but she does not have much in common with the elderly women who make up her husband's congregation. Further, her lively imagination, combined with a rather impertinent manner of speaking her opinion when it is not wanted, makes her suspect. She feels shut out, not accepted, and too closely scrutinized by others. From time to time Jane has an impulse to free herself from her life, exclaiming at one low point: "'Oh, I can understand people renouncing the world!'" (**JP** 130). At this particular moment, she has been thinking about men, their childishness and their obtuseness. But such impulses do not come over her often, for she is in general a gregarious, likable woman whose heart goes out to people like Prudence Bates, who she thinks ought to have a husband. She is delighted when Miss Doggett comes to ask her advice about Jessie Morrow and drops everything to go out in a pouring rain to confront Fabian and Jessie. Jane is sensitive to the loneliness of other people as well, such as when, after a gathering of the literary society to which she belongs, she watches the group of writers dispersing and observes: "Once outside the magic circle the writers became their lonely selves, pondering on poems, observing their fellow men ruthlessly, putting people they knew into novels; no wonder they were without friends" (**JP** 120). So keen is Jane to help relieve some of the loneliness in the world that she busies herself with finding potential mates for her friend Prudence.

Prudence Bates at 29 lives alone and likes it very much. Her chief occupation, as Jane wryly observes, is her love affairs, or more precisely, her idealized idea of them. As *Jane and Prudence* opens, Prudence is wallowing in an unrequited love for her boss, Dr. Grampian. She had first become aware of her "love" for him at a time of "a temporary emptiness in her heart" (37). Prudence has a strong tendency to dramatize everything, a characteristic that makes her feel great sympathy for complete strangers but rather unsympathetically of those she knows well. She has a striking inability to form genuine emotional attachments to others. Prudence's relationships are apparently more often platonic than physical. When Jane, overcome by curiosity, asks her if she is Fabian's mistress,

Prudence's reply is noncommittal, but later, after Fabian and Jessie announce their engagement, Jane concludes that they had not been lovers. Prudence's dislike of humanity in general, her preference for playing at love rather than actually loving, indicates that Prudence is unlikely ever to establish a lasting love relationship. She prefers the dramatic posture to the truly felt experience and seems destined to live her life alone.

Prudence reminds one of the young Barbara Bird in *Crampton Hodnet*. Barbara "had cherished many impossible, romantic passions for people she scarcely knows" (68), prefers the *idea* of love to the actual, and almost fears the physical expression of love which Francis Cleveland seems to be insisting on. She does not like to be kissed, and when she finally agrees to run off with him to Paris, she ends up panicking and abandoning him in Dover. Barbara prefers a platonic love, a spiritual harmony between man and woman. Deciding to leave Francis at Dover, she sees herself as free: "She was sure she would never marry now, and there came into her mind the comforting picture of herself, a beautiful, cultured woman with sad eyes" (190). One can imagine her having a series of just such relationships in a pattern very like that of Prudence Bates. This connection is not accidental, for Pym obviously had *Crampton Hodnet* in mind when she wrote *Jane and Prudence*. Not only do we have Jessie Morrow and Miss Doggett again, but Barbara Bird shows up at a literary gathering. Jessie Morrow describes unrequited love in exactly the same terms as Prudence does: "the sort of love that lingers on through many years, dying sometimes and then coming back like a twinge of rheumatism in the winter, so that you feel it in your knee when you are nearing the top of a long flight of stairs" (**CH** 204, **JP** 37). Pym seems to have been interested in tracing this character type through several decades: Barbara Bird is only twenty years old when she becomes involved with Francis Cleveland, but Prudence Bates at twenty-nine seems no more mature than Barbara. These two women bear a remarkable resemblance to a still older woman, Leonora Eyre.

132

Leonora's self-absorption and overweening sense of propriety and decorum make her increasingly removed from real emotional commitment. She is unusual for Pym, the coldest of any of the characters, repeatedly described in terms such as "cool," "icy," and "remote," though she might also be seen as an extreme example of what might become of Barbara Bird and Prudence Bates. As the novel opens, Leonora has been perfectly content with her lifestyle. Happy to return to her home on the day of the book auction at which she grew faint and was "rescued" by Humphrey and James, for example, she imagines the loneliness of her friend Meg in contrast to "her own tranquil solitude" (**SDD** 16). She tells James that she lives alone by preference and truly seems to enjoy it. Deriving great pleasure from artistically arranging her possessions, she carefully cleans them, removing any with imperfections so as not to spoil the perfect elegance she has created. Leonora needs very much to control all aspects of her life. Even one's death, she thinks, could be "as elegant as one's life, and one would do everything possible to make it so" (**SDD** 18). Her use of "one" instead of the first person pronoun is not only part of her image of elegant gentility and refinement but one more indication of her emotional reserve.

As Leonora grows more involved with James and then is rejected by him, however, she becomes increasingly distressed by signs of her own aging and horrifyingly aware of her isolation. Although Leonora believes that one should not show emotion, for such a display is bad manners, one evening, alone in bed with a headache, unable to reach James, she weeps. These tears come as somewhat of a surprise and reveal a vulnerability in Leonora that has not been apparent before. Her other signs of weakness--feeling faint, tiring easily and needing assistance--are all part of Leonora's carefully maintained facade of fragile sophistication. But these tears are not shed for anyone's benefit; they reveal real emotion. They come after a conversation on the telephone with her friend Meg. Leonora is crying not only because of the brown spots on her hands, sure signs of age, but because of her faint consciousness that her relationship with James might in some perverse way parallel that of her friend Meg with Colin. These are tears of self pity for the aging, lonely Leonora.

As James becomes fully involved with Ned and moves from the flat in Leonora's home, Leonora finds her days empty in a way they had never been before. She fills her lonely hours by washing her china and cleaning her silver "obsessively," for "she had always cared as much for inanimate objects as for people" (**SDD** 182). The new mirror Humphrey finds for her to replace James's fruitwood mirror does not reflect her as "ageless and fascinating" the way James's mirror had done, and "now her reflection displeased her, for her face seemed shrunken and almost old" (**SDD** 182). Viewing some jewelry at Christies, she is overcome by a profound sense of her own unhappiness. Tears come to her eyes "not only for herself but also for the owners of the jewellery, ageing now or old, some probably dead" (**SDD** 183). In her confusion, she finds herself in a self-service restaurant and sits alone, offended by the elderly woman clearing tables, whom she asks to remove her tray of dirty crockery from Leonora's table. Leonora has reached her lowest point. She feels "debased, diminished, crushed and trodden into the ground, indeed 'brought to a certain point of dilapidation'. I am utterly alone, she thought" (**SDD** 184-85). Leonora does not wallow in self-pity, however. Rescued at this point by her cousin Daphne, she starts to find strength again, a strength that arises out of disdain for other people.

For a time, Leonora's increasing unhappiness ironically had made her more tolerant of the feelings of others. At Keats's house, for instance, where she has gone with Ned and James, Leonora at first experiences her usual feeling of contempt when she sees a middle-aged woman carrying a shopping bag full of books, a frozen dinner on top. But then, she imagines the woman going home to a "cosy solitude," preparing her dinner without fuss, having the company of her books and the memory of her afternoon in Keats's house. It is not an unpleasant image, Leonora thinks, and she is not surprised to see tears of joy on the cheeks of this woman. Earlier, she has been annoyed that a saleswoman in an antique shop repeatedly addressed her as "madam" despite their being social equals: "Does one then seem so cold, proud and formidable, she asked herself, when one is none of these things?" (**SDD** 121). Leonora has perfected icy elegance to such a degree that, even though she denies it to herself, she is impenetrably remote. At one point, when she is particularly distressed over James's relationship with Ned, she thinks she might let Humphrey kiss her, but her manner is such that he regards her detachedly and patronizingly, leaving her feeling "cheated of something, a warmer show of affection, the kiss she had expected and had decided to allow him. They might even have ended up in bed and it could have been cosy and comforting for her" (**SDD** 167-68). This thought is so out of character that it indicates a certain desperation in Leonora's thinking. She has long found the idea of sex disgusting, and she has never loved anyone deeply--even James astonishes her when he uses the word "love" to describe his feelings for her. This notion that she might charitably allow Humphrey to kiss her is mere fantasy. She undoubtedly considers it a way of continuing to control Humphrey by giving him a small liberty, but it would never occur to Humphrey now to press for anything more than a kiss on the cheek. Having once tried unsuccessfully to have a sexual relationship with her and having been badly rebuffed, he is not likely to try again. Even her friends Joan and Dickie Murray see her as frigid. When she spends the weekend at their cottage, Dickie tells his wife that Leonora is "'so cold and inhuman.... I always feel I'd like to.... '" Joan's giggling response is, "'Now, darling, don't be beastly about Leonora,'" to which Dickie says: "'But suppose one *did*.... That's really just what she needs. Do you think Humphrey ever has?'" (**SDD** 177). Joan cannot imagine Leonora's having sex with anyone, and the two of them enjoy a laugh together at Leonora's expense.

Leonora not only finds sex offensive and unthinkable, but any human contact becomes disgusting to her. As she emerges from her depression over James's involvement with Ned and rejection of her, she insulates herself from all feeling whatsoever. Pym brilliantly chronicles Leonora's journey into despair and then her recovery from it by giving a chilling account of Leonora's emotional detachment. The anguish she feels over James is connected with her refusal to admit that she is aging, a condition she denies by choosing mirrors and soft lighting that flatter her reflection, scorning and shunning old people, and generally acting as if the experiences of everyone else cannot possibly apply to her. Although Leonora briefly entertains the thought that she and Humphrey might have a sexual encounter or momentarily feels sympathy for other people, by the end of the novel she has become even more cold and remote than at the beginning. After the kindness of her cousin Daphne when she was feeling utterly alone, her thought is that the women's club Daphne had taken her to is unbearable. Then, returning a cat to her friend Liz, she thinks: "One would hardly want to be like the people who fill the emptiness of their lives with an animal" (**SDD** 188). Spring brings with it a renewal of spirits and a determination to remain in control of her life. She evades Ned's hands when he reaches out to take hers, and when Meg consoles her by putting her arms around her, Leonora finds "the contact distasteful" and tries to shake her off (**SDD** 202). She finds Meg's soothing gestures embarrassing and ridiculous. Finally, she is so cold when James comes to visit her in the final chapter that it is clear she has refused to become like Meg with her homosexual friend Colin. As Humphrey approaches her house in the final scene, she is thinking of how perfect, how "absolutely correct" are the peonies he is bringing her (**SDD** 208).

Leonora's story has been a study of the void that results when one refuses to connect emotionally with other people. Having always insisted on being in strict control of herself and her collection of carefully selected admirers, Leonora chooses to insulate herself from any passion. Rather than having spent all her passion, like Belinda Bede, she appears never to have had any to expend. Her compensations for emotional deprivation are an excessive interest in perfect things, the elegant arrangements of furniture and Victoriana, and an uncluttered emotional life. Refusing to be like Meg, she will remain like one of her faultless pieces, untouched, perfect, absolutely cold.

Pym described *Quartet In Autumn* as "a study of isolation told with humor and detachment" (**MS PYM** 165, fol. 101). This novel evolved as Pym herself was reflecting on aging, illness, and death. Her journal entries from the early seventies record observations which she incorporated into the book: "Sitting at lunch in the help yourself in B & H I think, why, those women are like lunatics in some colour supplement photograph of bad conditions in a mental home. Twitching and slumping or bending low over their food like an animal at a dish"; "As one gets older--the difficulties of being a guest helping and not helping, doing and not doing"; "Living at Finstock with no permanent base in London now! O strange life and in the heat of Monday (24th July) [1972] feeling quite ill at Paddington and having to be 'careful'" (**MS PYM** 70). Recording on 4 May 1973 that a friend had died in the night, Pym is prompted to write a description of a scene which becomes one of the "upsetting sights" Letty observes in the Underground platform in *Quartet In Autumn* (**MS PYM** 71). In 1974 she suffered a stroke which resulted in a stay of two and a half months in the hospital and then had temporary aphasia during which she could not remember things nor spell. Over this period of several years, she developed the idea of four characters who work in an office and face retirement.

All four of the central characters in *Quartet In Autumn* live alone, and their disconnectedness from one another is stressed over and over again, beginning with the opening paragraphs which describe them all going to the same library on the same day at different times. The librarian recognizes that they all belong together, but it takes retirement and Marcia Ivory's death for them to realize it themselves. They have no contact with one another outside the office and on the few occasions any one of them thinks of visiting or telephoning another, the idea is quickly dispensed with. Even Letty Crowe, the most adventurous of them all, routinely fails to make contact even in the most natural of all places, over lunch at a table shared with another woman. Letty recognizes the pathos of their isolated lives by comparing a small gesture of solicitude she makes toward Marcia to pigeons picking insects off one another: "Perhaps this is all that we as human beings can do for each other" (9). Through their experience with Marcia's illness and death, however, Letty, Edwin Braithwaite, and Norman (whose last name we are never told) develop a bond that seems likely to continue to get stronger.

Three of the four central characters are social people who at least attempt to maintain contact with other people, and it is this connection with others that suggests their futures will be much more promising than Marcia's unhappy end. While Edwin's involvement in the church, owning his own home, and having a family all keep him occupied, Norman and Letty have their own problems with aging and loneliness. Norman is angry, resentful, and irritable almost all of the time. An irascible little man who complains about just about everything, he nevertheless does not know what to do with himself when alone. He cannot fill up his holiday with any useful activity and finally returns to the office early, the few days he has left sure never to be needed but, instead, "would accumulate like a pile of dead leaves drifting on to the pavement in autumn" (QA 52). He has no relatives other than the husband of his dead sister and lives in a bed-sitting-room.

As for Marcia and Letty, at the retirement party in their honor, people cannot imagine what horrible fate lies ahead for Marcia. Letty, however, is neatly pegged by the other office workers as the "typical English spinster" who will retire to a country cottage and occupy herself with the usual activities of church, gardening, and needlework. Letty's retirement brings complications she had not anticipated, however, when, first, she is informed that Marjorie will marry and that she cannot live with her and then that her landlady has sold her house. These developments trouble Letty, who reacts to them with the same sort of sensation she imagines a drowning person might have. While she has accepted retirement courageously, as if beginning another new adventure, her confidence is shaken. Confronting Mr. Olatunde with the request that he and his family not make so much noise, she becomes embarrassed when he asks her to join them. Wondering what Edwin, Norman and Marcia would have done under the same circumstances, she thinks that Edwin probably would have joined in and that even "Norman and Marcia, usually so set in their isolation, would in some surprising way have been drawn into the friendly group. Only Letty remained outside" (QA 67). Her new living arrangements, a bed-sitting-room in the home of eighty-year-old Mrs. Pope, are not much better. She studiously avoids Mrs. Pope, seeing her even less in her retirement than before. Letty's sense of isolation is deepened further when she walks past her old office building and then later visits her old office. She has a sensation of nothingness, as if she and Marcia had been swept aside, "as if they had never existed" (QA 128). Still, she continues to take care of herself, having her hair done regularly, dressing in her best clothes when she goes out, eating well, and embarking on a reading program.

Marcia Ivory is disconnected not only from her fellow office workers but from everyone except her physician, Dr. Strong, whom she has elevated to the status of a god. Except for her fascination with Dr. Strong, however, Marcia has no patience with nor interest in any other relationship. She resents the social worker Janice Brabner and would rather not answer the door when Janice calls nor speak to her when asked a direct question. She ignores the friendly overtures of a woman sitting beside her at Dr. Strong's clinic. Although she is grateful for Letty's offer to make her tea, she can never forgive her for burdening her with a milk bottle from a company different from those in her collection. Having ignored Letty's postcard with its invitation to get together for lunch, she surprisingly agrees to join her with Norman and Edwin for lunch, but her behavior and her appearance on that occasion indicate that she is dangerously close to madness. Further evidence that she has become totally isolated and detached from the people she worked with is that, although she had shared family-sized tins of instant coffee with Norman in the office, she scornfully tells Janice Brabner after she has seen Norman watching her from across the street: "'That was just somebody I used to work with. I don't want anybody like *that* coming to see me'" (QA 148). This denial of Norman combined with the subsequent revelation that she has willed him her house suggests the degree of Marcia's mental instability and confusion. It is grimly ironic that the attention and excitement Marcia has always been fascinated by, including an ambulance ride to the hospital and the attentions of Dr. Strong, are all but lost on her. She is unconscious during the ambulance ride, and Dr. Strong sees her only for the most crucial of events--her breast removal surgery and her dying moments--while at all other times she is attended to by interns or assistants. Marcia's starvation and death are physical manifestations of her withered emotional state, her isolation not only a symptom of her madness but also a cause of it.

Pym has foreshadowed Marcia's death early on with the old woman slumped over on the Underground platform, refusing help, and with other references to old people dying. Attempting to explain what has happened to Marcia, Janice Brabner concludes that she is the result of a "lack of liaison" that might somehow have prevented her death (QA 187). Dr. Strong's slightly stern rebuke-- "'Haven't you been looking after yourself properly?'"--has implications that go beyond the usual remark a doctor might make to a patient who has not followed directions (QA 175). Marcia has not been looking after herself at all, and the institutions normally responsible for looking after people have somehow not made the right connections. Everyone has been trying to look after Marcia, but Marcia has rejected their efforts. Not her neighbor, her office coworkers, her doctor, nor her social worker can be "blamed" for Marcia's death. Yet the troublesome, nagging thought remains that surely someone might have done something. While the State provides basic needs and social services looks after the elderly, Marcia is one of those people who have truly "'fallen through the net of the welfare state'" (QA 21). She is the real social problem, but no one seems capable of dealing with her. Her neighbors think they ought to help her but are ineffectual in the few things they offer to do for her; Letty makes an effort by inviting her to meet for lunch, but Marcia ignores her; the persistent social worker Janice Brabner does what she is paid to do and complains about the ingratitude of people like Marcia. Even Norman and Edwin make efforts in their own way, tentative and incomplete as they are. Edwin occasionally stops at the end of her road and contemplates dropping in but never does; Norman actually stands opposite her house at one point, sees her, but leaves without speaking to her. Discussing that incident later, the two men feel that something definitely ought to be done about Marcia, but unable to arrive at any satisfactory plan, end up joking and laughing together: "Nervous reaction, perhaps, but why nervous, Norman wondered. Something in the subconscious, Edwin suggested, but that set them off into more laughter" (QA 158-59). The doctors assume the State is taking care of Marcia; the State makes its effort but fails. The problem goes beyond anything social workers or doctors or well-meaning neighbors can do: Marcia has no real emotional ties to any other human being, and the lesson implicit in her death is chilling.

Marcia's death, ironically, has the effect of bringing Letty, Norman, and Edwin together in a way they had never imagined as workers sharing the same office. For Letty, Marcia's death has brought a "sense of desolation," an acknowledgment of how completely alone she is, despite the fact that she and Marcia had never been particular friends (QA 189). Edwin names himself Marcia's next of kin at the hospital, feeling, perhaps, a responsibility that transcends the circumstance of his happening to be present when Marcia was found slumped over her table. Norman is deeply moved by Marcia's death, a response that, taken with other small clues, suggests that their peculiar relationship had more meaning than either of them would have admitted. This is borne out by the surprising revelation that Marcia had willed Norman her house. When Letty, Norman, and Edwin gather in Marcia's house to sort through her possessions, it is clear that theirs has become a friendship that will last. Norman's toast as they are about to drink the sherry they have discovered in Marcia's cupboard is "'Here's to us, then'" (QA 217). Their sense of being a group of friends who can look forward to a future of shared activities will prevent their having to experience the isolation and loneliness that characterized Marcia's life.

Despite the odds against them, most of Pym's characters manage to "make do" remarkably well. Conscious that they have had to settle for something less than they would like, they have nevertheless managed to adjust; aware of the problems inherent in human relationships, they make the effort to establish them nonetheless. Many discover that autonomy is ample compensation for the drawbacks of solitude. Those who fail to adjust, that is, those who remain emotionally out of touch and therefore doomed to a permanent disassociation from any meaningful interaction, are those whose inner lives have withered. This is most forcefully illustrated in Leonora Eyre and Marcia Ivory. Pym's admirable women-- Jessie Morrow of *Crampton Hodnet*, Belinda Bede, Mildred Lathbury, Jane Cleveland, Dulcie Mainwaring, Catherine Oliphant, Letty Crowe, and Emma Howick--are willing to take risks and have a fully developed capacity for hope and a cheerful resignation to the realities of present day England. Their ability to look upon themselves and their surroundings with detachment gives a misleading impression of their emotional depths, but all are deeply feeling women who have developed a way to live in a confused and disappointing world.

SIX

INFINITE POSSIBILITIES

At the end of *Quartet In Autumn*, Letty is musing over the unlikely prospect that any romantic attachment could develop between her friend Marjorie and either Edwin or Norman. The last sentence of the novel reads: "But at least it made one realise that life still held infinite possibilities for change" (218). Despite its surface optimism, the statement comes at the conclusion of a novel filled with images of decay and death, and the prospects for change that Letty is thinking of are anything but infinite. Still, the statement is typical of Pym's affirmation of life and cautious optimism in the face of inevitable shifting circumstances that she never abandoned, even when conditions were at their bleakest in her own life. From her early disappointments in love through the bitter blow of fourteen years of rejection by publishers, Pym managed to maintain a stoical cheerfulness about the future both personally and in her fiction. It is a trait shared by many of her characters, who look forward hopefully even in the bleakest of times. Furthermore, changing circumstances provide the impetus for many of her plots, and almost all of the novels' indeterminate endings hint that change is about to occur. The prospect of change is not always embraced, however, for many characters prefer to keep things as they always have been, some of them living in their memories of days gone by, others wishing literally that they had lived in another age. The subjects of the past, change, and the future are treated with the same complexity that characterizes Pym's treatment of other themes. Some characters are frightened by change, having accepted the routine of their lives so thoroughly that they do not want to alter it for any reason. Others find change disconcerting because they truly believe the old ways were simpler or better than the new ways. Finally, some welcome change for the possibility that their futures will be brighter, fuller, or freer than their pasts. Pym became increasingly interested in the subject over the several decades she was writing, so that by the time of her last two novels, *Quartet In Autumn* and *A Few Green Leaves*, the theme becomes central.

Even *Some Tame Gazelle*, which gives the impression of being completely insular, makes many observations about people's connections with the past as they try to live in a changing world. Begun when Pym was only twenty-three, it was revised over the next fifteen years, during which time England was being devastated by a war and rebuilding itself. While the novel does not directly discuss the effects of the war, some of its characters remember vividly the pre-World War I days and mourn the passing of that period. Others, having experienced the larger world, now live a quiet life in the village. Miss Liversidge, for example, has traveled abroad extensively and had done relief work among the refugees in the Balkans during the first World War. Ricardo Bianco is an Italian count who for some inexplicable reason has settled in this village, and his friend John Akenside was killed in a riot in Prague. Most of the central characters are university-educated. From the world outside the village come Bishop Grote, an African priest; Nicholas Parnell, a friend of Belinda's from the university and head librarian there; and Nathaniel Mold, the deputy librarian, who has made an extensive tour of Africa. It is these strangers who pose the threat to the familiar routine of Belinda Bede, for in this novel, change is resisted wholeheartedly and viewed as something of an evil in itself.

The entrance of strangers into Belinda's cozy village is not new, for young curates arrive regularly, much to her

144

sister Harriet's delight. The comfortable routine of their lives is indicated in the first chapter when, as Harriet, Belinda, and the new curate settle down for a comfortable evening in the drawing room after supper, Belinda thinks of how this is just like countless other evenings they have spent with other curates. She has a curious mixture of responses to that thought: "There was something almost frightening and at the same time comforting about the sameness of it all" (**STG** 16-17). This opening scene sets the stage for the conflict of the novel, and while Belinda never fully explores sameness from its frightening perspective, at least that aspect of the static life occurs to her. With her life-long unrequited love for Archdeacon Hoccleve, her love of "our greater English poets," and her sister's zeal for young curates, she is perfectly content. Belinda has never for a moment considered the curates or Count Bianco's routine marriage proposals as anything other than amusing diversions for her sister. But when strangers come with marriage proposals, Belinda senses danger. Genuinely upset by the possibility that her sister might accept a marriage proposal, for instance, she finds herself in an uncharacteristically melancholy mood, thinking of the way things change. Realizing that "the fine madness of her youth had gone," Belinda reflects:

> *Change and decay in all around I see ... All, all are gone, the old familiar faces....* Dear Nicholas was back in the Library, John Akenside was in heaven, while his earthly remains rested in an English cemetery in the Balkans, and if Harriet married Theodore Mbawawa, even she would be gone. (**STG** 160)

Thoroughly comfortable with life as it has been, she wants nothing to change.

Nor does Belinda expect or even want the Archdeacon to return her love. While she expresses hope for the future, it is never in terms of her actually being loved by the Archdeacon, for that would mean his wife Agatha's somehow disappearing from the scene. It would be a monumental change she does not feel capable of dealing with: she simply would not know what to do if their circumstances were to change. Toying briefly with the idea of knitting a pullover for Henry, for instance, Belinda is sure that she will do something "safe and dull" like a jumper for herself. Knitting for the Archdeacon would take the "fine courage of youth" and was "too fraught with dangers to be attempted" (**STG** 83-84). She has lost the intensely passionate energy she had when young and now prefers the mellow contentment of her middle years. Experiencing a flush of pleasure when Henry thanks her for mending a hole in his sock, she is so unnerved by the feeling that she wonders aloud to Harriet what it must be like to be a pillar of salt: "'I should imagine it would be very restful ... to have no feelings or emotions'" (**STG** 80). Although she thinks of hope as a wonderful thing, even if nothing comes of it and she does not know what she would have done without it, her hope now would be simply that things would return to the way they were before Mr. Mold and the Bishop had come to the village.

At the novel's end, with the disturbing Grote and Mold gone, Belinda looks forward to everything continuing as it had before. She does not look too far into the future: "she could only be grateful that their lives were to be so little changed.... Dr. Johnson had been so right when he had said that all change is of itself an evil" (**STG** 251). Belinda's strong resistance to change is a large part of the reason some critics finds this novel almost unrealistic, its characters frozen in some idyllic world that never existed. But Belinda is no different from countless other people in the real--or fictional--world who have long settled for the sure comforts of familiar routine. Her reality is no less valid than the reality of people who actively seek and wholeheartedly accept change. Her personal crisis when she is confronted with the prospect of a major upheaval in her life is as traumatic for her as it would be for anyone else. For Belinda Bede, if the static life is at times frightening, it is at least familiar; the unknown is much more of a threat.

Excellent Women examines the effects of change on the quiet domestic life from a different perspective. Here, change brings unprecedented emotional possibilities for Mildred Lathbury, a prospect she finds appealing despite its unsettling nature. Again, as in *Some Tame Gazelle*, the novel opens with the arrival of newcomers who disturb the daily routine, in this case Helena Napier and, shortly, her husband Rocky. The Napiers represent a different kind of threat from that of the outsiders who come into Belinda and Harriet's world proposing marriage, however. Not only are they worldly, but they are also glamourous, at least to Mildred. More importantly, Mildred's infatuation with Rocky causes her for perhaps the first time to examine her life closely and question it. Mildred sees the possibility that her life could be different, that she does not necessarily have to be drab and colorless. Smitten by Rocky's charm, not caring that it is superficial and largely insincere, she senses a potential for passion in herself that she had never before suspected. Unlike Belinda Bede, Mildred rather enjoys her newfound feelings and thinks it is better to have had them than never to have had the experience at all. Responding to spring and her strange new feelings for the vibrant Rocky, she begins to make noticeable changes herself: she begins to wear more make up, to arrange her hair differently, and to select less drab clothes, all the direct result of meeting the Napiers. She finds it upsetting that William Caldicote wants her to remain exactly as she is, an observer of life, an excellent unmarried woman. "'Life is disturbing enough,'" he tells her (**EW** 69). Change for William is not at all welcome for rather peculiar reasons. When Mildred discloses her feeling that she might like not being herself, the fussy, old-maidish, self-absorbed William is prompted to remark petulantly that he has been moved to a new office and does not like it at all because "'different pigeons come to the windows'" (**EW** 71). In contrast to William's stolid preference for keeping things as they always have been, Mildred finds the prospect of being "'unlike oneself occasionally'" a pleasant one (**EW** 71). Buying mimosa on impulse, selecting "Hawaiian Fire" lipstick, and questioning the necessity of tea all indicate the degree to which her world is being altered.

In addition to the Napiers, another person new to Mildred's small world threatens to disturb the status quo. Allegra Gray, the attractive widow who moves into the upstairs flat in the vicarage, soon has Julian and Winifred Malory enraptured by her charms, at least for the time being. The first hints of Allegra's influence are Julian's holding her hand and then Winifred's plans to have a smarter summer wardrobe with Allegra's tasteful advice. Emissaries from the larger world such as the Napiers and Mrs. Gray, it would seem, are more attuned to what is fashionable and attractive. That all is not well in the Malory vicarage becomes apparent when Mildred overhears Allegra and Winifred arguing over the proper flower arrangment for the altar. At one point later in the novel, after Julian and Allegra are engaged and Helena has left Rocky, Mildred and Winifred openly express their feelings about how these new people have changed their lives. Mildred tells Winifred that she almost wishes the Napiers had not come to live in her house: "'Things were much simpler before they came'" (**EW** 165). Soon, Winifred blurts out the truth that she sometimes wishes Allegra had not come to live there either. Both women find the complications brought about by these newcomers unsettling.

Excellent Women concludes with Mildred still single, but it hints that she might marry Everard, as indeed we learn in *Jane and Prudence* that she does. Marrying Everard will not be the romantic event Mildred had imagined in her fantasies of Rocky, however. Instead, Everard is rather stuffy and staid, despite his good looks. He is conventional, telling Mildred to stay just as she is, and traditional, viewing wives as persons whose job it is to proofread and index for their husbands. The "change" in Mildred's life will not be a marriage of love and romance. Rather, it has to do with the variety of the work she will perform for Everard, as he assures her that she could learn to do his proofreading and even help him with the index: "'The index would make a nice change for you,'" he says

(**EW** 255). Her response is jaded and resigned: "'Yes, it would make a nice change,' ... And before long I should be certain to find myself at his sink peeling potatoes and washing up; that would be a nice change when both proofreading and indexing began to pall" (**EW** 255). This sentiment is echoed in Dulcie Mainwaring's observation in *No Fond Return Of Love*, when Neville Forbes tells her that change is good for everyone: "'Well, yes, but there are changes and changes'" (258). The kind of change Mildred anticipates, as Everard's excellent helpmate, is not particularly positive. Subsequent references to Mildred in other novels indicate that Mildred's life as Mrs. Bone involves a great deal of secretarial and editorial work.

At the end of *Excellent Women*, Mildred is actually thinking of both Julian Malory and Everard Bone and the prospect of having her "'full life'" after all in protecting and helping the two of them (256). Mildred does have a choice, at least, but it is not much of a choice. Rocky is out of the question for her, so she is left with two men who pale by comparison. Again one is reminded of Dulcie Mainwaring in *No Fond Return Of Love*, when she compares the freedom to select what one wants for tea to life: "'Except that there you can't always choose *exactly* what you want'" (75). Though people make conscious choices all the time, often, as Dulcie points out, the choices are not precisely what one might like. Although Mildred tells Mrs. Morris that she cannot change now and says to Rocky, "Let me stay as I am.... I'm quite happy'" (224), she later observes that "'nothing can ever be really the same when time has passed,'" adding, "'even if it appears to be from the outside'" (234). While it might seem as if Mildred remains the same as she always has been, it is clear that she has undergone a change; and while she believes that things were simpler before the Napiers arrived, she does not regret having had the experience of knowing them.

Early on, Mildred has acknowledged that at least the experience of knowing Rocky has enriched her life. Returning from the Old Girls' Reunion, she and Dora meet a former Wren officer who had known Rocky in Italy. Later, when Dora remarks that they have' had a lucky escape in not having come under Rocky's influence, Mildred, seeing it quite differently, says: "'Perhaps it's better to be unhappy than not to feel anything at all'" (**EW** 115). This remark is a sharp contrast to Belinda Bede's reflection on the tranquility of not having any feelings. While Belinda is frightened by what she believes is the evil of change, Mildred has had enough of comfortable familiarity to welcome even the pain of previously unfelt experience. Perhaps she eventually marries Everard for the change it brings, though the only difference marriage to him would make is that she would gain in social status, a consideration that Mildred is keenly aware of but not particularly driven to attain. Mildred has from the first been dissatisfied with her life, and that feeling grows throughout the novel. At its conclusion, she seems almost desperate for a change, the prospect of the two spinsters living in the flat vacated by the Napiers singularly depressing. Her infatuation with Rocky has brought closer to the surface a dissatisfaction with her life that she had long ago buried or may never had been aware of had it not been for his glittering charm and winning ways. Superficial and fickle though he is, Rocky brings zest and color with him, suggesting dazzling possibilities for a woman whose world has been void of those things. But Mildred's life seems ironically destined to be more of the same, despite her strong desire to the contrary. Life as Everard's wife promises to be little different from life as a spinster. Mildred is wise enough to recognize the limited possibilities for someone with her background and experience. Although we can never know why Mildred marries Everard, the ending of *Excellent Women* suggests that she is quite willing to accept whatever changes come her way.

Reading the posthumous novels, one discovers characters and themes which Pym used in the novels published in her lifetime. One can safely assume that she "recycled" those characters, themes, and even identical passages which she felt were particularly well conceived. Thus, the two characters Miss Doggett and Jessie Morrow from *Crampton Hodnet* are fully employed in *Jane and*

Prudence. Nor is it surprising that the same lines Belinda Bede remembers in her moment of worry that Harriet might leave her appear at the end of *Crampton Hodnet*: "'Change and decay in all around we see,'" say Michael and Gabriel, adding, "'but not *here*'" (216). Miss Doggett and Jessie Morrow concur in the closing sentences that one is not likely to find change or decay in Leamington Lodge. The fact that the concluding chapter is virtually a mirror image of the opening chapter reinforces this suggestion that things do not change in this North Oxford town. Jessie Morrow has neither Belinda Bede's fear of change nor Mildred Lathbury's desire for it. When the novel begins, Jessie is not nearly as resigned to her unchanging life as she is at the end, however. Indeed, tidying up after the tea party which opens the novel, Jessie is impressed by a young student's handling of a potentially awkward situation. His skill makes her think that he might after all have some bright future ahead of him, and that discovery in turn fills her "with hope even for herself" (11). In the course of the novel, Jessie occasionally feels impulses that might be pleasant to follow but on the whole accepts that any possibility of excitement in her life is gone. Aware that things might have been different had she accepted Mr. Latimer's proposal, marriage to him would have been a most unsuitable change. She is happy with herself, neither burdened by unrequited love nor regretting her decision.

Unchanging circumstances often represent stability, not stagnation, as they do for Belinda Bede in *Some Tame Gazelle*. Pym had always been interested in the idea of comfort in sameness, as the thoughts of several characters in the very early work *Civil To Strangers* indicate. Speaking of the unsettling nature of Stefan Tilos's influence on their village, Mrs. Gower tells Cassandra that she thinks his coming has not been a good thing. Cassandra agrees, looking forward to the time when he will be gone, and feeling "glad of the stability of things, of the pattern of her life in Up Callow" (113). Likewise, Mr. Gay, upset by events Mr. Tilos's presence has precipitated, regards Mrs. Gower as "the only stable thing left in a changing world" (125). Although Deirdre Swan in *Less Than Angels*

151

complains that her neighborhood is boring and her mother's meals predictable, the conventional lives of Mabel Swan and Rhoda Wellcome create exactly the sort of environment Catherine runs to when she is emotionally devastated over Tom's death. There is no danger of anything changing in their household. When Deirdre wishes her mother would fix something different for supper, her aunt suggests an egg. Deirdre has a more exotic meal in mind: "'Some rice, all oily and saffron yellow, with aubergines and red peppers and lots of garlic.'" Her mother's relieved response is, "'Oh, well, dear, it's no good wishing for that sort of thing *here*'" (38). Deirdre's criticism of the unimaginative and uninteresting suburb she has grown up in is typical of the young. On the other hand, Catherine Oliphant, ten years older than Deirdre and without close relatives, embraces the cozy world of Mabel and Rhoda, for whom each day is a repetition of all their previous days. They are only slightly different versions of Belinda and Harriet Bede.

In some of the novels, certain characters cling to their memories of the past for the comfort they provide in an uneventful present. In *Civil To Strangers*, for instance, Stefan Tilos's Hungarian aunt, Miss Hunyadi, spends her lonely old age recalling the happy months she spent years before at Leamington Spa with her good English friend, whom she met when her friend was a governess in Budapest before the war. At the end of the novel, plans have been made for Miss Hunyadi to visit the Marsh-Gibbons in the fall, where she "could spend long evenings knitting and remembering the past" (164). *Gervase and Flora* ends with Flora's thought that traditional things give the most comfort, while in the *Home Front Novel*, Lady Nollard constantly laments the changes in her life following her husband's death, particularly the passing of those days when she had entertained frequently and brilliantly. Count Ricardo Bianco of *Some Tame Gazelle*, one of whose chief topics of conversation is his childhood in Naples, is principally occupied with bringing out an edition of the letters of his long-dead friend John Akenside. In the same novel, Connie Aspinall, a "kind of

152

relation" of Miss Liversidge who has been taken in by that imposing woman, has seen better days as a companion to a lady living in Belgrave Square. Playing at a concert in the church hall, "poor Connie" at her harp reminds Belinda of another time: "Her thin, useless hands, her fluttering grey dress, ...even the instrument itself with its Victorian association, made Belinda think of past glories, of more elegant gatherings than this one, at which Connie might have played" (43).

Another character like Connie Aspinall is Miss Prideaux in *A Glass Of Blessings*, who has "vivid memories of life as a governess in Europe in the grand old days. Miss Prideaux appeared to remember only the best parts of her life, so that she was sometimes accused of exaggeration or even of downright lying" (28). Miss Prideaux now resides in a bed-sitting- room cluttered with souvenirs and photographs of people from those glorious days. She could be one of Mildred Lathbury's distressed gentlewomen, or rather, the type whose loss William Caldicote believes he understands so well: "'The great house in Belgrave Square with the servants bringing up trays from the basement, the Edwardian country house parties with visiting foreign royalties, the villa at Nice or Bordighera for the winter months... '" (**EW** 68). Dulcie Mainwaring's neighbors in *No Fond Return Of Love* seem frozen in this kind of past, Mrs. Beltane somewhere in the England of the 1920s and Senhor Macbride-Pereira, Sao Paulo of the 1890s. Though their company leaves Dulcie feeling a "sense of unreality," she thinks it "one of their chief charms, their being so out of touch with everyday life" (28). These people dreaming of older, better days provide a marked contrast to the people, mostly young, who make the transitions required by shifting social changes of the nineteen-fifties and -sixties. As Pym herself got older and especially when she was regarded by some as being outdated, she made a conscious effort to include more references to contemporary life. But from the first Pym was aware that for many people, change is not necessarily good. She often implies that she agrees with those characters for whom the past was clearly better than the present, as she does in

Quartet In Autumn and *A Few Green Leaves*, for instance. Further, she demonstrates the ways in which recalling the past, which cannot change, is one way to cope with unwelcome changes in the present.

This is especially evident in *A Few Green Leaves*. Miss Olive Lee never tires of reminding the village folks of the old days in the manor when Miss Vereker had been governess to the de Tankerville girls and how things were better then. Older village women cherish the memory of Miss Vereker because she is their link to that pre-war past, when there was still an order and formality to life that is missing now. The governess, of their own social class but with the privilege of providing a service to the de Tankerville family inside the manor, was their link to the life of the gentry that cannot possibly be maintained by the agent of the current inhabitants. It is not the same now, Miss Grundy laments, recalling that Miss Vereker had always wanted to live in the cottage in the woods but now lives in London with her nephew. Once Miss Vereker had every reason to think that she would one day retire to that cottage, but circumstances are changed now. Even though Miss Lee reminds her that "'we can't expect to get everything we want.... We know that life isn't like that'" (159), it is Miss Lee herself who most often reminisces about Miss Vereker and the past. When the discussion turns to the fact that they had no need of hunger lunches in the old days, for example, Miss Lee points out: "'We looked after our own people out there [Africa] in those days.... Things aren't the same now'" (159-60). It is a lament that forms the refrain of the novel. Indeed, when Miss Vereker actually returns to the village to surprise her old friends and see the manor once again, she gets lost and is found wandering in the woods. Sheltered for the night in Dr. Shrubsole's house, Miss Vereker is so disturbed by the changes she has already seen in the village that she is not at all sure that she wants to visit the manor, "with all the changes and her memories. But she was sure of one thing-- tomorrow she would pay a visit to the mausoleum. That was always the same" (228).

154

It is not only some odd, spinsterish women who long for the past. Leonora Eyre of *The Sweet Dove Died* is another such character. Although she is unmarried, she does not fall into the same category with Miss Olive Lee and Miss Prideaux because she is sophisticated, financially independent, and admired by men. Accused of being behind the times, Pym was trying in this novel, written during the long period when she was not being published, to become more contemporary. As a result, she not only included sex scenes but made James bisexual, an interesting response to the charges that she was outdated. At the same time that she was attempting to be trendy, she created a character whose personality is unlike any of her previous central characters, with the possible exception of Prudence Bates, but who has a deep affinity for an entirely different age. Cold, aloof, self-centered and manipulative, Leonora collects Victoriana--"'I adore them. Somehow I feel they're me'"--and would indeed have preferred living in Victorian days (23). She says of Virginia Water: "'All those trees and distant ruins, so much *me*'" (48). She likes the fruitwood mirror James lends her because when she looks in it in a certain light, she sees the reflection of "a woman from another century, fascinating and ageless" (87). Like Henrik Ibsen's Hedda Gabler, she finds the realities of life, particularly aging and sex, loathesome.

Leonora's vicious treatment of the elderly Miss Foxe is evidence of her own fear of aging, and she seems almost to refuse to acknowledge the modern age she lives in. She has never learned to drive and romanticizes the taxi drivers on whom she must rely, referring to them as "sweet." On one occasion, the "warm soft voice" of her Black taxi driver leads her to "imagine herself as a beauty of the Deep South being handed from her carriage or as a white settler in the days when native servants were humble and devoted" (SDD 16). On her bedside table are books of poetry by Arnold and Browning, smelling salts, a bottle of pills, and "presiding over all these the faded photographs of a handsome man and a sweet-faced woman in late Victorian dress. Leonora had long ago decided that her grandparents were much more distinguished-looking than her father and mother whose photographs had been hidden away in a drawer" (**SDD** 17). Leonora's childhood having been spent in various European towns, she too is fond of recounting the memories of her romantic past, so fond that people have found her a bit tedious on the subject. She is curiously out of place in the world of James and even that of his uncle Humphrey, for while Humphrey is an antique seller and appreciates Leonora's sophistication and culture, he is not pleased with her remoteness. He tries without success to turn their relationship into something sexual, but she will have none of it. She is frigid, wanting nothing to do with sex in a time when everyone seems to want it. At one point Humphrey tells her that she has too romantic a view of both the past and the present, to which she responds: "'One doesn't look so far ahead'" (**SDD** 92). Leonora wants not to look too far ahead because she is getting old, and that reality hits her forcefully in the course of this novel. Leonora belongs to another age, with her smelling salts, her fainting fits, and her pristine elegance.

Kitty Jeffreys and Wilmet Forsythe are like Leonora in the respect that they, too, seem to belong to some elegant other era. Kitty cannot "bear anything sad or coming to an end" and manages to endure living in a small English university town by recalling her glorious past on a Caribbean island (AQ 3). Like Leonora, she dresses with impeccable taste. Her chief occupations now are selecting appropriate attire for social occasions and resting in order to preserve her beauty and energy. She cannot bear talk of aging or death. In *A Glass Of Blessings*, Harry sends Wilmet a little heart-shaped box of the Regency or early Victorian period and, thinking it is from Piers, she feels "like the heroine of a Victorian novel," hiding it in her dress pocket and fingering its inscription (96). That same Christmas, Professor Root gives her an early Victorian mourning brooch because it seems appropriate to her style of beauty which, he says, "'is happily not quite of this age'" (104). She becomes melancholy when looking at old photographs because of the changes over time they represent: "'It all seems such a long time ago ...--from that to this, whatever it may have been or is now'" (110). Wilmet's identification with another age has the effect, as it does with Leonora, of making her seem cool and unapproachable not only to Piers but to her husband Rodney as well. Both Wilmet and Leonora are good at flower arranging, which, we are told, is "a fashionable modern pastime for a certain type of woman--a hobby for the gentler sex, almost like the accomplishments of a Victorian young lady" (**FGL** 75). Although flower arranging is a relatively recent English activity, they are skilled at it in the way accomplished Victorian women were expected to be skilled in some other genteel pastime. Kitty Jeffreys disdains gardening but does like to sit among the flowers, as if she herself is "arranged" there. In contrast to Wilmet, her mother-in-law Sybil, who is very much of this age with her avid interest in social work and the problems of contemporary society, has no skill whatsoever in flower arranging, and Daphne Dagnall of *A Few Green Leaves*, who lives only for today, realizes that she hates flower arranging.

Time and again, Pym contrasts the way things are with the way they used to be. More often the old times are viewed as having been better--or at least simpler--than the way things are today. For example, Rhoda Wellcome tells Dulcie Mainwaring that young women are much cleverer than they were in her day but that they were not necessarily happier: "'Life was simpler then. We made our own pleasures. Perhaps in some ways we were more serious--felt our responsibilities more'" (**NFRL** 75). This sentiment that life was simpler for the older generation than for the younger is a view presented in *Less Than Angels* as well. Professor Mainwaring, peddling Edwardian musical comedy tunes on the pianolo, wonders to the young anthropology students gathered at his home for the research grant competition why people are not as lighthearted as they were in his youth. Mark Penfold's reply resounds with solid reasons: "'Two wars, motor-cars, and newer and more frightful bombs being invented all the time.... One feels there is something not quite right in being gay'" (211). This sobering observation points out a

157

very real reason why one might long for the past. For both men and women in the mid- nineteen-fifties, the spectre of war means the possibility of death, and advances in technology mean more complicated lives than in the long gone era of gaiety that Professor Mainwaring recalls. The series of murders Rhoda reads about, with bodies of young women being discovered in an unsavory part of London, Mrs. Foresight's chauffeur reading a Communist newspaper, and the political uprisings in Africa which lead to Tom Mallow's violent death are reminders of the less-than-halcyon present.

After *The Sweet Dove Died*, Pym wrote two drafts of a novel which was posthumously published as *An Academic Question*. That novel also indicates Pym's attempt to be contemporary, acknowledging recent social changes by having characters who engage in recreational sex and live together without being married. While in *Less Than Angels* Tom Mallow and Catherine Oliphant live together, it is almost as if they are brother and sister rather than lovers. In *An Academic Question*, Caroline Grimstone's sister not only lives in London with her boyfriend Gary Carter but also has an abortion. There is a student rebellion on Guy Falkes Day that ends in a fire in the university library, and people have written obscenities on a campus statue which itself borders on the obscene. Pym found this novelistic effort to be unsatisfactory, but there are elements in it which made their way into her two subsequent novels. A kind of free-floating anxiety pervades the novel, reflected in Caroline's wanting an occupation which will make her life more meaningful than it is as wife and mother, in the efforts of the elegant but effete Coco Jeffreys and his mother Kitty to avoid fatigue and aging, and in the student unrest at the university as well as references to larger social problems in London's squalid districts.

An Academic Question also indicates Pym's interest in aging, death, and possibilities for change which she fully explores in her last two novels. Caroline Grimstone finds one use for her time at the retirement home, Normanhurst, in reading to old people. When Mr. Stillingfleet, whose manuscript is crucial to a central complication of the plot, dies, Caroline is deeply upset at his cremation, more because it reminds her of her father's death and of her own mortality than because of any warm feelings she had for him: "I wanted to say that I was not crying for Mr. Stillingfleet in particular but for the general sadness of life and for all of them [the old people at Normanhurst] who would so soon make the journey to this place [the crematorium]" (53). Although she says she is sad for the old people and their impending death, on her way home she runs into Coco and laments: "'Oh, Coco, it was awful with those poor old people. Shall we all get like that?'" Coco does not answer, for "it upset him as much as Kitty to think of age and death" (54). This theme of old age and dying runs throughout the novel. We see it in Dolly Arborfield's preoccupation with hedgehogs, her grief at their deaths, her refusal to go away from her home and her increasing isolation from human beings; in the discussions Caro has with her four-year-old daughter on the death of animals; in the retirement of Crispin Maynard, the impending retirement of Evan Cranton and their replacement by young academics with shoulder-length hair and revolutionary ideas; and in Esther Clovis's death and memorial service.

Pym explores the idea of change and possibilities in the character of Caroline Grimstone, who, at twenty-eight, has a kind of weariness about her: she seems at loose ends, unfulfilled, useless, drifting about for some kind of meaningful occupation to fill her time. Her feeling of uselessness is compounded by the fact that as a contemporary young woman, her role as wife is not as clearly defined as it is for Menna Cranton, for instance, who has four children and several grandchildren and "was an excellent housekeeper and cook and did all her husband's typing, this last skill dating from the days when it was regarded as one of the duties of an academic wife. Alan did his own typing and this seemed to cut [Caroline] off from his work" (AQ 7). There is an understated ominous air about Caroline's life, as if she has no right even to exist. On her way to confront Cressida, the woman whom Alan has gone to bed with, Caroline feels deeply

159

inferior. She has a recurring need for change: autumn becomes "a time for looking forward and perhaps even for making resolutions to alter and improve one's life" (**AQ** 137). A visit to her mother makes her keenly aware of how narrow their lives are and brings with it a sense that her own is becoming even narrower. Her volunteer work at Normanhurst does give her some small measure of satisfaction, and she finally becomes useful to her husband by gaining him access to the highly coveted Stillingfleet manuscript which leads to his publication in the most prestigious journal in his field. Thus she is instrumental in assisting her husband's career, opening possibilities for her own life: "I saw us moving on to other universities, perhaps even to America. Life suddenly seemed more full of possibilities" (178). Pym never returned to *An Academic Question*, leaving readers without the benefit of knowing how she might have revised it. Nevertheless, the novel serves to indicate her growing interest in the themes which become central in her last two novels: the passing of time, one's feeling of displacement in light of alarming social changes, the contrast of the present with the way things used to be, and how one functions with the knowledge of one's mortality. These and other subjects such as old age and retirement, dead animals, and symbols of change recur in both *Quartet In Autumn* and *A Few Green Leaves*.

Quartet In Autumn is Pym's darkest novel, but it was written at a time when she was bitter about what she saw as her failure as a novelist: no one would publish her rejected seventh novel, *An Unsuitable Attachment*, nor the novel she had written in the 1960s, *The Sweet Dove Died*. She had had a cancerous breast removed and had suffered a stroke which left her with temporary aphasia that prevented her from speaking or writing normally. Told by her doctor to retire after 28 years with the International African Institute, she had little hope of ever seeing again the kind of early success the flurry of publishing activity in the 1950s had promised. And so she wrote *Quartet In Autumn*, with no prospect of its ever being published, for her own pleasure. Letty's remark about infinite possibilities is particularly poignant in light of the grim

160

prognostication for Pym's own future, but it is prophetic as well. Pym's life turned around suddenly and dramatically in January 1977, giving in her last three years the kind of acclaim she had never dared hope for. When Larkin and Cecil named her one of the century's most underrated writers in *The Times Literary Supplement* article, Macmillan immediately accepted *Quartet In Autumn*, which Pym had sent to them after yet another Cape rejection. When she wrote to James Wright at Macmillan, after its acceptance, to describe what she had in mind for publicizing the book, she said that "the story, like life, ends inconclusively, though with hope for the future" (**MS PYM** 165, fol. 101).

Much is depressing about the book, despite Pym's claim to the contrary. Letty, Marcia, Norman, and Edwin all work in an office doing something so insignificant that there are no plans to replace Letty and Marcia when they retire. In fact, the whole department is being phased out and, once Norman and Edwin retire, will be obliterated. There will be no trace of the existence of these four people in the context of this office. Their conversations at work include discussions of the deaths of elderly people by hypothermia or starvation and other attendant ills of the aging. All four of them feel out of place and are constantly assaulted by signs of the changed social scene and reminders of their old age: the vibrancy of the young black woman in their office and the vitality and ebullience of the Nigerians who buy the house Letty lives in; Norman's "'psychedelic' plastic carrier, patterned in vivid colours" that contrast so decidedly with his personality (**QA** 22); the garish changes in Edwin's favorite tea shop, now decorated in a trendy orange and green with its monotonous and insidious background music; and even more distressing, the "stages towards death," as Letty calls them, that fifty years have brought about (**QA** 17). On the Underground platform, Letty sees an old woman who reminds her of a school friend slumped over and then witnesses her shouting an obscenity at someone attempting to assist her, and Marcia notices a violent message scrawled on a platform wall. Letty regards such incidents that she would not have seen when she was young as disturbing reminders of the potential for violence and dissolution in her rapidly changing world.

Norman's racism and his intense dislike of the automobile are symptoms of his deeper anger against changes over which he has no control. Visiting his brother-in-law in the hospital, he is unreasonably disturbed by and resentful of the urinal and vomiting pan he sees half-concealed beside the bed. Perhaps they are grim reminders of his own mortality or the frailty of humans in general. Enraged and irritable, he vents his anger on the automobiles zooming past him and blocking his passage. While the hospital is full, the church Edwin goes to that same evening is almost empty. Only a handful of people attend services anymore. Edwin does not like change at all, and while church is a real comfort, it too is undergoing disturbing transformations. When his good friend Father Gellibrand wonders if he ought to introduce the "Kiss of Peace--turning to the person next to you with a friendly gesture"--into the ceremony, Edwin advises against it, having visions of the young clergy in jeans and long hair and "himself trampled down by a horde of boys and girls brandishing guitars" (QA 15). He remembers with regret the old days when crowds of office workers filled churches at lunch time, and recalls one church in particular for which scandal "had put an end to the splendid services, the congregation had fallen away and in the end the church had been closed as redundant" (QA 203). That particular church had been replaced by a modern office building, one more ironic comment on contemporary life.

Edwin's quest for the church of the past is never-ending, but he has adjusted well enough to the present. Marcia, on the other hand, is lost somewhere in the past connected with the exigencies of World War II, stockpiling canned goods and milk bottles. Only Letty purports to live for today. She is not given to living in the past and remembers the post-war years only in terms of changes in fashion: "The New Look brought in by Dior in 1947, the comfortable elegance of the fifties, and in the early sixties the horror of the mini-skirt, such a cruel fashion for those

162

no longer young" (**QA** 26). Even so, after listening to a radio play about events in the life of an old woman, Letty dreams of people and times now gone, leading her to reflect on "the strangeness of life, slipping away like this" (**QA** 27). While she says she lives only for the present, Letty's dream suggests that, at least on a subconscious level, she is deeply aware of the irrevocability of passing time and the changes it has brought.

Despite the disquieting and often alarming signs of their mortality and the tremendous changes in contemporary life, these people still have hope for the future. The mad Marcia excepted, they manage to maintain a balanced perspective about aging and their future possibilities. Although Letty has a series of setbacks when her living arrangments are changed suddenly, not once, but twice, she manages to regain her even composure and self-assurance by the end of the novel. Earlier, having moved to Mrs. Pope's house and then learning that her friend Marjorie is engaged to marry David Lydell, Letty is wondering where she will live. Unwilling to spend the rest of her life in a bed-sitting-room in a North-West London suburb, she considers several options: "She told herself, dutifully assuming the suggested attitude towards retirement, that life was still full of possibilities" (**QA** 106). At this point, she is putting on a front, not at all convinced by what she is telling herself. But by the end of the novel, Letty seems to believe sincerely her confident observation about the infinite possibilities for change.

What does Letty have in mind when she has that thought? The immediate context of the statement is whether or not anything might develop between either Edwin or Norman, confirmed city dwellers, and Marjorie, who lives in the country. But Letty is thinking of more than just what might develop in her friends' lives: she is excited about the possibilities for change in her own life, a prospect intensified by her recent realization that she has a choice. When Norman and Edwin assume that Letty will be moving to the country to live with Marjorie now that Marjorie is not to be married, Letty tells them she has not yet decided. Norman encourages her to do exactly what she wants because it is, after all, her life, but Edwin protests that he thought she had always loved the country: "'I don't think I **love** it exactly,' said Letty, thinking of the dead birds and mangled rabbits and the cruel-tongued village people. 'It was just that it seemed a suitable arrangement when we made it. Now I feel that I have a choice.' She took a long draught of the sweet sherry and experienced a most agreeable sensation, almost a feeling of power" (**QA** 217). It is the possibility of control over her own life, the power to make a conscious choice, that accounts for Letty's optimism. By many people's standards, they are narrow choices, but for Letty, they are monumental. Norman, too, experiences an expansive awareness of possibilities when he inherits Marcia's house. Realizing that he has the power to affect the lives of Marcia's neighbors with his decision whether or not to live in the house, he feels "a quite new, hitherto unexperienced sensation--a good feeling, like a dog with two tails, as people sometimes put it--and he walked to the bus stop with his head held high" (**QA** 203). One is reminded of J. Alfred Prufrock, another lonely soul, daring to disturb the universe. Norman's and Letty's new-found feeling of power is exhilarating.

Pym's final novel, *A Few Green Leaves*, is filled with references to the past, to changing circumstances, and to the future as she presents an amazing array of observations on old age, death, the present and the past. The village manor is no longer inhabited by the original family, and so interest is "concentrated on the past" when, in the opening scene, the villagers go for their annual walk in the park and woods surrounding the manor (3). Emma Howick regrets having selected "the arid new town with its too obvious problems" for her sociological study and wishes instead she were studying the village (38). Beatrix Howick likes to look out her window hoping to see the kind of thing one would have seen a hundred years before, and her favorite way to fall to sleep at night is to recall her college friends of forty years before. The young rector Tom Dagnall is passionately interested in the distant past, though even the recent past would do: at one point he wishes he had been in the village in the thirties so that he could have rescued some of the documents of the de Tankervilles when they left the manor. His preference for a summer holiday would be a "quick journey back into the seventeeth century by time machine" (121). Young Dr. Martin Shrubsole specializes in geriatrics while old Dr. Gellibrand, who believes things were better in the old days, dotes on the young, particularly the pregnant young. Old village men in a pub are "obscurely hostile" when Emma attempts to start a conversation with them by commenting on the flower festival, for "they never had such a thing in the old days" (85). Only Tom's aging sister Daphne, who resents his interest in local history, lives "entirely in the present with no memory of any kind of past" (118-19), but she does look to the future with a hopeful spirit: "'One goes on living in the hope of seeing another spring,'" she says with some emotion (4). However, as if to set the stage for this final Pym drama, characterized as it is by curious, unexpected twists, Daphne's fervor is dampened slightly when, the very next moment, she spies what she thinks is a patch of violets only to discover it is a piece of trash.

There are other, more significant instances of the unexpected. When we suspect that Miss Vereker will die as she makes her journey through the woods to the village, it turns out that she simply falls asleep, and then, without warning, Miss Lickerish dies, in a scene brilliant for its simplicity: "She boiled a kettle on the fire and then sat in her chair with a cup of tea at her side and a cat on her knees. But some time during those dark hours the cat left her and sought the warmth of his basket, Miss Lickerish's lap having become strangely chilled" (**FGL** 227). This death, along with reports of those of characters from previous novels, is a concrete manifestation of the preoccupation with change and dissolution that pervade the novel in such things as Tom's search for the ruins of the deserted medieval village and his interest in death and burial rites, but especially in the central position of the mausoleum as social gathering place.

165

References to characters and events from earlier novels are sprinkled throughout this one, a favorite practice of Pym which proliferates and has added poignancy in this final novel. There are reports of people's deaths, particularly those of Fabian Driver (*Jane and Prudence*) and dear Esther Clovis (introduced in *Excellent Women* but appearing most fully in *Less Than Angels*). Attending Miss Clovis's memorial service, Emma hears a eulogy delivered by Digby Fox and sees Deirdre Swan Fox, old Dr. Apfelbaum, and Gertrude Lydgate, all characters from *Less Than Angels*. Pym was determined to hold this memorial service: an almost identical scene appears in *An Academic Question*, which Pym had no way of knowing would ever be published. There are numerous other connections with and echoes of Pym's previous works. Dr. Gellibrand is the brother of Father Gellibrand in *Quartet In Autumn*. At the "bring and buy" sale, Emma notices that someone has brought marmalade which had been boiled too long and gone syrupy; in *No Fond Return Of Love*, Dulcie makes lemon marmalade which goes beyond the settling point and becomes syrupy. The pot of quince jam Christabel contributes to this same sale reminds readers of the delight Ianthe Broome's uncle Randolph expresses when Sophia Ainger offers him quince jelly in *An Unsuitable Attachment*. When she sees Graham Pettifer wearing a raincoat at the flower festival, Emma recalls the same lines Aylwin Forbes quotes to Dulcie Mainwaring when she is caught in the rain without a coat. There are references to Father Thames, St. Luke's, and Wilf Bason from *A Glass Of Blessings*, and to Miss Lee's Christian guest-house, the Anchorage, from *No Fond Return Of Love*. One can imagine the pleasure Pym had in remembering these characters and scenes from the earlier works. These poignant reminders of Pym's fictional past add considerably to the richness of this novel and reinforce a major theme: the way memory works to sustain us in the face of constantly changing circumstances.

Except for Daphne, who claims she is interested only in the present, all of the other characters find the past a source of pleasure and interest. Much of the action of *A*

Few Green Leaves takes place over the course of a summer, and with summer's end come many changes, on both personal and larger social fronts. Adam Prince, for example, formerly an Anglican priest who had become Catholic and now a food critic for a gourmet magazine, finds his summer ending in a series of disquieting experiences, all centered around the fact that familiar rituals and old customs have disappeared. Changes in the old ways of doing things are responsible for the impersonal, almost bland characteristic of modern life. Thus, Tom's group of history society ladies, attempting to record local anecdotes for future historians, are not getting the kind of vivid information he had hoped for, causing him to think: "Perhaps we were all flattened out into a kind of uniform dullness these days--something to do with the welfare state and the rise of the consumer society" (**FGL** 110) Not only were things simpler in the old days, but they were also more personal, more human. This idea is illustrated by the attitude of Dr. Shrubsole toward his elderly patients. Even though he is a specialist in geriatrics, his interest is "detached and clinical." When Daphne makes her enthusiastic comment about spring and hope, his response is to move away from her, disturbed: "He felt that the drugs prescribed to control high blood pressure should also damp down emotional excesses and those fires of youth that could still--regrettably--burn in the dried up hearts of those approaching old age" (**FGL** 5). While he gives prescriptions and takes their blood pressure, Martin Shrubsole's interest in the elderly is purely professional. He wants nothing to do with other aspects of their lives.

Unsettling responses to the changes brought about by modern life manifest themselves physically in some of the characters. Adam goes to Dr. Gellibrand for the tension he attributes to worrying over the disturbing changes he is experiencing in his job, and on the same morning, Emma seeks help from Martin Shrubsole for a rash on one of her hands, wondering if it might be caused by stress. To his inquiry if she has been under much stress lately, she replies: "'Well, who hasn't, come to that.... Life is full of stressful situations, isn't it?'" (**FGL** 210). Uncomfortable

167

with admitting it, though each has a reason, neither Adam nor Emma is willing to articulate the cause of their stress. This inability to be open with their doctor is further evidence of the breakdown of real contact between people that Adam laments.

The "hectic pace of modern life" has its effects in small villages and large cities alike. In *Quartet In Autumn*, for instance, Norman's brother-in-law is hospitalized with a duodenal ulcer brought about by the "worrying nature of life in general" and more specifically by the stresses of his job (11), and in *The Sweet Dove Died*, Leonora keeps on her bedside table a bottle of pills "to relieve stess and strain" (17). These characters are all suffering from the kind of emotional strain inherent in modern life. They may get a prescription for pills from their doctors, but the real cure is not to be found in a doctor's office. While Martin Shrubsole prescribes an ointment for Emma, Dr. Gellibrand writes Adam a prescription for something "more in the nature of a placebo" with the advice that he learn to accept the expediencies of modern life and the deteriorating quality of both food and service: "'Try not to be quite so critical--learn to like processed cheese and tea-bags and instant coffee, and beefburgers and fish fingers too--most of the people in this village live on such things and they're none the worse for it'" (FGL 208). His flippant attitude toward Adam suggests he, too, is unwilling to become involved in his patients' emotional or spiritual crises--that is an area better served by the clergy, presumably, though no one ever goes to the rector for help. It, too, indicates the deterioration of interest in and commitment to one's fellow humans that Adam Prince laments.

Dr. Gellibrand himself is not willing to accept wholeheartedly the changes of contemporary life nor face the fact of his own declining years. He regrets "the old days when he had seen patients in the more gracious surroundings of his own home" (FGL 17) and the days when patients used to walk to surgery from the outlying villages rather than be conveyed there in cars bearing all sorts of wild slogans. He does not like the elderly but loves "the whole idea of life burgeoning and going on" (**FGL** 18). When older people come to him for their ailments, he is more likely to fall back on old-fashioned remedies. Daphne, for example, prefers the young Martin Shrubsole to Dr. Gellibrand because all Dr. Gellibrand ever suggests for her complaints is that she buy a new hat. When Tom invites him to speak to the history society on the history of medical practices, Tom has in mind his beginning in the seventeenth century. He is disappointed when Dr. Gellibrand focuses his talk on the "'good old days' of the nineteen thirties before the introduction of the National Health Service" (**FGL** 243). His comments lead to a discussion of jogging for health and eating a proper diet. Dr. Gellibrand's "past" is the same as the past of Miss Lee, Miss Grundy, and Mrs. Raven--that within their memories. Tom's interest in death and dying in the old days, ancient burial practices, and ruined villages contrasts with the interest in the past shared by the old people of the village, who would prefer not to think of how close they are to their own ends.

Both Tom and the larger group of elderly who scoff at his preoccupation with the remote past share their conviction that life is not what it used to be. For both, life then was better than life now. For instance, Tom is struck by Anthony a Wood's August 1678 diary entry stating that "'The act for burying in woolen commences the first of this month.'" He realizes how difficult that would be these days: "One was probably buried in some man-made fibre-- Acrilan, Courtelle, Terylene or nylon, never in plain cotton or wool" (**FGL** 21), the latter fabrics being of better quality and longer durability than the man-made fabrics. It is the same general complaint of Adam Prince about the quality of service and food in the past being better than it is today. By the same token, discussing the manor and Miss Vereker, Miss Lee laments, "[W]e haven't got any kind of centre to the village now'" (**FGL** 116). The old days of paternalism and patronage are gone, and with them, as Magdalen Raven points out, "'perhaps the people have been swept away too'" (**FGL** 116). Like Miss Vereker, who can find "nothing to complain of in her present life, except that it was not the past" (**FGL** 205), the village women find that just about everything about the past was better, more meaningful, and preferable to their present lives.

A discussion of World War II leads to remarks that even those dreadful years had their charm. Magdalen Raven, whose son-in-law Martin Shrubsole has forbidden her to smoke cigarettes and have sugar, recalls fondly the funny cigarettes they used to smoke in those days. The general feeling is that things have never gotten any better since before the war, a view that characters in other novels express as well. As Mrs. Lyall in *Jane and Prudence*, tells Jane, sadly, "'[T]hings are not quite as they used to be. . . especially since the war'" (90). Memories of the war often prompt characters to recall highlights of their personal lives rather than the war's actual horror and devastation or to compare the present with the way things were before that catastrophic event. When Catherine remarks to Mrs. Beddoes in *Less Than Angels*, for instance, that her visit has been like a scene from *Traviata*, Mrs. Beddoes at once recalls that before the war she and her husband had always had a box at Covent Garden. In *A Glass Of Blessings*, Wilmet Forsythe remembers only the parties and camaraderie of the WRNS in Italy during that time, and in *The Sweet Dove Died*, Leonora Eyre is reminded of spring, before Normandy, with flowers in full bloom and brigadiers making passes and marriage proposals.

At one point, in a discussion of the passing of the days of the gentry and their having provided the center that held the village together, Emma suggests that the clergy and the doctors have taken the place of the gentry. In reality, it is only the doctors who have done so. Their waiting rooms are filled during surgery days, while the church is almost empty all of the time. The passing of the days when churches were full and the clergy were truly spiritual advisers is another change strongly noted in Pym's novels, especially in the last two. In *A Few Green Leaves*, the complaints the villagers take to their doctors are seldom serious, more often superficial physically, the real problem emotional or spiritual. Daphne Dagnall only wants someone to pay attention to her, Adam Prince is

170

distressed by changes he cannot control, and Emma's rash is presumably connected to vague stresses over her relationship with Graham Pettifer. The official spiritual provider for the village, Tom Dagnall, has few parishioners and seldom is sought out by troubled souls. He feels especially incompetent making hospital calls and believes that he has let down most of his people. The only time Tom is really useful, fittingly enough, is when Miss Lickerish dies. His passion for the distant past, in contrast to the elderly people's fond memories of the more recent past, suggests that he is out of touch with the needs of his parishioners, both in his official capacity and as a fellow human being.

Like Marcia in *Quartet In Autumn*, people go to their physicians rather than to their clergy. In fact, in that novel, the physician, at least in Marcia's view, replaces God, and "the chaplains were his ministers, a little lower than the housemen" (19). Edwin laments the fact that the church across the street from Marcia's hospital is not filled with doctors and nurses. He even has "grave suspicions that Mr Strong, Marcia's surgeon, was not any kind of churchgoer. Something he had said, some disparaging remark he had made about the chaplain... " (204). The physician, having replaced God in the eyes of many, has no reverence for another higher power. On the other hand, Marcia dies with a smile on her face because her deity has graced her bedside with his presence. That is more than all the chaplains in the hospital combined could do for Marcia Ivory.

It is fitting that Tom Dagnall, the nominal spiritual leader of his village, and Dr. Gellibrand, the physician, should meet in the mausoleum. Death is, after all, the great leveler, and *A Few Green Leaves* is very much about death. The mausoleum is the dominant symbol of the novel, connected as it is with the village manor, whose history "lay in the past, in the wall tablets and monuments in the church and in the mausoleum which had been erected in memory of the de Tankerville family" (41). For Tom, it represents a time when commemorations of the dead were done in elaborate, florid inscriptions in contrast

171

to the memorials of today, so that now it seems "an awkward anachronism in such a small and humble parish" (63). It also stands for a time in the village history that was simpler and more sincere: "We were more embarrassed nowadays or less insincere, he would not have liked to say which, for 'sincerity' was disproportionately valued today. It would be impossible, for example, to imagine anything like the de Tankerville mausoleum being erected now" (62-63). As he is having these thoughts, Tom meets the young Terry Skate, who has come to "tidy up" the mausoleum and has popped into the church to familiarize himself with the surroundings. In keeping with the juxtaposition of past with present that occurs throughout the novel, this young man, whose interest in the church is eventually shaken by something he sees on television, shows up at just the moment when Tom is reflecting on the past, for his appearance prompts the narrator to comment on "these days of sex equality and uniform dress and hairstyle" (63). Furthermore, the mausoleum was a favorite spot for the last governess of the de Tankerville girls, Miss Vereker, who frequently visited it to honor the memory of that family. Tom learns this information when he unexpectedly runs into Dr. Gellibrand in the mausoleum. Each feels at first slightly awkward to have discovered the other in this unlikely spot, but the meeting turns out to be almost "a social occasion" (107). It is a favorite spot for silent contemplation. When Daphne announces her imminent departure to live with her friend Heather Blekinsop, Tom's first impulse is to go there to think of the implications of this change for him and to meditate "on the end of all things" (137).

Despite all the emphasis on death and dying, burial rites and upsetting changes in contemporary society, the novel ends on a positive note. Life does indeed go on. Emma has rid herself of the wrong man and seems about to "embark on a love affair which need not necessarily be an unhappy one" (FGL 250). She and Tom will no longer be lonely, Emma's mother can stop being uneasy about having an unmarried daughter, and Daphne might even end up in Greece. Anything is, after all, possible.

172

Following the dissolution of her love affair with Gordon Glover, Pym filled two volumes of diaries in 1943 with her despair over Glover's loss and her determination to get over him. Although she indulged in self-pity from time to time, in general she maintained a "drearily splendid" determination to forget him. Joining the WRNS to help speed the process, she took control of her life in a way the best of her central characters do. One entry, dated 29 March, suggests Pym's hope for the future no matter how miserable the present:

> Oh mumbling, chumbling moths, talking worms and my own intolerable bird give me one tiny ray of hope for the future and I will keep on wanting to be alive. Yes, you will be alive, it will not be the same, nothing will be quite as good, there will be no intense joy but small compensations, spinsterish delights and as the years go on and they are no longer painful, memories. . . . Or it may not be like this at all. You don't know. Nobody does. (VPE 120)

There is the same element of hope in a remark Miss Grundy makes to Tom: "'A few green leaves can make such a difference'" (FGL 202). There must always be just one tiny ray of hope for the future because nobody knows what lies ahead. That is why Pym's final novel does not leave readers with a sense of doom, and why Letty in *Quartet In Autumn*, for whom the future might appear to be anything but hopeful, believes in the infinite possibilities for change.

SEVEN

BUT WHAT DOES IT LEAD TO?

Literature was a delight and comfort to Barbara Pym, who once told an interviewer that "'the Anglican Church and English literature'" were "'the two important things'" in her life.[1] The frequency with which her characters turn to literature, the way it affects their lives, and the many discussions of novelists and their imaginative powers attest to Pym's firm belief in the power of literature to speak to one's own experience, especially in matters of love. Her books are filled with references to poems, plays, novels, and hymns. Pym does more than just display her wide knowledge of literature, however, for her characters are fairly indiscriminate in their allusions. They have a fondness for minor, obscure poets, for example, or indulge themselves in "light novels by female authors." They are just as likely to allude to a half-remembered line or two from a poet now forgotten as they are to a Donne poem or an Austen novel. Beyond affirming the value of literature as a source of consolation and pleasure, Pym so frequently contrasts the social scientist with the writer that her novels make a compelling argument in favor of the liberating power of the imagination over the almost dehumanizing force of science. She is an excellent spokesperson for the value of liberal arts in a world committed to scientific inquiry and hardnosed practicality. Pym may never have had to defend herself as Dulcie Mainwaring does when challenged by Miss Lord in *No Fond Return of Love*: "'All this reading.... But what does it lead to, Miss Mainwaring?'" (24-25). Nevertheless, her novels can be seen as an extended, complex answer to that very question.

Part of the answer is supplied by observations on those who do not read: they are clearly missing the comfort that literature gives. When Flora presents Gervase with an anthology of poetry in the unfinished *Home Front Novel*, it is with the wish that it will give him comfort for many years to come. Emma Howick's mother Beatrix, a tutor in English Literature at a women's college, laments that Emma is "not better read in English Literature, with all the comfort it could give. A few sad Hardy poems, a little Eliot, a line of Larkin seemed inadequate solace" (**FGL** 165). Catherine Oliphant tells the anthropologist Alaric Lydgate that men would do well to look to literature, with characters such as Heathcliff and Mr. Rochester, for it is not only "'we poor women who can find consolation in literature'" (**LTA** 224), and in the same novel the narrator points out that had Elaine been much of a reader, she could have had "the consolation and pain of coming upon her feelings expressed for her in such moving words" as those of Jane Austen's Anne Elliot (**LTA** 186). This combination of pain and consolation in the narrator's assessment of the value of literature is consistent with Pym's own general philosophy: life is difficult and often disappointing, so one finds comforts where one can. When Mildred Lathbury turns to these lines from a Christina Rosetti poem as she is trying to cope with the grief and shock of Rocky's leaving: "*Better by far you should forget and smile/Than that you should remember and be sad ...,*" she is keenly aware of their painful implications for her own life: "It was easy enough to read those lines and to be glad at his smiling but harder to tell myself that there would never be any question of anything else" (**EW** 171). From *Some Tame Gazelle* to *A Few Green Leaves* Pym makes clear her belief that literature articulates emotions more eloquently than ordinary people are able to do, though the joy of finding one's feelings well expressed is often bittersweet.

176

This belief in the comfort of literature is illustrated by Pym's private papers as well. In a January, 1940, letter to Robert Liddell, for instance, she reports quite happily that a novel she is working on (*Crampton Hodnet*) has some of her best characters. After naming them, she adds: "I'm sure all these might be a comfort to somebody" (**VPE** 100). At Oxford she had begun her practice of filling notebooks with quotations from her favorite poets and novelists. One, labeled *My Love in Literature*, contains poems by such writers as Browning, Rossetti, Young, and the Earl of Rochester (**MS PYM** 83). She consciously searched for quotations that expressed her own experience, recording in her 1933 diary, for instance: "I ordered a copy of Ernest Dowson's poems in Bodleiana and spent some time in finding appropriate lines and poems. I'm beginning to enjoy my pose of romantically unrequited love" (**VPE** 27). This is an interesting passage, not only because it points to the practical use Pym made of literature, but also because of what it indicates about her coping mechanism for the pain of unrequited love. Many of the diary entries indicate a genuine anguish over Henry Harvey's cold and fickle treatment of her. In describing herself as striking a "pose," she can conceal the depth of her feelings by putting some distance between herself and her emotions. The passage thus anticipates the way her fictional heroines look with such detachment at their own silliness for loving men who are not worthy of them. The sentiment of this early diary entry appears in *Some Tame Gazelle*, the novel based on Pym's love for Harvey. At one point, Belinda Bede is thinking of her love for Archdeacon Henry Hoccleve and the fact that after all these years, the "fierce flame had died down, but the fire was still glowing brightly." This thought prompts her to quote a couple of lines from a poem and then to reflect: "How much more one appreciated our great literature if one loved, ... especially if the love were unrequited!" (189). For the young Pym, spending hours in the library copying out lines of poetry about unrequited love was a pleasurable activity and some compensation for the real pain of that love. Her novels imply the impoverishment of life without that consolation.

Ten years later Pym found herself in the excruciating throes of yet another unhappy love affair, this time with Gordon Glover. Her response then was to fill two volumes of journals in one year, detailing her feelings. Called "After Christmas," as if they were drafts of a novel, the journals chronicle her struggle to attain some sort of emotional peace. Filled with anguished remarks over her separation from Glover, they are intensely personal, intimate, and indulgent--unlike Pym's novels themselves, which are detached almost to a fault. The journals were an essential part of her healing process and reveal a great deal about the value Pym placed on writing as therapy. In one respect, the journals from this period resemble the "pose" Pym adopted when she was younger: she assumes the Victorian novel writer's practice of addressing her "readers," as in this entry from March 10, 1943: "Well, I ramble on and you Reader will wonder at it. But Gordon would understand." Later, on April 15: "It seems a long time since I read a good book or made an intelligent observation, doesn't it, reader?" (**MS PYM** 108). But these journals reveal a weakening in Pym's resiliency that the earlier journals imply. At twenty, Pym almost seemed to enjoy searching for poems that described the pain of unreturned affection. But at thirty, she wrote from a mature, jaded perspective, the bitter pain no longer an amusing opportunity to "pose" but a profoundly felt reality. Even though she adopted the novelistic form and the distance it provides, she was emotionally devastated. The journal became an extension of herself which she regarded almost as a confidante. The last entry of the first volume, dated May 30, 1943, describes the hot night after she has finished her exam for the WRNS and is trying to sleep in the home of friends, listening to the sirens and gunfire in the distance: "I lay awake thinking of Gordon, wondering where he was and longing hopelessly for him and panic came over me at what I had done and the life that was before me.... So this volume ends as it began on a melancholy note.... Goodbye dreary old book. I feel quite sentimental about you" (**MS PYM** 108). In these journals, a mature Pym shows herself capable of deep feelings, of overwhelming passion and a capacity for love that many of her characters do not begin to suggest they are capable of. At the same time, they are further evidence of Pym's high regard for the consolatory powers of writing. Many of Pym's characters are not surprisingly quite fond of literature and take great pleasure in reading. Dulcie Mainwaring, Belinda Bede, and both Jane Cleveland and Prudence Bates have degrees in English literature and are great novel readers. Emma Howick, who has a degree in anthropology and whose mother named her after Jane Austen's heroine, though she prefers to identify herself with Thomas Hardy's wife, contemplates writing her own novel by the end of *A Few Green Leaves*. Characters without university degrees also delight in remembering passages of a poem, a book, or a favorite hymn. Ianthe Broome is a librarian who sees herself as an Elizabeth Bowen heroine, and Letty Crowe spends her lunch hours in a library searching for suitable contemporary romances or biographies. Catherine Oliphant makes her living as a fiction writer and thinks of herself as looking like Jane Eyre. Those who are not otherwise noted as "great readers" at least demonstrate familiarity with works of literature: Mildred Lathbury, whose bewilderment at an anthropological lecture she attributes to her "lack of higher education" (**EW** 91), tells her story in the first person, assures readers that she is not at all like Jane Eyre, and reads Christina Rossetti's poetry; Leonora Eyre reads Elizabeth Bowen and keeps the poetry of Browning and Arnold on her bedside table, drawing comfort from the beauty of their images; and Wilmet Forsythe, herself possessor of a vivid imagination, has an idea of what Virginia Woolf might make of a scene she witnesses.

Numerous lesser characters in the novels quote half-remembered lines of poetry and allude to works of both great and obscure writers, and people are always reading fiction by their favorite woman writer. Even the most unlikely characters have a ready supply of apt or not-so-apt quotations. Tom Dagnall feels he has made a fool of himself when he impulsively quotes some lines to Emma: "'Leigh Hunt,' said Tom quickly, attempting to cover his foolishness. '*Not* a good poem'" (**FGL** 76). Geoffrey Manifold startles Prudence Bates by quoting lines from Coventry Patmore, and John Challow reads Tennyson at tea. Perhaps most surprising of all, Marcia Ivory has been known to allude to a poem. Wondering what to send Marcia in the hospital, Letty considers a book: "She was the kind of person who would say that she didn't have time to read—yet hadn't she once, surprisingly, quoted a tag of poetry, some left-over fragment of her school days that had stuck in her memory?" (**QA** 178). Later, going through Marcia's house, Norman discovers on her bedside table an anthology of poetry. The choice of what to send her is irrelevant to the dying Marcia, but it is not at all surprising that such a gift would occur to Letty. The response of her landlady is equally expected: "'A *book*?' Mrs. Pope's tone rang out scornfully" (**QA** 178). This imperious tone reminds one of the scorn in Miss Lord's query about what literature leads to. Dulcie's weak reply to Miss Lord, that she does not exactly know but that it gives her pleasure, is probably the best one could do in the face of such scepticism and is as good a justification for reading as any other reason. Barbara Pym herself explained that she wrote for her own pleasure and amusement with the hope that other people, however few, might like what she wrote ("Finding a Voice," in **CS** 386). But literature does far more than give pleasure and amusement.

One use of literature is that it supplies examples of behavior that might seem otherwise unusual or inexplicable. When Leonora Eyre fantasizes briefly about marrying James, she thinks that "surely life—and literature—were not without precedents for such a marriage?" (**SDD** 119). Leonora is not serious about marrying James—or anyone, ever, for that matter—but the thought that such a marriage is not beyond the realm of either the real or the imaginative is reassuring. Aylwin Forbes, on his way to propose to Dulcie Mainwaring, rationalizes his sudden change of heart by remembering the end of *Mansfield Park*, when Edmund falls out of love with Mary Crawford and realizes his affection for Fanny. Aylwin is sure that Dulcie would "know the novel well, and would understand how such things can happen" (**NFRL** 260-61). Like Aylwin, Ned in *The Sweet Dove Died*, attempting to evoke sympathy for James, calls on literature to make his point, telling Leonora that she surely would not let James come to her door and not open it--"'Like that scene at the end of *Washington Square*'" (200). Literature assures characters that their behavior is entirely reasonable. At the same time, it also provides some measure of credibility for Pym's own less plausible scenes, so that if readers find it unlikely that Aylwin should so quickly turn his affection from Laurel to her eminently more suitable Aunt Dulcie, Pym has succeeded in reminding us that it can and does happen.

Even unusual names of characters are given validity by their existence in literature. Aylwin Forbes's name comes from the novel *Aylwin* by Theodore Watts-Dunton, Wilmet Forsythe's from a Charlotte M. Yonge novel, and Ianthe Broome's from a Walter Savage Landor poem, for instance. Had one accused Pym of giving quirky names to some of her characters, she had only to point to literary precedent, though she is well aware that their existence in literature is probably the only place one would find them: in *An Unsuitable Attachment*, Ianthe Broome comments that Rupert Stonebird's name "'sounds like a character in fiction'" (33). Besides unusual names, Pym's use of more familiar allusive names invite readers to compare or contrast the people bearing them with their literary namesakes. Beatrix Howick, a specialist in eighteenth- and nineteenth-century novels, named her daughter after Jane Austen's heroine in the novel of that name in the hopes that she might herself possess some of the fictional character's best qualities. Emma, who has so far failed her mother in that respect, thinks not of Austen's Emma but of Thomas Hardy's first wife, "a person with something unsatisfactory about her" (**FGL** 9). In *The Sweet Dove Died*, the name "Eyre" for Leonora might suggest a parallel between the Bronte character and Pym's, but the two have little in common. As if to underscore their dissimilarity, a friend of Phoebe's is reminded of a combination of Beethoven's Leonora overtures and Jane Eyre: "'rather *disquieting*, don't you think?'", she asks Phoebe (85). By the same token, Phoebe Sharpe's name leaves Leonora with the same feeling of distaste when she first hears it: "The name evoked a memory of Gilbert and Sullivan (*The Yeoman of the Guard?*) and Thackeray's Becky Sharpe; a disturbing combination ... " (102). Pym purposely uses familiar names from literature and expects her readers to make the connections or note their incongruity.

One of Pym's favorite characters, Prudence Bates, is very much a creation of the Barbara Pym we know from her diaries, with her fondness for reading, her predilection for romance and her vision of herself acting a role. Although Prudence reads Coventry Patmore, whose poetry exalts the domestic status of women to its highest, she enjoys novels that are "not very nice," the kind that "described a love affair in the fullest sense of the word and sparing no detail, but all in a very intellectual sort of way," reading one such novel "into the small hours of the morning to the book's inevitable but satisfying unhappy ending" (**JP** 47). The books that Prudence reads are the books that she lives, for Prudence seems quite content with her own "satisfying unhappy" relationships. She is not genuinely upset by the news that Fabian will marry Jessie--she had only decided on Fabian because he was conveniently at hand when she conceived the notion that it was time to marry--but acts out the role of jilted lover for all of a weekend, writing a "sad, resigned letter, a little masterpiece in its way" that brings tears to the eyes of the guilty Fabian (**JP** 199). Prudence's relationship with Geoffrey Manifold is an indication of the way her future will continue to repeat her past, following the literary tradition of the romance novel. Although Geoffrey and Prudence are more evenly matched intellectually than she and Fabian--over dinner they find that they are so familiar with the plots of foreign films that they do not need to see the new one at the Academy--this relationship, too, is doomed. She tells Jane: "We shall probably hurt each other very much before it's finished, but we're doomed really'" (**JP** 217). Prudence has become so much like the characters she reads about that she anticipates the inevitable ending of her own "plot." Jane, reminded of a

Marvell passage, concludes: "How much easier it was when one could find a quotation to light up the way" (**JP** 217). It is a sentiment shared by many of Pym's characters and, of course, by Pym herself.

Pym's early works are more heavily filled with literary references than her later ones, perhaps because she was so close to her years at Oxford as an English major and still very much influenced by what she was reading. In "Finding a Voice," a 1978 radio talk in which she discusses the influence of other writers on her work, Pym says of her first novel, written at 16, that it has "all the 'best' or at least the most fashionable names are dropped, from Swinburne and Rupert Brooke to D. H. Lawrence and Beverly Nichols" (**CS** 382). That novel, *Young Men in Fancy Dress*, was never published, but *Some Tame Gazelle* came into print in 1950. It was her first published novel, begun when she was an undergraduate and polished and refined over the next fifteen years. Its central character, Belinda Bede, is patterned after Pym herself and is therefore inordinately fond of literature. Indeed, on the opening page of the novel, we are told that Belinda still "retained some smattering of the culture acquired in her college days. Even now a light would shine in her mild greenish eyes ... at the mention of Young's *Night Thoughts* or the dear Earl of Rochester's *Poems on Several Occasions*" (7). Belinda's horrified response to seeing a dead caterpillar in the cauliflower cheese she has served her sewing woman Miss Prior--"It needed a modern poet to put this into words. Eliot, perhaps" (51)--suggests the degree of confidence Belinda places in the imaginative powers of poets.

In addition to her overt fondness for literature, Belinda has harbored a quiet, abiding love for Henry Hoccleve, a self-centered, pompous curate whose own love for obscure literary references is a bore to everyone in his congregation except the faithful Belinda. While Belinda finds comfort and reassurance from her favorite poets, Henry uses literature to display his erudition. Members of his congregation grumble about his penchant for reading lengthy passages from difficult writers. His famous Judgment Day sermon, largely a string of obscure quotations with very little explanation from the Archdeacon, loses everyone almost immediately, and finally even Belinda cannot follow his point. Edith Liversidge, who had once walked out in the middle of one of Henry's sermons, echoes the feelings of the congregation when, later that day, she complains in her usual blunt manner that the sermon had too many quotations. The Archdeacon's preference for literary sermons reveals a lack of originality, for, as Belinda notes, he is not particularly clever theologically. This observation is borne out when, in *Excellent Women*, the Archdeacon delivers that same Judgment Day sermon to an equally disgusted and unimpressed congregation as a guest speaker during a Wednesday noon Lenten service attended by Mildred Lathbury. Yet he is envied by Father Plowman, who, having failed to take Honours in Theology, listens jealously to the Archdeacon's explanation of the history of the rare word *dingle* and thinks rather defiantly that he could do the same. His jealousy is a measure of his own lack of imagination, while Belinda's adoration of Henry's literary self-indulgence is an indication of how modest are her needs, how unassuming her expectations. Both the Archdeacon and she like the sound of his voice. One of the happiest times in her life is the hour he spends reading to her aloud from *Faerie Queen* and *The Prelude*: "Just one evening like that every thirty years or so. It might not seem much to other people, but it was really all one needed to be happy" (STG 158). It is the combination of the pleasure of Henry's company and his reading poetry to her that has provided the magic for Belinda.

Pym capitalizes on Belinda's love of a good quotation by making it the source of humor in a very comic scene. When he proposes to Belinda, Bishop Grote first mistakenly attributes a line about beauty not being everything to the wrong poet and then unwittingly insults her when he refers to *Paradise Lost*: "Belinda interrupted him with a startled exclamation. *'Paradise Lost!'* she echoed in horror. *'Milton* ... '" (STG 224). Pym's female characters do not think much of Milton and his treatment of women, and this ill-timed allusion to him puts an end to

184

Grote's proposal. Belinda does admit that she cannot marry him because she loves another, and when the Bishop assumes this beloved has died, he hints that Lord Byron had said something particularly appropriate, leaving Belinda to wonder, "Could Lord Byron have said anything at all suitable?" (STG 224). When she cannot imagine what it could be, she is more interested in the literary point than in the actual matter at hand, but the bishop leaves without enlightening her. At the end of the novel, the offensive intruders to her quiet life having gone away, Belinda is greatly comforted by the prospect that life will go on just as it always had, and she will continue to find consolation in the greater English poets and her love for Henry Hoccleve.

A degree in English literature does more than just give consolation and pleasure, however. It can also lead to feelings of inadequacy, especially when the women who hold those degrees measure themselves against standards set in fiction. Jane Cleveland is a great novel reader who finds that life as a clergyman's wife is not as it is pictured in Victorian novels. Nor has she produced enough children to match the standard of a Charlotte M. Yonge heroine. By the same token, she can justify playing matchmaker for Prudence by comparing herself with Emma in Jane Austen's *Emma*, forgetting the trouble that Emma gets into for her efforts. Jane is selective in the way she applies literature to her own life, judging herself a failure as curate's wife on the one hand and finding encouragement for meddling in Prudence's life on the other. On the whole, however, Jane's training in English literature has led to little more than disappointment: she is too imaginative to fit in well with the usual lot of women in her husband's congregation, but she will probably never return to her research begun at Oxford and abandoned when she married. She can scarcely remember what she once had in mind to do. So Jane is caught in a double bind--too bright for the parishioners, who cannot appreciate her imaginative qualities and view her as somewhat of an oddity, but not energetic enough to ever finish her research now after all these years. When she does finally dig out her notes from the attic, the pages, yellow with age, fall apart in her hands.

Other women who read English literature at college experience this sense of not having quite fulfilled themselves. Belinda Bede, not so clever as her sister Harriet, with her degree in the classics, nor quite on the same level as Agatha Hoccleve, admires those engaged in obscure research and feels that what she does is "'rather useless'" (**STG** 68). After three decades, Belinda is still conscious of being in competition with Agatha. When Henry recites some lines from Gray's *Elegy*, both Agatha and Belinda listen with interest. They "did not say 'Oh, *quite*' when he had finished but enlarged intelligently on the charming theme. Agatha was reminded of Piers Plowman, Belinda of the poetry of Crabbe, which she could not remember very exactly, but she felt she had to be reminded of something out of self-defence, for Agatha had got a First and knew all about *Piers Plowman*" (**STG** 65). Despite, or perhaps because of, her superior success as a student, Agatha Hoccleve now envies her niece Olivia Berridge, who is doing research on some aspects of *The Owl and the Nightingale*. She wishes she had the opportunity to do scholarly research again, having once been a medievalist herself. Both Agatha and her niece Olivia Berridge have achieved one measure of success by obtaining husbands, both having, apparently, proposed marriage rather than wait for their intendeds to ask them. But for all their cleverness, what use has been their education? Agatha has been a competent archdeacon's wife, though, like Jane Cleveland, she is noticeably deficient in certain domestic areas. Olivia appears to be quite suitable for the role of curate's wife, but one cannot help wondering if she will join the ranks of women whose half-finished research lies moldering in the attic, her work on the obscure passages of *The Owl and the Nightingale* abandoned. Will she rather, like Agatha Hoccleve, in thirty years remember wistfully that she had once done some research, and like Jane Cleveland, not remember exactly what it had been?

Education for women does not lead to the kind of professional acclaim that it does for men. Dulcie Mainwaring, who had gone to Oxford because of her "sentimental penchant ... for the poetry of Marvell, Keats, or Matthew Arnold" in combination with "an ambitious English teacher and parents who, rather bewildered by the whole thing, could afford to send her," now finds herself "making indexes and doing bits of research for people with more original minds than herself. What, as Miss Lord would ask, did it lead to?" (**NFRL** 42-43). In this same passage, Dulcie is musing over her niece Laurel's telling Monica Beltane that her favorite subjects at school are English and history. Dulcie cannot help thinking sardonically of all the young girls, like herself, who must have said the same: "And what answer should a girl give now when asked what had been her favourite subjects at school? Russian and nuclear physics were perhaps too far advanced, as yet, but English and History would hardly do" (**NFRL** 43). Dulcie is well aware that women's education is more suited to prepare them to be men's helpers than anything else. Viola Dace, once a Ph.D. student in English at the University of London, now too makes indexes and lies to Dulcie about having written articles and planning her own book. It is Aylwin Forbes's book Viola indexes. Unlike Viola, Aylwin finished his Ph.D., is employed as an editor of a learned journal, makes decisions about the fate of its contributors, and is invited to deliver papers at learned conferences. In *An Academic Question*, Caroline Grimstone had gone straight from the university to marriage and now has little to occupy her time, even with a four-year-old daughter, toward whom she does not feel particularly maternal. The result is that she feels very much the way Wilmet Forsythe in *A Glass of Blessings* sees herself, useless and unfulfilled. Caroline believes a number of influences are responsible for her uneasy feeling: "Fiction, journalism and the conversation of other university wives, some of whom had part-time jobs, tended to make me see myself as a frustrated graduate wife" (**AQ** 4-5). But the crux of the problem is that, as a modern woman whose husband is more domesticated than she and

187

who does his own typing, she feels cut off from his work at the same time that she does not have a career that her university training should have prepared her for.

Alone among the college graduates, Prudence Bates has a career that she makes no apologies for--as assistant to Dr. Grampian, seeing his books through the press. She is in reality just like other educated women, notably Dulcie Mainwaring and Viola Dace, who end up in secondary roles, doing the typing or indexing for men's works that women with no higher education, like Mildred Lathbury, perform so excellently. But Prudence enjoys her career, annoyed only occasionally by the fact that she is called upon to defend it from time to time, especially at old students' reunions, where Miss Birkinshaw, herself unmarried and stuck with an unfinished manuscript on a minor English poet, feels compelled to comment on the fact that only three in her year did not marry. Prudence is annoyed by the remarks of Miss Birkinshaw and a couple of clergymen's wives, one of whom says, "'I dare say you write quite a lot of his books for him.... I often think work like that must be ample compensation for not being married.'" Prudence's response indicates her comfort with her position: "'I don't need compensation.... I often think being married would be rather a nuisance. I've got a nice flat and am so used to living on my own I should hardly know what to do with a husband'" (**JP** 10). It is not likely that Prudence will ever have to do anything with a husband, but more importantly, she is not likely to ever be much more than the glorified assistant she is to Dr. Grampian. Education, then, is a mixed blessing for women and certainly does not make them any more wise in their relationships with men.

Pym often blurred the distinction between literature and life. She implies that her characters have a life of their own outside the realm of her fictional world and sometimes suggests that those in the "real world" are more like fictional characters. A case in point is the scene in which Dulcie Mainwaring has a conversation in *No Fond Return of Love* with Wilmet Forsythe from *A Glass of Blessings*. Here, Keith and Piers, still together, are on

188

holiday with Wilmet and Rodney, all four perfectly in character and exactly as we remember them from the earlier book. In a brilliant, ironic stroke, Viola says of them: "'What odd people they were! Like characters in a novel'" (**NFRL** 197). Of course they *are* characters in a novel, but here is another character in a novel reacting to people in the "real" world of the novel as if they were fictional people and too odd to be true. That Pym felt the line between fiction and reality was a thin one is illustrated by a journal entry she made on December 28, 1945: "Your spinster in two ages—first as a governess in a large family house, perhaps in Warwick Square. Then later in a modern re-incarnation about which you know quite a lot. Is this book to be a novel or a clever sort of commonplace book—fiction—autobiography—..?" (**MS PYM** 84). Pym implies the interconnectedness of reality and fiction so firmly that it was almost a matter of how one chose to label it.

Perhaps because it is about academics rather than anthropologists or village inhabitants, *No Fond Return of Love* is one of Pym's fullest explorations of the uses of literature and the subtle interconnectedness of fiction and reality. Like Viola, who comments on the *Glass of Blessings* characters, Dulcie and Aylwin have read extensively, are influenced by what they have read, and often see themselves or others as if they were fictional. Aylwin, who takes James's *Portrait of a Lady* with him to Italy and comes back talking like a James character, can justify turning his attentions to Dulcie because that very thing happened in an Austen novel. Dulcie is especially inclined to think in terms of the interrelatedness of fiction and life. For example, when she finally speaks up in a most forthright manner to Aylwin, indignantly berating him for entertaining the hope that her niece Laurel might return his affection and then lashing out at him for selecting unsuitable wives, she thinks: "She was by no means at her best this morning, though if it had been a romantic novel ... he would have been struck by how handsome she looked when she was angry" (229). The sentiment of this observation is repeated in *An Academic Question*, when Caroline Grimstone, lunching with her former Byronic-looking first love tells us: "I wished I were in a novel or even some other person's life where we could have gone back to his flat or to a hotel, sleazily romantic with heavy dingy lace curtains" (96). But Caroline is unable to live out her fantasy, nor does Aylwin notice how romantic Dulcie looks.

Furthermore, Dulcie's tendency to think of her prying into people's lives as if she were viewing a film or play indicates how highly she regards the role of detached observer: "It seemed ... so much safer and more comfortable to live in the lives of other people--to observe their joys and sorrows with detachment" this way (**NFRL** 105). The emotional danger lies in becoming too involved, as Dulcie finds out. By the time she has travelled to Tavistock to spy on Aylwin's mother, her position has shifted from detached observer to actor in a drama: events, she feels, will unfold with the "inevitability of a Greek tragedy" (**NFRL** 181). Not only can she imagine herself as a character in a novel or an actor in a play, but she also sees herself in the role of creator, expressing her disappointment in Viola in terms of that role: "In a sense, Dulcie felt as if she had created her and that she had not come up to expectations, like a character in a book who had failed to come alive, and how many people in life, if one transferred them to fiction just as they were, would fail to do that!" (**NFRL** 169). This particular observation is an indication of Dulcie's powers of imagination. Well read and educated, she is sensitive to what makes characters and real people "come alive."

Like Barbara Pym the novelist writing down overheard bits of conversation, her characters sometimes view the world as if they too were writers. A chance phrase might be a book title; an unusual situation, the plot for a novel. Aylwin Forbes, frustrated by the news that his mother-in-law is conducting a jumble sale in aid of the organ fund when he has come with flowers to make up with his wife, is indignant about the way women treat men. When the organist tells Aylwin that the ladies will be expecting him, Aylwin thinks of the enthusiasm they will no doubt greet him with: "Like all men connected with the Church--his

190

own brother Neville included--the organist would be at ease with the ladies. He could see the phrase--*At Ease With Ladies*--as the title of a novel or even a biography" (**NFRL** 79). Pym characters everywhere seem to have this imaginative quality. The curate Mark Ainger in *An Unsuitable Attachment*, for example, amused by Father Anstruther's reminiscing about the delicious fairies someone used to make for bazaars, says to Sophia: "'A bond of fairies.... Obviously a title for something'" (66). Even Mildred Lathbury, referring to Everard Bone's mother's eccentric interests, thinks: "Birds, worms, and Jesuits ... it might almost have been a poem, but I could not remember that anybody had ever written it" (**EW** 151). When Dulcie Mainwaring and Viola Dace are in the dining room of a hotel and overhear a clergyman remark that this place must be "'a change from Uganda,'" Dulcie whispers to Viola: "'What a lovely title for a novel that would be ... and one can see that it would be almost easy to write. The plot is beginning to take shape already'" (**NFRL** 178). It is no accident that Pym chooses this moment to bring onto the scene a woman who can be none other than Barbara Pym herself: "[S]he was a woman of about forty, ordinary-looking and unaccompanied, nobody took much notice of her. As it happened, she was a novelist; indeed, some of the occupants of the tables had read and enjoyed her books" (**NFRL** 179). Besides the delight of dropping into her own novel, Pym must also have taken great pleasure in including among the books on the shelf in Dulcie's bathroom a copy of *Some Tame Gazelle* (**NFRL** 67). Examples of this type abound throughout the novels.

It is an intriguing device, this toying with what is real and what is fiction. It seldom seems forced. Like so much in Pym, its cumulative effect over all the novels is to imply some basic truth about the complicated mystery of life. We are all actors, she suggests, and the plot possibilities are endless. Just months before the end of her own life, Pym wrote in her diary that she had found herself "reflecting on the mystery of life and death and the way we all pass through this world in a kind of procession. The whole business as inexplicable and mysterious as the John Le

191

Carré TV serial, *Tinker, Tailor, Soldier, Spy*, which we are all finding so baffling" (**VPE** 331). How absolutely fitting that she compares the deep mystery of life with the complications of a spy novel. She herself, fascinated by the potential for any "real" life situation to be turned into fiction, had been a kind of spy, looking for the raw material that she could use in her novels, shedding her own insight into the "inexplicable and mysterious" meaning of life. Good writers of fiction and poetry, she always intimated, have the power to distill the significant meaning from ordinary reality.

Catherine Oliphant, herself a fiction writer of short stories for women's magazines, is an ingenious representation of Pym's belief in the power of art to make meaning of life. Catherine has had the bad luck to witness her lover Tom holding hands with another woman at the table they always sit at in their favorite Greek restaurant. In *A Glass of Blessings*, Wilmet and Rowena, sitting under hair dryers, discuss the fiction in the magazines they are reading. Commenting on a story by Catherine Oliphant, Rowena says it begins with a man's former mistress watching a man and a young woman holding hands in a Greek restaurant. Wilmet protests: "But what a far-fetched situation.... As if it would happen like that! Still, it must be dreadful to have to write fiction. Do you suppose Catherine Oliphant drew it from her own experience of life?" Rowena, laughing, says "I should hardly think so!" (152). Thus, Catherine in *Less Than Angels* struggles over how to write a convincing short story, thinking rather sceptically that it is difficult to get women to read beyond the first page and imagining them sitting under a hair dryer, flipping through pages of a magazine. Then she has the painful experience which, we learn, she turns into the short story referred to in *A Glass of Blessings* and which is reacted to in just the way Catherine imagined it would happen. Pym not only legitimizes the use of even the most unlikely coincidence in fiction but suggests the therapeutic power of writing about one's experience. Pym might very well have seen herself in the character of Catherine--trying to write convincing fiction based on painful personal

192

experience. Literature is cathartic for both writer and reader. Pym focuses on this relationship between the writer and her creative process by creating a character who does exactly as she does in her own life.

It seems a logical step for Pym to write the kind of fiction which her characters themselves would turn to. Pym's extended treatment of the unmarried woman provides a literary model that is largely missing in fiction before hers. In *Quartet in Autumn* Pym directly states this neglect of spinsters when she describes Letty's reading habits: "She had always been an unashamed reader of novels, but if she hoped to find one which reflected her own sort of life she had come to realise that the position of an unmarried, unattached, ageing woman is of no interest whatever to the writer of modern fiction" (3). But Pym, in fact, writes the novel Letty could not find. Interestingly, when Letty abandons "romantic novels" because she cannot find what she needs in them, she turns to biographies. "And because they were 'true' they were really better than fiction," Pym writes. "Not perhaps better than Jane Austen or Tolstoy ... but certainly more 'worth while' than the works of any modern novelist" (3-4). Pym cannot resist championing the great writers of fiction over the writers of "reality" for their ability to point to essential "truths" more skillfully than writers of "true" works. Later, in her retirement, Letty returns to reading novels, a fact the snooping Mrs. Pope has little respect for when she discovers that the only book beside Letty's bed is a novel.

The argument in favor of fiction writers is made nowhere so forcefully as in Pym's treatment of the contrast between anthropologists and writers. While anthropologists and writers of fiction are often linked, particularly in their technique of detached observation, the contrasts are marked. Pym makes a clear distinction between the two methods of recording human behavior. Literature is an inquiry that makes no claims to objectivity; indeed, the real power of literature is the imaginative freedom it gives both reader and writer. The only claims to validity that literature makes are personal: it is a subjective interpretation of human experience that, if well done, strikes a chord of recognition and touches the heart. Catherine Oliphant expresses this difference well when, saddened by Tom's departure for Africa, she takes a bus to wherever it leads, gets off, and enters a large restaurant, where the people seem without direction, in need of someone who will guide them not only in their selection for a meal but also "to the deeper or higher things of life." Who would supply this need, Catherine wonders: "The anthropologist, laying bare the structure of society, or the writer of romantic fiction, covering it up?" (**LTA** 194-95). In the same novel, Professor Mainwaring shocks the young anthropologist Digby Fox when he reveals that he has given all of his anthropological books to the research center, for they are "'not the kind of reading to see me into my grave'" (**LTA** 209). Instead, he is reading Shakespeare, the Bible, and Anthony a Wood.

One of the best examples of the value of humanities over science is in *A Few Green Leaves*. Like Pym herself, who learned the technique of detached observation from the anthropologists she worked with at the International African Institute, the anthropologist Emma Howick takes notes on the village and its inhabitants in just the way a novelist might, listing characters and behavioral traits and describing situations, but she finds herself thinking more and more as a novelist than as a social scientist. While Everard Bone, the anthropologist, would see the writer and the social scientist as doing the same thing--"'After all, both study life in communities'" (**UA** 127)--Emma notices a decided difference between the two. She prefers the cozy term "village" over the more scientific "jargon word 'community,'" for example (**FGL** 38), and at the end of the novel she may very well be planning to write a novel, not an anthropological tract, on her observations.

Pym has prepared readers for this rejection of science in favor of art from early on, when, for instance, acting on impulse Emma writes to Graham Pettifer, scarcely "marking the distinction between fact and fiction" (**FGL** 12) and, later, thinks after her lunch with Graham that if she were a novelist, there might be "some material in his story that she could use, but a sociological survey of modern marriage, under whatever title you gave it, would find the whole affair very commonplace and predictable" (**FGL** 37). Her discomfort with the scientific view of human behavior becomes increasingly marked. For instance, while Graham Pettifer and Robbie and Tamsin Barraclough muse on the sociological implications of the flower festival in the cycle of village life, Emma's thoughts turn to the significance of the festival in "a different, less scientific, light. Flowers in a beautiful setting and a meeting with an old lover suggested a romantic novel rather than a paper for a learned society" (**FGL** 86). At this point she is not at all sure that she could write a novel: "[S]he had never thought of writing fiction, had, indeed, tended to despise her mother's studies of the Victorian novel" (**FGL** 86). Some time later, when this same group is assembled in the cottage Graham has lived in over the summer to write his book, Emma is irritated by their "arid academic chat" (**FGL** 174) and wishes that she were home doing some household task. In fact, when Robbie asks her about her work, Emma tells her that it is changing directions, "thinking as much of the bramble jelly as the notes she had made on the village" (**FGL** 175). In the course of the conversation, when Graham tells the Barracloughs that Emma could find a new approach to writing about village life, "'even if she had to make it up,'" Robbie protests that she could not do that: "'After all, we're not novelists,' he added, smiling in a superior way into his beard" (**FGL** 175). This is the point at which Emma finds the conversation and the company of these sociologists unbearable. Leaving the group, she meets Tom Dagnall and shortly finds herself sitting at her kitchen table, sharing a drink with him, minding her blackberry jelly, and chatting about domestic things.

Ianthe Broome's defense of novelists is particularly apt, for she points out to a party of anthropologists that because life can be interpreted in so many ways, the novelist has the advantage, letting her imagination roam where it will. She is thinking of her own seemingly insignificant experience in John Challow's room when: "'Even the most apparently narrow and uneventful life' she began thoughtfully, then stopped, uncertain of what she was going to say next. What did it mean for *her*--that little episode--what was its significance in the pattern?" (UA 127). While both the writer and the social scientist record human behavior and attempt to explain its larger implications, the writer of fiction has the freedom to interpret any way she wants. Furthermore, she is more interested in the emotional ramifications of human interaction. Literature has a liberating, humanizing component missing in science, with its mission to classify and codify.

Less Than Angels has two excellent examples of this contrast between literature and science in the characters of Tom Mallow and Alaric Lydgate. Tom, who left his village to study anthropology in London and then do field work in Africa, returns for a visit to his childhood home and finds himself reminiscing with his first sweetheart, Elaine. When she reminds him that he had once quoted poetry to her, Tom "found himself mourning the young man of those days, who went for long country walks and quoted poetry. Now he went into Regent's Park and talked about his thesis. He wondered if the change was for the better" (185). The implication is that it is not, and that point is made even more forcefully with Alaric Lydgate. Plagued for eleven years by a trunk full of field notes he is unable to write up, Alaric regards himself a failure and sits alone in his room at night wearing an African mask--how much easier life would be if one could hide behind a mask and not have to actually look people in the eye, he thinks. The scientific observer of human behavior wishes to cut himself off from social intercourse and its attendant difficulties. It is the fiction writer Catherine who liberates him from his crippling inability to make human contact by suggesting that he might not have to write up his notes. At first visibly shaken by the idea, he later jubilantly burns his notes. It is a wonderful scene, Alaric now free of his burden, confronted by the outrage of anthropologists Esther Clovis and Gertrude Lydgate. When Miss Clovis snatches burning pages of kinship tables from the fire, Alaric pokes them back in with his stick. The anthropologists are horrified at the loss to the scientific world as he throws bundles of papers into the fire, but Catherine responds to the aesthetic quality of the scene: "'Oh, *pretty* ,'" she cries (229), as "some of it, eaten by white ants, fell away like a shower of confetti" (228). When Alaric's sister demands to know what he will do now, he tells her that of course he will go on writing reviews of scholarly books--he cannot give up his scientific training entirely--but also that he may very well write a novel. Catherine's remark that "'he has the most wonderful material'" refers to his own experience in Africa, not his scientific recording of other people's experiences (229). It is a powerful affirmation of the potential for literature to free the spirit, in opposition to what science can do to the human element.

It is not only the greater English poets or novelists who put their fingers on the pulse of human behavior. Pym is no snob: her characters make references to not only the greater but the lesser writers, and they are just as likely to think of snatches of commercial jingles or lines from hymns as they are to quote from the writers one would read at Oxford in an English Literature course. Pym read all sorts of novels and counted among her favorite writers Charlotte M. Yonge and Ivy Compton-Burnett. Furthermore, she was always aware of what was going on in popular culture, such as what songs, movies or novels were hits, according to her sister, Hilary Walton.² Some of her characters feel they ought to be reading "better" literature or even "more important" things like science or politics, but they find it tough going. In *Quartet in Autumn*, Letty, whose reading preference had been romantic novels and then biographies when she could not find what she wanted in popular fiction, tries to do some "serious" reading once she retires. On the first day of her retirement, she goes to the sociology shelves of the library, having been attracted by "the idea and the name of 'social studies'" (114). What a disappointment the books turn out to be. Within a week she comes to the conclusion that "sociology was not quite all that she had hoped for.... She had imagined herself revelling and wallowing--perhaps these words were too violent to describe what she had imagined--in her chosen subject, not frozen with boredom, baffled and bogged down by incomprehensible jargon" (117). When she returns the books to the library, feeling guilty and inadequate for what she sees as her failure, she alleviates her guilt somewhat by reminding herself that she is supposed to enjoy retirement, and that if reading novels and listening to the radio are what she wants to do, she has every right to do so. Literature in whatever form, Pym seems to say, has its own intrinsic value far greater than that of the sciences.

This belief is expressed time and again, implicitly as often as explicitly. For example, in *Excellent Women*, Rocky and Mildred, attending the Learned Society meeting at which Helena and Everard are to give their paper, discuss the titles of books in the bookcase they are standing by. When Rocky wishes that "'people still wrote books with titles like [these] . . . --we have become too depressingly scientific,'" Mildred suggests he write his own book about his adventures in Italy. He could come up with whatever imaginative title he wanted and not be limited by the restrictions of science. A short time later, Mildred, finding herself completely incapable of following Helena's lecture, lets her eye wander to the open window, noting the details of square gardens on this lovely spring day. The passage is a wry comment on the stuffiness of such meetings, with the Americans taking notes furiously while Mildred rebukes herself mildly for not having used her time more wisely reading up on the subject instead of buying a new hat.

Pym reworks this scene in *An Academic Question*, when Caroline Grimstone, the university-educated wife of an academic anthropologist, attends a lecture that promises to be interesting: "For what could be more fascinating than a study of a community one actually knew? ... But after a very few minutes it became apparent that the dead hand of the sociologist had been at work" (77). Her attention strays to a detached study of the appearance of the lecturer and she manages somehow to endure the next twenty minutes of horrifying boredom. Mildred Lathbury, on the other hand, feeling inferior because everyone else in the room seems to be listening intelligently to Helena, draws some comfort from seeing that an old woman in the front row has been sleeping. This same woman is the wife of the President of the Learned Society. Pym follows up on this seemingly small matter when, at the death of this man, his widow gives his collection of anthropology books and images to the Society and is apparently free to do the things she really enjoys, gardening and reading novels. Elsewhere, Rhoda Wellcome and Mabel Swann, vaguely conscious that they ought to be worried about the larger problems of the world, sometimes write down titles of books they feel they ought to read but are "secretly relieved when each time they went to get a book the librarian handed out yet another novel" (**LTA** 40-41). Pym would be the first to say that the "greater English poets" and novelists are the most astute at seeing the larger truths and grander meanings of life, but she would never deny the sheer pleasure of reading for its own sake or writing as a form of imaginative expression. She has no pretensions in this regard, celebrating the cozy delights of elderly women reading popular novels any day over the baffling coldness of sociology and political science.

While the characters in Pym's first published novel, *Some Tame Gazelle*, are so obviously drawn from life, Pym continued the practice of turning real people and events into fictional characters and scenes. Reading the journals, one is sometimes confused about which events actually took place and which are Pym's rendering of them for possible inclusion in her fiction. She had the habit of writing something down as if it were a scene in a book, such as this first entry of a new notebook with a picture of a cat on the front: "In her notebook, with a picture of a marmalade cat on the cover, Miss ____ the middle aged spinster is making notes for her 'great' novel on homosexuals. She is a rather comic character" (**MS PYM** 85, fol. 1). Not only would she cast herself in a fictional scene, but she also recorded bits of conversation, comic scenes, anthropological findings, and headlines from articles--"Bishop's Lost Wife Was in Attic"--and then used them in her novels, sometimes word for word. At one point Pym records: "Today I wrote Sandy a note telling him what the milk situation was and it occurred to me, why should not a masterpiece consist of such notes, for after all it is *Life!*" (**MS PYM** 84, fol. 5-6). Hazel Holt recounts in *A Very Private Eye* that at the International African Institute, Pym found a rich source of comic material for her novels in the anthropologists and linguists whose papers she edited for the journal Africa, "embroidering the few facts she knew about the various authors and reviewers into a splendid fantasy so that it was often difficult to remember what was real and what was not. ('I couldn't ask W. if his Mother was better because I couldn't remember if we'd invented her.')" (183). Elsewhere, in a 1964 notebook entry which she later sent to Richard Roberts as a letter, Pym turns a little scene which apparently occurred between the two of them into a short vignette, adding: "So you see, my dear, how with a little polishing life could become literature, or at least fiction! I hope you get its poor little message, or that it at least entertains you for a moment" (231). This practice of taking real events and turning them into fictional events that give real insight into their meaning is evidence of Pym's imaginative powers.

There is another sense of imagination as well, that which, rather than turn fact into a fiction that is in a way truer than life, distorts reality. This is fantasy. In *A Glass of Blessings*, Wilmet Forsythe's powers are in this imaginary realm, and it is exactly her inclination to fantasize that leads to humiliation but ultimately to self-knowledge. Wilmet repeatedly envisions things that turn out to be not true; she misjudges just about everyone she knows. The furniture depository represents this tendency in her: she sees it as having some noble purpose and is awed by its vastness, picturing the rooms filled with great shrouded furniture. Piers points out the reality: it is covered with bird droppings on the outside and is an ordinary storage building, probably decaying inside. Near the end of the novel when Wilmet inquires about the condition of Mary Beamish's furniture stored in that same depository and is assured that it came out just fine, she remembers her walk past the depository with Piers, and their "wild imaginings--the dramatic decay, the baroque horror of it all. It would not be like that in reality, and perhaps it was just as well" (253). Reality is not as Wilmet had imagined and the novel is a revelation of just this point: her life has been a fantasy from which she must move in order to become a mature adult.

Other characters also have truly vivid imaginations, a characteristic which has the potential to be dangerous if allowed to get out of control. In *A Glass of Blessings*, an overly imaginative mind leads to personal humiliation, but that humiliation is necessary for Wilmet's emotional growth. In *Excellent Women*, an active imagination is an important part of Mildred's own initiation into life. Lunching with William Caldicote, Mildred examines the label of the wine he has ordered and exclaims that "'Nuits St. Georges ... conjures up the most wonderful pictures, armour and white horses and dragons, flames too, perhaps a great procession by torchlight'" (67). William's response has implications larger than it at first appears. He tells her that Nuits St. George is simply an area where there are vineyards and that a wine bearing a label from there is not necessarily of the best quality: "'It might,' he said seriously, 'be an *ordinaire*. Always remember that. *A little learning is a dangerous thing*, Mildred'" (67). Like Wilmet Forsythe, Mildred has had very little experience with anyone beyond her fairly limited circle of friends. The novel is a record of her increased experience, her realization of her own potential for passion, and her ultimately settling for less than she might have desired. Her imagination had elevated Rocky to romantic proportions before she even met him, and at the time of this scene with William, she is quite infatuated with him. Rocky himself is *ordinaire*, superficial and glitzy, but Mildred is captivated all the same. Having had only "a little learning" about love and glamorous men, she is vulnerable to his charm and finally deeply pained by his departure.

Jane Cleveland has an imagination that is charming and endearing, even if it does make her seem a bit odd: people do not appreciate her outspokenness nor her fantastic turn of mind. She is curious to know about personalities, eager to hear all about the people in their new village from Mrs. Glaze and Father Lomax. Furthermore, she often thinks metaphorically, as when Mrs. Glaze is telling her about some of the church people: "Mr. Mortlake and His Friends ... A Lion Above the Bird ... but these are the titles of new novels still in their bright paper jackets, thought Jane with delight. And they are here in this parish, all this richness" (**JP** 20-21). Similarly, Belinda Bede's imagination sustains and comforts her. After her wonderful evening with the archdeacon, she thinks of her love for him as a kind of "warm, comfortable garment ...certainly something without glamour or romance. All the same, it was rather nice to think that Henry *might* prefer her to Agatha, although she knew perfectly well that he didn't. It was one of the advantages of being the one he hadn't married that one could be in a position to imagine such things" (**EW** 157-58). Imagination is a comfort and a resource, and characters with imaginative minds are at an advantage over those without them for precisely that reason. Having too powerful an imagination, particularly when it spills over into the imaginary, results in disappointments, as characters frequently find the contrast between their expectations and reality quite marked. Seldom is the real as good as the imagined. Pym enjoyed the process of imagining what might happen almost more than the final result: the actual recording of scenes, quotations, scraps of conversation in her notebooks was "often more of a pleasure than the actual writing. To jot down an idea for a scene and then to imagine it filled out is immensely satisfying, but, as everyone knows, the final result invariably falls short of the original conception" ("Finding a Voice," in **CS** 386). This attitude is frequently expressed in the way her characters mentally construct people and situations the way they want them to be, only to find that the way they really are does not measure up to their fantasies. Thus Dulcie is disappointed because Viola is not the way she had created her, and Sophia Ainger is distressed that Ianthe is engaged to John: "'I never thought of her as getting married--it seems all wrong,"' she tells Rupert Stonebird. 'I wanted her to stay as she was, almost as if I'd created her"' (UA 247). In *Excellent Women*, after Rocky has told her that he and Helena have reconciled, Mildred feels "flat and disappointed, as if he had failed to come up to my expectations," though what her expectations had been, she cannot say exactly because what she might have wanted is "too unreal to contemplate" (226).

Memory distorts in this way as well, so that characters are always being disappointed when someone they had embellished in their minds turns out to be very different. Flora Palfrey, in the *Home Front Novel*, has long thought herself in love with Edward Wraye, largely because there was no one else to be in love with. When he appears at her door, with flowers plucked from a garden and an enlarged photograph of himself, to bid her farewell as he goes off to war, she is pleased by his attention but disappointed: "It was altogether just the situation she had always dreamed of between them, and yet, now that it was happening, she was conscious of a feeling of anti-climax. Surely he was not as *tall* as she had always thought him. He had a spot on his forehead and his manner was really rather *affected*" (CS 256). A similar disillusionment occurs in *So Very Secret*, though here the memory has been held for many years. When Cassandra Swan meets her beloved Adrian once again, he does not even recognize her, while she is stunned: "Was this the man whose memory I had cherished for so long? This blank, wooden personality with only a certain facile charm, which could be switched on and off as required?" (CS 301). It is a common occurrence among Pym's characters, and in keeping with her general theory that the imaginary is almost always better than reality. In *The Sweet Dove Died*, James and Phoebe experience the same reaction when James drops in on Phoebe after their first meeting at a crowded party: "[W]as this the face ... that had seemed intriguing in the candle-lit restaurant?" thinks James, while Phoebe "seemed disappointed too, as if he had not come up to her expectations, whatever they might have been" (41). Laurel in *No Fond Return Of Love*, drops in on Paul Beltane at his flower shop and thinks, "A pity he's so dumb," feeling that he looks "younger and more callow than she had remembered" (64). Emma, in *A Few Green Leaves*, feels a "sense of anticlimax" when Graham Pettifer, whom she has not seen for years, arrives for lunch, while he is struck by her thinness and recalls--rather crassly--that she was "more attractively covered in the old days" (33-34). Penelope Grandison finds her interest in Rupert Stonebird intensifying after their first meeting, "mainly because she had not seen him again and had therefore been able to build up a more satisfactory picture of him than she had been able to check with reality" (**UA** 54). And, indeed, when she finally meets him again, he turns out to be "less interesting than she had remembered" (**UA** 83). Wilmet Forsythe experiences this sort of thing all the time, once her self-centered fantasy world begins to crumble. Having imagined herself as Piers's beautiful savior, she feels "an air of unreality about the whole scene" when she first meets Keith (GB 193), for nothing from then on turns out to be as she had fantasized, from where Piers lives to the reason for his new-found cheerfulness. But while imagination can distort reality, leading to disappointment, the imaginative mind is far preferable to the unimaginative mind.

Only occasionally is the imagination something to be wary of. When Phoebe observes of James's mother's photograph that she looks even more remote than the Victorian age, James, "fearing, not for the first time, the power of Phoebe's imagination" cuts her short (SDD 79). It is an interesting point, for what James fears from her apparently harmless musings on his mother's looks is the potential of a mind capable of far more than his is capable of. James is easily swayed by whoever he happens to be with at the moment. People like Phoebe and Ned have a power he lacks. Leonora, who is neither reflective nor a very deep thinker, senses almost immediately that Ned is more of a threat to her relationship with James than Phoebe could ever be, thinking there is something ominous about Ned's quoting from the Keats poem from which the novel's title is derived. She tells Ned he must go see Keats' house, "agitation rising in her, for now the harmless little poem seemed almost to have some obscure and unpleasant meaning. But that was fanciful and ridiculous, surely" (146). Ned, the clever American working on his dissertation on Keats, does eventually get the better of Leonora. In this case, what Leonora had dismissed as fancy turns out to be fact.

In contrast to Wilmet Forsythe, who weaves fantasies out of her limited world view and finally comes to a jarring realization about herself, and Mildred Lathbury, whose imagination opens the door to increased self-knowledge, Dulcie Mainwaring's imagination has a worldly turn to it. Her imaginative powers keenly and positively developed, she is given to imagining all sorts of scenarios, but she manages to hold her fancy in check. Early in *No Fond Return of Love*, she gives money to "a new and particularly upsetting beggar selling matches; both legs were in irons and he was hugging himself as if in pain. She had given him sixpence and walked quickly on, telling herself there was no need for this sort of thing now, with the Welfare State. But she still felt disturbed, even at the idea that he might be sitting by his television set later that evening, no longer hugging himself as if in pain" (31). Near the end of the novel she sees this very "beggar," walking briskly down the street, wearing a good suit. Far from being upset by this confirmation of her early vision of him, she thinks it must be an omen of something but cannot articulate what it is at the moment. Dulcie, aware of life's inconsistencies and unfairnesses, knows that there are larger implications to this experience; for she typically is able to draw larger connections from seemingly trivial things, such as when she compares having one's choice of cakes at tea with Life, pointing out the distinct difference that one does not have the same freedom in Life as at tea. Or, feeling sympathy for Miss Lord's upsetting experience at a cafeteria, when she did not get baked beans but the man behind her did:

"Yes, I know, that's what life is like. And it *is* humiliating. One feels a sense of one's own inadequacy, somehow, almost unworthiness," said Dulcie thoughtfully. "But then life is cruel in small ways, isn't it. Not exactly nature red in tooth and claw, though one does sometimes feel ... And what will you have for pudding today?" she asked, jerking herself back to reality by a sudden awareness of Miss Lord's pitying look at her vague philosophizings. If this is what education does for you ... she seemed to imply. Well might one ask, "But what will it lead to?" (84)

"All this reading" has led Dulcie Mainwaring to a sensitivity to the plight of others and to a greater understanding of her position in the grand scheme of things. It makes her more attuned to the "higher meaning" of a choice of cakes or the availability of baked beans.

"All this reading" also makes Dulcie in some small way like Barbara Pym herself, who had the imaginative power to turn life's seemingly insignificant events and people into not only highly readable and immensely pleasurable material, but to make of them meaningful observations on the human condition. Pym would no doubt wholeheartedly agree with Anton Chekhov's observation that the function of literature is not to solve the problems of humanity but to state them more clearly. Pym implies both explicitly and implicitly the important uses of literature throughout the novels: it gives consolation and pain, it helps people "connect" with one another, it can liberate the spirit, and it ultimately makes those with knowledge of it more compassionate humans.

NOTES

CHAPTER 1: SOME ASPECTS OF THE NOVELS

1. For a comparison of Jane Austen and Barbara Pym, see especially A.L. Rowse's "Miss Pym and Miss Austen" in *The Life and Work of Barbara Pym*, pp. 64-71, and Janice Rossen, *The World of Barbara Pym*, pp. 7-9. Robert Emmett Long summarizes the controversy among critics in *Barbara Pym*, pp. 201-206.

2. For a thorough analysis of the way in which Pym consciously structured her novels, see Robert J. Graham's "The Narrative Sense of Barbara Pym" in *The Life and Work of Barbara Pym*, pp. 142-55.

3. Interview with Hilary Walton, 25 February 1988, Oxford, England. Mrs. Walton also observed that she thinks some scholars are treating her sister with a bit too much gravity: the one dominant characteristic of Barbara's novels, she said, is their lightheartedness.

4. For detailed discussions of the portrayals of single women in novels, see Dorothy Yost Deegan, *The Stereotype of the Single Woman in American Novels*, and Merryn Williams, *Women in the English Novel, 1800-1900*.

5. Qtd. in Dale Spender, *Mothers of the Novel*, p. 162.

CHAPTER TWO: RIDICULOUS, REALLY, THE RELATIONSHIP BETWEEN MEN AND WOMEN

1. *Women in England 1870-1950: Sexual Divisions and Social Change*, p. 14.

2 *Women In England*, p. 4.

3. *Women In England*, p. 3.

CHAPTER SEVEN: BUT WHAT DOES IT LEAD TO?

1. Caroline Moorhead, "How Barbara Pym Was Rediscovered After 16 Years Out in the Cold," p. 11. For a full discussion of Pym's treatment of the Church of England in her fiction, see chapter four, "High Church Comedy," in Janice Rossen's *The World of Barbara Pym*.

2. Interview with Hilary Walton, 25 February 1988.

WORKS CITED

Auchincloss, Eve "Surprises of Comedy and Sadness." *New York Times Book Review*, 1 Feb. 1981, p. 9.

Burkhart, Charles. *The Pleasure of Miss Pym*. Austin: University of Texas Press, 1987.

Deegan, Dorothy Yost. *The Stereotype of the Single Woman in American Novels*. New York: King's Crown Press, 1951.

Lewis, Jane. *Women in England 1870-1950: Sexual Divisions and Social Change*. Bloomington, Indiana: Indiana University Press, 1984.

Long, Robert Emmet. *Barbara Pym*. New York: Ungar, 1986.

Moorhead, Caroline. "How Barbara Pym Was Rediscovered After 16 Years Out in the Cold." *The Times*. 14 September 1977, p. 11.

"Reputations Revisited." *The Times Literary Supplement*. 21 Jan. 1977, pp. 66-68.

Rossen, Janice. *The World of Barbara Pym*. New York: St. Martin's Press, 1987.

Salwak, Dale, ed. *The Life and Work of Barbara Pym*. Iowa City: University of Iowa Press, 1987.

Spender, Dale. *Mothers of the Novel*. London: Methuen, 1986.

Williams, Merryn. *Women in the English Novel, 1800-1900*. New York: St. Martin's Press, 1984.